WALSINGHAM WAY

WALSINGHAM WAY

COLIN STEPHENSON

DARTON, LONGMAN & TODD
London

© Colin Stephenson 1970
First published in Great Britain in 1970
Reprinted 1970
by Darton, Longman & Todd Limited
85 Gloucester Road, London SW7
Printed in Great Britain by
Cox & Wyman Limited
London, Fakenham and Reading

ISBN 0 232 51137 3

For
MEL AND UVEDALE
under whose most hospitable roof
most of this book was written.

Contents

List of Illustrations

Preface

So many are the facets of Walsingham, and of Father Hope
Patten's work, that speaking or writing of it is like a lucky dip.
I mind a day when I drove away from the shrine with a Pres-
byterian friend. 'It's done me more good than harm,' he said.
I mind a young Jewish friend, ailing terribly, who appreciated
the offerings made for him at the shrine. 'Hope you don't
think it's cheek of me to pray for you, too.' I mind a former
fellow war correspondent, tough as they come, one of the London staff of the American United Press, with whom till I told
the tale of Walsingham I had never discussed religion. Before
we left he crept into the Holy House: 'Is it all right if I light a
candle too?' and afterwards: 'Whatever else may be said, this
is a happy place.'

On and on one could write about this extraordinary site, a
modern brick church, architecturally debatable according to
some experts, but a place about which none can be indifferent.
A lapsed Roman Catholic woman, with a difficult history: 'I
haven't prayed like that since I was fourteen,' she said as she
left the Holy House aged 45.

How easy it is to say that all this is mere religiosity; then
what about the Children's Home? What about the prep-school
at Harrow? What about the Retreat House loaned to the
Diocese of Bradford, loaned by the shrine from its Yorkshire
properties? What about the lady who had read about the shrine
in the papers (*The People* as it happened): 'I came a year ago
with my idiot son and swore that if he were cured I'd be back
next year with twenty pounds . . . Here's the money,' and she
disappeared.

There are holy and happy places all over Christendom and to members of the Anglican Church one of the great joys, perhaps to some of us the very greatest, during the past thirty years, has been the sign that the Mother of God favours the endeavour to restore her honour and veneration in our Church. One may visit Lourdes; one may visit Tinos in Greece, or Maria Lach in the Rhineland, or Sopacani by the Serb-Albanian border where sheep grazed and there was no roof half a century back; one finds the same sense of happiness.

This book is a story, with all its twists of common humour, of how one man became the agent for remaking one of the happy places of God's earth. Father Hope Patten was a terrifying person to all at some times and to some at all times; but whatever his idiosyncrasies, whatever the strange vagaries of performance – as chairman of a committee of Guardians for instance – whatever one's anticipatory alarm at the innovations to be discovered on one's next visit, he was a priest for ever and one knew, at once, that he had been meant to be a priest for ever.

Here is a story, then, against the rather curious background of the Anglican Church revival in the past century, of a great priest and a great shrine. Whatever the archaeologists may say, and whatever the sentimentalists may wish to believe or discredit about the original historic site, things happen at Walsingham. Those who go to ask God's help and accept his chastisement, get the latter as well as the first; but they grow, and this is a place where men may drink deep of the waters of solace.

There is a story in this book about the Chapter of the College of Guardians (who are trustees for, and in company law owners of, the shrine) and of a debate that began with such tenseness, yet ended in common accord and a clear sense that the Holy Spirit had literally directed the gathering. The author is one who knows least of what I now write. But before Fr Patten's death there was concern about his successor and at a critical moment in Chapter Fr Patten forced the issue by, without warning, directing that we elect a 'Vice-Chairman' to take his place in an emergency. The author of this book did not grasp till a couple of years later what was being done to him; but his name was in a flash proposed and seconded; in a flash it was carried *nem con;* for we knew without debate what and who was needed.

For the rest of that day Fr Hope Patten wore a happy and grateful smile. To follow Hope Patten was a privilege and a pain; this author, to whom, too, the shrine owes much, was, unbeknown to himself, at the time warmly welcomed by the Restorer as his Successor.

All who have been closely involved bless the day of that Chapter and will thank Fr Colin Stephenson for his humour and fun, as well as scholarship and detachment, in giving us this happy book.

The Earl of Lauderdale

Foreword

LIKE MANY BOOKS, this one turned out to be rather different from the book I intended to write. It is simply an account of the Shrine of Our Lady of Walsingham and what we know of its foundation and restoration. It makes no pretensions to scholarship and therefore I have made no notes of sources nor my authority for making some statements which I am fully aware are not accepted by everybody.

My intention has been to provide a readable account for the non-specialist, and most of the historical facts have been taken from Waterton's *Pietas Mariana Britannica* and J. C. Dickenson's *Shrine of Our Lady of Walsingham* Any conclusions drawn are entirely my own. I have tried to be objective, but obviously I cannot help being biased in some directions.

The account of the restoration of the shrine is, of course, mostly a biography of Father Hope Patten, because one cannot fully understand how it took place unless one knows something of his background and character. I admired him enormously and he had a great influence on me when I was a young man, but I have tried to present the facts from a completely neutral point of view, because I consider the work he accomplished to be far more remarkable if one knows something of his limitations.

A great deal of the work in collecting material about his early life was done by the Rev. Frederick Smith, and my use of this saved me much labour. I am also grateful to Dr Joseph Brice for a lot of help and advice and to Miss Ella Waydelin who from long experience of my handwriting and spelling undertook to type the manuscript. Of course any book of this sort owes much to the kindness and interest of many people and I would like to thank them all. Walsingham is a place loved by a variety of different people, and I hope it will be obvious that I am one of them.

I

The Lady Richeldis
and the Foundation of the Shrine

WHEN THE WIND BLOWS in from the North Sea across the
salt marshes of the Norfolk coast its full fury is not felt in the
small valley through which the river Stiffkey flows. Inland
about five miles from the coast a Saxon hamlet had grown up
dependent upon a Manor owned by a family of Norman origin
called de Faverches.

It may well be wondered why a Norman family was established in this remote part of England before the Conquest, but
it was in fact quite usual for families to cross the Channel and
settle here. They acted as a kind of 'fifth column' when William
the Bastard, later known as the Conqueror, made his rather
dubious claims to this country.

The place was not of any great importance, for East Anglia
was full of great landowners and the de Faverches are not
mentioned in the Doomsday Book. It was indeed known as
Walsingham Parva to distinguish it from its grander neighbour,
Walsingham Magna.

The place-name may originally have been Woelsingham,
from the son of Wulfgyo called Wolkytel whose brother Kytel
is mentioned in Doomsday.

The manor house of the de Faverches was probably on the
rising ground behind the present parish church of Little Walsingham, where ancient cellars have been found, thought to
have belonged to some large house of that period.

It was almost certainly a very simple community centred upon the Manor House and engaged largely in the cultivation of the land and the production of food and clothing for its own needs. It would be governed by the feudal system which gave the Lord of the Manor extensive rights and powers. Amongst his dependants there would be craftsmen of various sorts engaged in building and repairs, whose successors still do the same sort of work for the Walsingham Estate today.

This part of England had been evangelised almost four hundred years before by St Felix who established his Cathedral at Dunwich. It had seen the blood of martyrs flow when in 870 the Danes used Edmund, the King of East Anglia, as a target for archery practice. By the time the de Faverches settled themselves at Walsingham the cathedral was at North Elmham not far away. The name of the bishop was Stigand and he had a very colourful career. He was known as 'Cnuts priest' and on the death of Bishop Aelfric in 1038 he had more or less intruded himself into the vacant see. There was some discontent about this and so Stigand was thrust out and Grimbatel appointed in his place. Stigand was not taking this without reaction and got a charge of simony brought against Grimbatel, who was removed. Stigand then moved in again himself.

Stigand seems to have been a man whose ambition was matched by his energy, for when Canterbury became vacant he got himself elected without giving up Elmham, and then added the bishopric of Winchester for good measure. This was too much for the King who made him resign Elmham and promptly appointed Stigand's brother Aylmer. When William the Conqueror came in 1066 both Stigand and Aylmer were deposed in disgrace and William's chaplain Herfast was appointed to East Anglia and moved the see to Norwich. Things cannot have been very happy in the diocese in 1061 when the happening took place which was to make Walsingham Parva a focal point of holiness.

There are great difficulties about the date 1061 and it cannot be verified, but it is not entirely outside the bounds of possibility. Sir Geoffrey de Faverches, the Lord of the Manor, was married to a lady called Richeldis and, as we know her son to have been alive almost a century later when he founded the Priory, she must have been a very young girl in 1061 and quite elderly when her son Geoffrey was born. As in the East today, girls were then betrothed in infancy and married at the first sign of puberty. The exact date is not really very important for we are concerned with a chain of events which grew out of something, and it does not much matter when exactly it all began.

The happening was religious and there can be little doubt that the Lady Richeldis, whatever her age, had a reputation for piety. She lived at a time when even the undevout went often to Mass and performed religious exercises which today we should think rather ostentatious. Large numbers of men and women took religious vows, from hermits and anchorites to members of regular orders, some austere and some mixed with a considerable amount of worldliness. Those who did not take vows themselves, if they were wealthy enough, founded monasteries and churches. There was a good deal of pious 'keeping up with the Joneses' and to some extent the saints held the interest and popularity accorded by the modern world to film and football stars. In any case, to have the reputation for being devout in such a society would have involved a considerable commitment to works of religion.

Whatever else piety at this time may have contained, it is fairly certain that devotion to the Mother of the Lord played a great part in religious exercises. It has often been implied that this particular devotion was a late development of Christianity, but it can be shown to belong to its earliest substance and in the Catacombs at Rome there are paintings of Mary with small figures at her feet asking for her prayers. This developed into a cultus which was beginning to play a larger and larger part in worship, until by the twelfth century it broke out into a wonderful artistic exuberance. It would be possible to trace some of its later luxuriance in England to the influence of the lady of the manor of Walsingham Parva.

Her piety was not only in exterior acts, she was a mystic and a visionary. There is so much more we would like to know, but the only recorded facts are that she was devout and that she had a vision.

The dreaming of dreams and the seeing of visions have played a great part in every religion and Christianity is no exception.

The experience of Mary at Nazareth, which we call the Annunciation, came within this category and both the Old and New Testaments are full of similar phenomena, while the lives of the saints record many such things in various forms. An interesting feature is that so many visions have involved the appearing of the Blessed Virgin herself, and this has been a fairly constant happening throughout the Christian centuries and not confined to any particular place or time. It might almost seem a continuation of the Blessed Virgin's own experience at Nazareth, she herself playing the part of the Archangel Gabriel as a messenger of God. Each appearing has been a type of Annunciation which has brought a message of some kind with a command for its proclamation.

There are, of course, those who would doubt the validity of any experiences of this sort regarding them as purely subjective, and it cannot be denied that some visionaries are the victims of psychological disorder. But they cannot all be dismissed in this way and there have been enough reliable witnesses to prove the point. It has been unusual for more than one person to experience the full apparition, yet others in smaller or larger numbers have seen surrounding phenomena which have convinced them that a supernatural happening was taking place. In the long run it has been left to the visionaries to prove by their own integrity that this thing was of God. Lucia, the only survivor of the three children who saw Our Lady of Fatima in Portugal, is alive today and lives as a Carmelite nun. Bernardette of Lourdes, whose experiences led to the foundation of the greatest place of pilgrimage in the world, lived only a hundred years ago and every detail was carefully recorded. In her lifetime she converted some of her severest critics and has been canonised as a saint. It is an astonishing thing that her human remains did not corrupt in the grave and can still be seen exposed in the chapel of the Convent at Nevers, where she died. Photography had been discovered in her childhood and so we can compare the rather dense-looking little peasant girl with the serene and refined beauty of the young nun, and it certainly helps in understanding why her contemporaries became convinced that she had seen the Blessed Virgin, as she claimed.

Many visionaries have had a hard task in convincing their

contemporaries that what has been revealed to them has not been a figment of their own imagination or a deceit aimed at drawing attention to themselves. Many, like Bernardette, have been peasant children who have been subjected to a great deal of pressure and bullying in an attempt to make them admit that they have been mistaken. The authorities of the Church have often behaved in this way because they have feared to be made ridiculous by the exposure of a fraud, but there have been others made angry because they started from the premise that such things do not happen and that anyone who claimed such an experience must be a fool or a liar.

It is unlikely that Richeldis would have suffered any of these indignities. She lived in an age which was anything but sceptical and which expected these things to happen. In addition to this she had a privileged position. She may have been young, but she was the wife of the Lord of the Manor and could expect a certain deference from authorities of both Church and State. It is interesting that, in contrast with many other similar appearances of Mary, which involved very uneducated peasant children, this English version was from the beginning rather a patrician affair.

We know nothing whatever about the circumstances of her vision. She may have been alone and later told her confessor or her husband, or she may have been seen by others rapt in a trance. They may well have recorded incidents which had convinced them that something supernatural was taking place. Tradition says that the vision was repeated three times, so that it would seem to have been a series of happenings, as is recorded of the apparitions at Fatima and Lourdes. In both these cases the Virgin is supposed to have appeared in a particular place and little pieces of the holm oak, over which she was seen hovering at Fatima, are preserved as precious relics. When Erasmus came to Walsingham in 1511 he records an interview which he had with the Augustinian Sub-Prior, during which the monk 'drew out of a bag a portion of the wood cut from the beam on which the Virgin Mother had rested'. He gives no other information except that it had a wonderful fragrance, but it may well have had some connection with the vision of Richeldis, as the holm oak had at Fatima.

. . .

A vision is something that cannot be put under a microscope, and even if we knew far more about what happened at Walsingham we should find it difficult to sort out the authentic facts. What we do know for certain is the outcome, which was the building of a little wooden house, which came to be claimed as a replica of the house at Nazareth in which Mary received the Annunciation, and where later she lived with Joseph and her divine Son. Whether the house at Nazareth was a cave dwelling or an ordinary peasant's house we cannot know, but what was built at Walsingham was never claimed as the original house. Much later, in 1295, the Holy House of Loreto appears in Italy according to a 15th-century writing, but this is said to be the very house from Nazareth, transported by angels. Although the house at Loreto was slightly smaller than Walsingham, it seems to have been similar in shape, and one cannot help wondering, since few people still believe in its aeronautical exploits, whether its construction was not influenced by the already famous English shrine.

If 1061 was indeed the date of these revelations, then it was soon after the Holy Land and Nazareth itself had become almost inaccessible to Christian pilgrims, so that Peter the Hermit, trying to visit Jerusalem in 1093, was so appalled by the condition of the Holy Places that he raised the cry which led to the Crusades. The miseries of pilgrims trying to visit the Holy Land of Palestine may give some clue as to why the Blessed Virgin appeared in this place at this time and why Walsingham so soon became known as England's Nazareth and those who went there called it the Holy Land.

It is hard for us to understand the intense devotion men of that time felt for the place of Christ's birth, ministry and death. Being cut off from these places stirred up feelings which found poetic expression in a yearning for the heavenly Jerusalem. Such hymns as 'Jerusalem the golden' and 'Jerusalem, my happy home' belong to this period. Richeldis was sure that she had been taken in spirit to the place where Christ had lived, and that His mother herself had shown her the very house and commanded her to take particular note of its measurements, so that she could cause it to be reconstructed exactly. She had the resources, both men and materials, at her command and there was no one except her husband that she needed to convince. The ecclesiastical authorities must have been consulted at some point, but it is not likely to have bothered the bishop at North Elmham in quite the same way as the apparitions at Lourdes and Fatima tormented the lives of the bishops in whose dioceses they took place. Her main problem was where exactly she should build this little house, and while she was pondering on this question a strange phenomenon was observed. In the meadow where she had seen Our Lady two plots remained absolutely dry after a heavy dew had fallen, and both were exactly the size needed for the house she intended to have built. Springs of water had welled from the ground and she chose the site which was nearest to two of these. When, however, they began to build everything went wrong and it seemed to the workmen that they could make nothing fit, and so they abandoned the work in despair. Richeldis was dismayed at this and spent the whole night in prayer hoping to get further guidance from Our Lady. When the day dawned a great miracle had taken place, for the misshapen house was now perfectly completed, and it had been moved without the aid of human hands to the other site which was two hundred feet away from the first, and was obviously where it was intended to be.

This legend comes from a ballad of the fifteenth century printed by Richard Pynson, the only copy of which is now in the Pepysian Library of Magdalene College, Cambridge. It talks of the pilgrimages as having gone on for four hundred years, which shows that its composition must have been late, but it may well preserve many earlier traditions which had been handed down. There is no other record and so we are forced to rely on it for any consideration of what may have happened. We know from other examples how anxious religious houses were to push back the date of their foundation as far as possible, and this tends to make one the more suspicious when one finds records of Richeldis' son being still alive in the mid-twelfth century.

The story of the miraculous moving of the house is interesting because it does not seem to have much point in the legend as we have it. By the time the Pynson ballad was written the extraordinary history of the flying house of Loreto was being spread around Christendom and the Abbot of Glastonbury, who had recently been to Italy, had a Loreto Chapel built on the north side of his Abbey Church. At first one is tempted to think that the writer of the Pynson ballad has put a bit of flying into the legend to keep up with Loreto, but it may well be the other way round, and that the travels of the Loreto house were based on the much earlier legend of the moving house at Walsingham. If this is so, then the event recorded in the Pynson ballad might cover the deliberate removal of the house from one site to another. This need not have been a conscious attempt at fraud, for pilgrims finding the position of the house changed would be likely to account for it by some story of supernatural intervention.

This possibility becomes the more interesting in that there has been some controversy about the original position of the holy house at Walsingham. If the Saxon foundations on which the present Anglican Shrine has been built were indeed those of a covering Chapel to protect the little house Richeldis had erected, then at some point it must have been moved and placed alongside the Church of the Augustinian Canons in the Priory grounds, where it undoubtedly seems to have been at the time of its destruction. Recent excavations on the Abbey (as the Priory is now called) site have shown that there are no earlier foundations and that those unearthed of the covering Chapel must be 'the new work' of which William of Worcester wrote when he visited Walsingham in 1479. When Erasmus came there in 1511 the windows were still unglazed, while the porch was in the process of being built at the time of the dissolution, which took place thirty years afterwards. It would seem that either the house stood uncovered for over three hundred years, or that it was moved at some time from its original position for some special reason.

It is improbable that we shall ever know the answer to these queries, as records have disappeared and all is a matter of speculation. If it was moved, there is a possible explanation of the reason in the fact that, until fairly recent years, the River Stiffkey was much given to flooding. Photographs taken in 1911 show a man in a boat rowing around the area where the Anglican shrine now stands. If such flooding took place from time to time it is not surprising that the Canons decided to move the house to a more convenient and safer position beside their Church. The grotto at Lourdes has suffered from similar floods;

though it is not possible to move a mountain, they have made attempts to divert the river. The house at Walsingham was probably a type of 'prefabricated' wooden building and shifting it would not have been difficult. It sounds a rather impious thing to do, but their veneration was for the house rather than the site, and by this time a mystique was growing around the image within the house which was becoming the centre of the cult. When the Pynson Ballad was written the move would already have taken place and the fact that there had been two sites was translated into legend.

When Richeldis built the house it was a work of private devotion and it would be fascinating to know how it became an object of public pilgrimage. We have plenty of records of the development of Lourdes and Fatima, and in both cases word passed from mouth to mouth that something strange was taking place and the great crowds which gathered soon became a most serious problem. Human nature has not changed much in this respect, and there can be little doubt that what was happening at Walsingham would be passed on the same way and that men and women would want to go and see for themselves. At Lourdes and Fatima it was not long before miracles of healing began to take place and then the gospel scenes of the sick being carried there were soon being re-enacted.

At Lourdes the healing was associated with the spring of water which appeared, and it is strange that the gift of water has so often been combined with a vision of Our Lady. Water plays a great part in Christian symbolism. Moses brought water out of the rock, and it flowed from the side of Our Lord when He was pierced by a spear after His death upon the Cross. It became the outward and visible sign in baptism, and holy water is used to drive away evil and to bless people and things. Yet the water which has been left as a gift by Mary must surely remind us that during her earthly life she was a Palestinian peasant girl to whom, as even to this day, the gift of pure water would be the greatest boon. It is interesting to note that both at Ephesus and Nazareth there were holy wells associated with Our Lady.

Water plays a part in the Walsingham legend, for the ballad tells of twin wells beside which the house was first built, and

although there is no record of its use in healing, there seems
little doubt that it was regarded with particular veneration.
Thomas Gatele, who was sub-prior at the beginning of the
fifteenth century, is recorded as having fallen into 'the well of
Blessed Mary' when a boy and his survival was regarded as a
miracle. There are still in existence some small lead flasks,
known as ampullae, which are marked with a crowned W and
which were used by pilgrims to carry away the precious liquid.
In 1967 one of these ampullae was washed up on the Yorkshire
coast, obviously having been dropped overboard by some returning pilgrims and having remained a very long time on the
sea bed. It was sealed and there was still liquid inside it which
smelled faintly of roses. Near twin wells in the grounds of what
was the Priory there is an open stone tank about which there
are no records, but it would seem that at some time pilgrims
bathed in the waters as they do at Lourdes, perhaps encouraged
by the youthful experience of Dom Thomas Gatele.

Richeldis probably welcomed and encouraged visitors to the
Holy House, as she had built it as an act of devotion and in
obedience to her vision and not as a private oratory. She must
have made known her spiritual visit to Nazareth and her
intention to reproduce the Holy Land in England, because
almost from the first Walsingham pilgrims were called 'Palmers', a name usually reserved for those who brought back
branches of palm from Palestine as evidence that they had
reached their destination. Pilgrims to Compostella in Spain,
where the body of St James the Apostle was venerated, picked
up scallop shells on the sea shore and stuck them in their hats.
This became almost a general pilgrim badge and stone scallop
shells have been found built into several houses in Walsingham.
Most pilgrim shrines developed their own tokens or badges
and Walsingham had a variety of these, the best collection of
which can be seen in the Museum at Kings Lynn where one
variety has the only known representation of the Holy House.
This makes it appear to have been a building with two storeys
and a steep gable end.

We have no means of knowing when Mass began to be said
within the little house, but the de Faverches would have had no
difficulty in getting permission for this and would almost certainly have had their own chaplain. It is probable that when she

had the little house built Richeldis did not think of it as a chapel, particularly if it was constructed, as seems probable, with two storeys. At Lourdes and Fatima the crowds which came to the place of the apparitions demanded that Mass should be said for them, and at Walsingham it may have been much the same.

It seems evident that at first the centre of the cult was the Holy House and it was to this that men and women came on pilgrimage, but at some time an image of the Virgin and Child was set up in the house on the right side of the altar, which had already become part of its furniture. Little by little it was this image which became the chief object of devotion when men spoke of going to salute Our Lady of Walsingham. The idea of England's own Holy Land still persisted, but when the reformers took away the statue in 1538 and burned it in London they considered that they were striking at the heart of what they regarded as a vain superstition.

With the complete lack of records we do not know where this image came from or when it was put into the Holy House. It may have been one which belonged to Richeldis or that she had carved, perhaps from the beam on which Our Lady appeared, or it may have been given to her for the purpose. It is doubtful that she made any attempt to portray Our Lady as she had seen her in the vision, for it was of the house that she was particularly instructed to take note. We cannot be certain that the image which appeared on the seal of the priory was a copy of that which was set up in the Holy House and which Erasmus thought small and undistinguished. Because of the shape of seals a seated figure suited the design and was often so used, and there are many examples of this. Yet it would seem probable that the Canons at a place like Walsingham would chose their own venerated image to place upon their seal. The fact that the image shown on the pilgrim token, thought to represent the Holy House, is similar to that on the seal makes it fairly certain that this is what in fact they did. The Virgin is represented seated upon a high-backed throne and holding the infant Christ upon her knee. With her other hand she holds a foliated sceptre like a lily and the Child is holding a book which may be the scriptures or the book of life. Our Lady wears a simple crown and as shown on the seal she is covered by a canopy with curtains looped back at each side and being agitated by the wind. This may be an embellishment by the artist or it may be a record of its setting within the Holy House.

Images of Mary are symbols which represent the many strands of devotion belonging to the cult which has arisen around the Mother of the Lord, but there can be little doubt that the whole cult derives much from the pre-Christian tradition of the Mother-Goddess. This should not surprise Christians, as there are many primitive ideas, such as Sacrifice, which have found their fulfilment in Christ. Having this in mind, it is interesting to see in the Museum at Paestum in Italy a whole case of statues which appear at a distance to be of Our Lady of Walsingham, but are in fact of Hera, the queen of the sky and celestial virgin in Greek mythology, who was regarded as Woman deified.

Today it is quite common to copy cult images and set them up as shrines, but it is difficult to know how far this was a practice before the Reformation. The image in the Red Mount Chapel at Kings Lynn is thought to have been of Our Lady of Walsingham and there is in the Victoria and Albert Museum a statue which, although much mutilated, must have been very like that depicted on the Priory seal. At North Elmham, not far from Walsingham, there is a fragment of mediaeval glass high up in a window of the north aisle which may well have been intended as a representation of the figure of Our Lady in the Holy House.

It is very unlikely that there was any sort of pilgrim organisation for a long time: people came simply to visit the place, said their prayers and made offerings, probably burning wax tapers in the little house. The lighting of candles at places of pilgrimage has always had a strong psychological appeal and there have always been candles burning in the Grotto at Lourdes since the apparitions took place, even when it has been flooded and they have stuck up like bullrushes out of the water. In the time of Richeldis a wax taper would have been a very valuable offering and not lightly regarded.

There are many things one would like to know about this Saxon lady with a Norman name who was the medium through whom a great force of spiritual energy was released, but it is unlikely that any historical facts will come to light. There are visionaries

who have been formally canonised and their names preserved
in the calendar of the Church, but we do not even know when
Richeldis died or where she was buried.

There are, of course, those who think that the date 1061 is
impossible and who would like to place the whole thing a
hundred years later. Even today institutions like to push back
the date of their foundation as far as possible, and this may well
have been the case at Walsingham. The whole legend could
have arisen from the influence of the Crusades, when the wife
of a Norman knight was so fascinated by his tales of the Holy
Land that she devised the idea of building a Holy House of
Nazareth as a domestic chapel. It would be natural for the
story to get around that she had done it at the prompting of a
vision. The historical fact is that the house was built and became
a place of pilgrimage, and we have plenty of evidence for this.

Richeldis' son seems to have been called Geoffrey, like his
father, which has led those who think the foundation was later
to speculate as to whether this Geoffrey was in fact her husband
who got left behind when the vision of Richeldis was claimed
for 1061. If he was her son he showed a certain filial piety in
his desire to establish the shrine on a firm basis, for he made a
grant of land for the founding of a religious community. It is
not surprising that, having been born at England's Nazareth,
he had a desire to make a pilgrimage to the Holy Land in Palestine, but before setting out on this long and hazardous journey
he gave a charter to 'Edwy, my clerk, for the institution of a
religious order which he will provide'. For the endowment
of this he made over 'the Church of All Hallows, in the same
village, with all its appurtenances'. We do not know what Edwy
did about it, for the Priory of Augustinian Canons was not
founded till sometime between 1146 and 1174 and by that time
the manor had passed into the hands of the de Clare family.
It may be that Geoffrey died in the Holy Land and Edwy also
died before he could make a foundation. Roger, Earl of Clare,
confirmed the charter but speaks of 'my clerks of Walsingham,
Ralph and Geoffrey', and it is significant that the first prior of
Walsingham was named Ralph. He also adds the benefice of
St Peter, Walsingham Magna, to the endowment. Already
the Parva is swallowing up the Magna. A later charter which
Robert de Brucus addressed to the Bishop of Norwich gives

grants to 'God and St Mary, and the Canons of Walsingham
... of all the possessions which that church held on the day when
Geoffrey de Faverches set out on his journey to Jerusalem'.

It may well be that Ralph, the clerk of Walsingham,
gathered together a small community and then later joined
it to the Order of St Augustine. In any case the choice of
Canons of St Augustine as guardians of the shrine was a good
one, for they were priests living under a rule drawn up for his
household by St Augustine of Hippo which enabled them to
have a common life without being burdened by the full weight
of monastic observance. Their way of life had received official
approval at Lateran Synods in 1059 and 1063, so that they were
very much contemporary with the shrine, and in the following
century when they came to Walsingham were establishing
houses all over England. Augustinian priories were founded
about this time at Creake, Weybourne, Coxford and West
Acre in the immediate vicinity of Walsingham and ultimately
there were seventeen houses in Norfolk. They would seem to
have had a good deal of success in recruitment from the locality,
for lists of the brethren at Walsingham reveal that many had
been born in the surrounding villages. We hear such names in
the early lists as Snoring, Barsham, Burnham, Sheringham,
Warham, Walsham, Wighton and Lynn, as well as recruits
from Walsingham itself.

The problem of making a foundation was always the question
of how it was to be supported. Wealthy patrons played a great
part in this, for the founding of monasteries and building of
churches were amongst the most highly indulgenced good
works. Yet there was something more than self-interest in the
enthusiasm to create places of worship and a genuine desire
to have God served. Noble patrons took a real interest and
pride in their foundations. The Walsingham priory began with
an advantage, for it not only had wealthy patrons but the shrine
was already known and venerated, so that a steady income from
pilgrim offerings could be expected.

Splendid monastic buildings were being erected in the
vicinity. The Benedictines at Binham and the Cluniacs at
Castle Acre were engaged in extensive work, and the early
Priors at Walsingham must have determined that their house
should lack nothing in size and splendour. They built an

extremely large church, the great east window of which still stands as a record of its size. There must have been a long time during which pilgrims to the shrine became accustomed to the sound of axes and hammers as the various buildings of the priory were put up.

We do not know when the Holy House was covered with a protective chapel, but it may have been done when the Priory was built. If the house was a wooden building it would soon deteriorate unless it was covered in some way. The Holy House of Loreto, which came flying into history at the end of the thirteenth century, was soon covered by a large church, and so was the tiny chapel of St Mary of the Angels which was much venerated for its connection with St Francis. If the Holy House at Walsingham was uncovered when the Canons came to build their church, it is surprising that they did not incorporate it as at Loreto and Assisi and this would seem to indicate that it was already enclosed by the time the Priory was founded. On the reverse side of the seal which had the figure of Our Lady there appeared a cruciform church of Norman style, with a central tower and two smaller towers both at the east and west ends. The roof may have been covered with pantiles, which were made quite plain in the earlier seal, but the later one made them look like a low parapet of intersecting arches. Pantiles being such a feature of Norfolk architecture, it would be nice to think they covered the original house. In the later seal there are faces shown through the windows and one would like to imagine that one of them was intended to be Richeldis, but they all appear to have beards and are probably the early benefactors, including Geoffrey de Faverches and Roger de Clare.

There are those who think that this building is intended to represent the Priory Church. It is true that such portrayals were often simply formal and not meant as anything more than a rough impression of the building. We know that the Priory Church had a central tower and the male benefactors peering from the windows support this theory. On the other hand, the Saxon foundations unearthed in 1937 when the Anglican Shrine Church was extended do look, even to an unpractised eye, like a ground plan of the building on the seal. One can see the foundations of the round towers and the two porches on either side.

Perhaps, when so little is known with certainty, it is easy to indulge in wishful thinking, but it would an attractive thought that one was looking at the small chapel built over the Holy House, through the porches of which streamed a rising flood of men and women from all levels of society still able to experience the awe and wonder which our sophisticated world has in a great measure lost. Nor does it seem surprising that, since the Canons had come to Walsingham as guardians of the shrine, they should put on their seal the building upon which visitors should fix their eyes with the greatest devotion.

Certainly with the arrival of the Augustinian Canons the reception and organisation of pilgrims must have been put on a far more professional basis. We know later that a member of the Community was always in the Holy House, dealing with offerings and probably directing pilgrims in their devotions. Being members of an established and flourishing Order they had a wide influence and the means of being adequately represented at Rome, where the final seat of authority lay. They were soon making plans to get their house and the shrine an independent charter which would free them to a large extent from the authority of the bishop of the diocese.

Monks and nuns are ordinary human beings and suffer from the usual failings of mankind. Sometimes the fact that they have made personal sacrifices makes them the more possessive as a corporate body. The Canons at Walsingham were not at all pleased when they discovered in 1345 that Elizabeth, Lady Clare, proposed to establish a house of Franciscan Friars almost on their doorstep. The situation was made more delicate by the fact that the de Clares were great benefactors of their own house.

The Friars first came to England in 1226 and established themselves at Canterbury, London and Oxford, and became at once immensely popular. They were very much a new thing and, in spite of a partial surrender to the establishment, they still retained enough of the spirit and freshness of their founder to make them immediately attractive. Pious founders came forward in large numbers because the friars, with their great devotion to poverty and the wide dispensations they had to beg, made it possible to establish a spiritually profitable foundation at a very reasonable price. The fact that they were great preachers, at a time when sermons were something of a rarity, made them seem to be a great asset in a place where pilgrims gathered in large numbers. The Canons certainly did not agree with this, and one can imagine them gathering in their Chapter House to discuss this menace to their security. They acted at once and drew up a petition against this intrusion of the Friars. It was a very uninhibited document, in which they stated quite baldly that such a foundation with a hostel erected so close to the shrine was bound to diminish the income they obtained from Mass Stipends, burial fees and other tithes. In fact they made no attempt to hide the real reason for their objections which was the fear that the Friars would get hold of the pilgrims and leech them before they ever got to the shrine.

There must have been great chagrin in the Chapter House when the Canons learned that their petition had been rejected and that the Friars were to be established at the very entry of the village. It is to be feared that when the Franciscans arrived they were made only too conscious that, as far as the custodians of the shrine were concerned, they were unwelcome guests and there are records of constant friction between the houses. At Lourdes the same kind of situation arose between the parish priest and the Order of the Immaculate Conception which had been sent to develop the shrine.

However, whether the Canons liked it or not, the Friars built themselves a convent of more modest style than their neighbours, but with an extraordinarily large church in the nave of which pilgrims probably slept as well as listened to a type of preaching with which they were not familiar, and the simplicity of which made an immediate appeal to them.

Thus Walsingham Parva now had three large churches, for besides the two conventual buildings there was the fine parish church of All Hallows. Walsingham Magna had allowed its earlier church of All Hallows to fall into ruins and a new and splendid church dedicated to St Peter had been built, but that village had already become a much smaller and less important place. Clearly defined routes began to be traced from all over England, and to be known as the Walsingham Greenway or Palmers' Way, all converging on the small wooden house built by Richeldis and now recognised throughout the kingdom as England's Nazareth.

2

Procession along
the Walsingham Way

THE GREAT UPSURGE OF DEVOTION to the 'Mother of
God', as the Council of Ephesus in 431 had said that Mary
might be called, which took place throughout Christendom
in the twelfth century has been ascribed to various causes. The
rise of the Troubadours, the romantic allegory of love and the
glorification of virginity all played their part, as well as the
enormous personal influence of St Bernard who turned all this
romantic energy into a theological exaltation of the Mother of
the Lord. The Cistercian Order, which had founded five hundred and thirty Abbeys by the end of the twelfth century,
undoubtedly played a great part in developing the liturgical
expression of this devotion. What has not been so frequently
recognised is that veneration of Mary had already started in
England before the mellifluous tones of St Bernard had been
raised. It was about this time that England began to be called
'Our Lady's Dowry' although it is not certain how this title
arose. It may be connected with a legend told of St Simon
Stock, the English Carmelite, which claims that the Blessed
Virgin appeared to him and said that she was taking England
for her dower. This idea gripped the popular imagination and
there was no other country which began to build churches and
chapels in honour of Our Lady with such exuberance. As the
shrines of the great English saints developed there grew up with
each one of them an associated Marian cult. St Thomas at

Canterbury had the Shrine of Our Lady Undercroft, St Edward at Westminster had Our Lady of Pewe, while there was a venerated image at Lincoln near the Shrine of St Hugh and Glastonbury later built a Loreto Chapel, having had from its foundation a strong Marian bias. This impetus has sometimes been explained as a reaction against the strong paternalistic society of the time, and there may be an element of truth in this; but it would seem that in Marian devotion England had somehow attained a special place in the eyes of Europe, and it may not be too fanciful to attribute some of this to the influence of Walsingham.

With the difficulties which the rise of a militant Islam had made for pilgrims to the Holy Land there was a great boom in domestic pilgrimages in England. The Anglo-Saxons had a special reputation for making pilgrimages and there was a hostel built for them in Rome near the tomb of St Peter. The possible origin of the verb 'to roam', which came into the language at this time, implies that there must have been a lot of them who made the journey to Italy. The martyrdom of Thomas à Becket at Canterbury in 1170 set in motion a great wave of pilgrims towards that city, but pilgrims had already been coming to Walsingham for over a hundred years before that time.

There is a very human element behind the religious act of pilgrimage, for men and women have always loved to go and see places where wonders have taken place. Mohammed, in establishing the pilgrimage to Mecca, was simply using a form of devotion which was already firmly established in Christianity. The Church did its best to encourage this practice by granting indulgences to those who undertook such journeys, and there were many temporal advantages to be gained such as a suspension from paying taxes while on pilgrimage and immunity from arrest. The latter privilege encouraged debtors and minor criminals to take the pilgrim path in great numbers, which was one of the reasons why pilgrims began to get a bad name.

Wycliffe and the Lollards saw the abuse of religion in all this and pointed out that God is present everywhere, adding for good measure that 'it is a vain waste and idle for to trot to Walsingham rather than to each other place in which an image of Mary is . . .'. John Langland in the *Vision of Piers Plowman* wrote:

> Heremytes on an heape with hoked staves
> Wenten to Walsingham. . . .

counting it amongst the many abuses which he saw in the church around him. But official sanction and encouragement was given, and the Sarum Missal has a form of blessing for the staff they carried as well as a Mass for Pilgrims. Once a man had received this sign of a pilgrim his property was secure from confiscation or injury and he was above all law except ecclesiastical. Yet alongside these attractions there was a strong element of penance in the motive to make pilgrimages, and they were undertaken to implore God's mercy and to turn aside His wrath. Famine and plague played a terrifying part in the lives of men and women at that time and they were encouraged to think of them as manifestations of Divine Wrath at their sinful complacency and religious backslidings. Some made their pilgrimage more penitential by walking barefooted, just as today one can see old peasant women approaching the sanctuary of Fatima on their knees.

Pilgrimages could be performed by proxy, but this was a privilege of the important and wealthy. Often it was left in a will that a pilgrimage should be made after the death of the testator. Thus in Katherine of Aragon's will provision was made 'that some personage go to Our Lady of Walsingham on pilgrimage and distribute twenty nobles on the way', which was quite a large sum.

Pilgrims got a bad name with puritans because for many it was a chance of sight-seeing and became a very cheerful outing. There was a lot of loud laughter and singing as they went along. When a Wycliffite complained about this, Archbishop Arundel replied that it was a good thing for them to have singers and pipers because, if they were barefooted and struck their toe against a stone they needed something to cheer them up. Thomas Thorpe, on trial before the same Archbishop, was not so kindly answered. He was accused of saying that 'those men and women who go on pilgrimages to Canterbury, to Beverley, to Walsingham and to other such places are accursed and made foolish, spending their goods in waste'. 'Ungracious lousel,' replied the Archbishop, 'thou favourest no more truth than a hound. Since at the rood at the north door at London, at Our

Lady at Walsingham and many other divers places in England, are many great and praisable miracles done, should not the images of such holy saints and places be more worshipped than other places and images where no such miracles are done?'

But these unhappy controversies lay in the future; in its early years the shrine at Walsingham developed steadily and peacefully. From the finances of the Priory it might seem that things only really boomed in the fourteenth century, because they do not show any particular signs of wealth till then. On the other hand, we do not know that the offerings and bequests to the shrine were not kept separate for some years. There are so many silences in the story of Walsingham and it is always unwise to draw too many conclusions from silence. It would seem possible that Walsingham released a great tide of domestic pilgrimage in England, for from the time of its foundation pilgrimages grew in an extraordinary way and shrines of saints and relics began to appear all over the country.

An example of how shrines could profit from the proximity of Walsingham is given in the record of the small Cluniac Priory at Bromholm, which was founded in 908 as a dependency of Castle Acre on the bleak easternmost tip of Norfolk, where the monks lived in great isolation and poverty till about 1220 when they acquired a relic of the True Cross, which was highly miraculous and achieved wide renown as the Holy Rood of Bromholm. There can be little doubt that being close to Walsingham was a great factor in its development as a shrine, and we later hear of many famous people visiting both sanctuaries in one pilgrimage. In Langland's *Vision of Piers Plowman* for example they are placed together:

> But wenden to Walsingham, and my wife Alis,
> And byd the roode of Bromholm bring me out of debt.

In the Reeve's Tale in Chaucer the miller's wife cries out, 'Help, holy crois of Bromeholme', which shows how well known it had become; but it is possible that it would never have been heard of if it had not been so close to Walsingham.

There can be little doubt that until the rise of the cult of St Thomas of Canterbury, Walsingham was the greatest pilgrimage shrine in England, and even then the two were spoken of together. The fact that Chaucer chose Canterbury as the destination for his pilgrims has concentrated attention on that shrine. The importance of his work is that he created real and vivid characters, but they might equally well have been pilgrims to Walsingham as to Canterbury and he has provided us with a view of a wonderful cross-section of the type of people who went on pilgrimage. Some were good, some were rogues, and all had very mixed motives for making the pilgrimage, but in Chaucer's story they are living human people and his power of observation is remarkable. Particularly does he provide a vivid and authentic description of the kind of clothes the pilgrims wore, and they came from all ranks of society. So often in the annals of Walsingham there are the records of the great and mighty coming on pilgrimage that it is important to remember that the largest part of the crowd was made up of the Commons of England, the record of whose doings has been less carefully chronicled.

The Kings of England were amongst the most devoted pilgrims to Walsingham, but we have no certain record of who was the first to come. Tradition says that it was Richard Coeur de Lion, but there is no evidence for this and he spent so much of his reign out of the country that he would seem to have had little opportunity. When he returned from imprisonment in 1194 he is known to have made a journey through his realm and this would seem to have been the most likely opportunity for him to have made a pilgrimage to Walsingham, if he did so. He had such a romantic connection with the Holy Land as a crusader that it would seem appropriate that he should be the first English King to visit England's Nazareth.

His brother John spent much of his time at loggerheads with the church and clergy and therefore it does not seem strange to find no record of his having made a pilgrimage. Indeed, he might well have had a rather cool reception had he done so. Yet he came to Lynn, which is not far away, and so once again it is unwise to make a definite assertion from negative evidence.

Henry III was the first great royal patron of Walsingham whose many pilgrimages are documented. He paid his first visit in 1226 when he went on to Bromholm to venerate the relic of the Cross, which they had only recently acquired. From this time he made regular pilgrimages and Walsingham seems to have played a great part in his religious life. He demonstrated his interest by granting the Priory the right to hold a weekly market and a two-day fair on Holy Cross Day, and later another fair lasting six days for Our Lady's birthday in September. As the years passed Henry's visits became more frequent and he began to make gifts far more personal than the formal offerings which were to be expected from one of his rank. He gave oak trees for building, vestments for the church, and in 1246 he provided for a golden crown to be made for the image. Mrs Jameson, in *Legends of the Madonna* – a famous Victorian work on Marian art – ascribes the crowning of images to the influence of the Jesuits, but most of the famous mediaeval images of Our Lady were provided with rich crowns and Our Lady of Walsingham was no exception. There is evidence that as early as the eighth century this custom had started in Rome.

Henry was also exceedingly generous in his gifts of wax and tapers and in 1241 he provided for 3,000 tapers to burn in the Holy House on the feast of the Assumption, which must have made quite a blaze in that small space. In 1251 he spent Lady Day at Walsingham, which must have added great excitement to this Feast of the Annunciation, which was always kept as the feast of title at the shrine. The Canons had come to regard him as a personal patron because for many years he made them an annual grant of 40s., rather like a regular subscriber to a religious community today. His last visit was in 1272, when he came on from Norwich where he had been in person to settle a serious riot between the monks and the citizens. He was at Walsingham on 26 September and went on to Bury St Edmunds, where he became ill and was carried home to London and died on 6 November. He was buried in the tomb from which he had caused the relics of St Edward the Confessor to be translated in 1269 to the shrine where they still remain, and his own bones lie as their escort.

His son, Edward I, was probably the most devoted of all the monarchs to the Norfolk shrine. He had obviously been greatly influenced by his father and regarded Our Lady of Walsingham as his special protector, for when during his youth he was playing at chess in a vaulted room, and, having just moved away, a great stone fell from the roof above where he had been sitting, he ascribed this seemingly miraculous escape to the intervention of the Virgin of Walsingham. From this time he was not only an almost annual pilgrim, but he was particularly generous in his gifts to the shrine. It would be tedious to recount all the many visits which he made, but at Candlemas 1296 he caused a treaty to be sworn with the Count of Flanders in the Holy House itself, which must have been a memorable occasion for those who witnessed it. After his mother entered the nunnery of Amsbury he went to visit her there and came on at once to make a pilgrimage to Walsingham, which he regarded as the home of his heavenly mother. Unlike his father he does not seem to have had a great devotion to the Holy Rood of Bromholm for, in spite of his constant pilgrimages to Walsingham, he is only recorded as having gone on from there to Bromholm twice.

In 1289, having landed with the Queen at Dover after three years abroad, Edward made straight for Walsingham pausing on the way at Bury St Edmunds. He must have looked back with nostalgia at this pilgrimage, for the following year Queen Eleanor was struck down by a fever at Harby near Lincoln and her body was taken back to Westminster on a thirteen days' progress. In his grief the king erected a memorial cross at every place where the cortège stopped for the night. It is not surprising that we find him at Walsingham two months later for the Feast of Candlemas which he loved to celebrate at the shrine. East Anglia is often blanketed with snow at just that time of the year, so that it displays something of his resolution as a pilgrim that it was this feast which brought him most frequently to Norfolk. In fact that year the country suffered from a great drought and there were special penitential processions made, asking for rain. In 1294 the king spent three weeks in the vicinity staying for some of the time with the Benedictine monks at Binham. In 1296 his temper was obviously getting very bad and during his pilgrimage he seems to have hurled a coronet into the fire while in a rage, for there is an entry of a payment 'to make good a large ruby and an emerald lost out of the coronet when the King's grace was pleased to throw it behind the fire'. In September 1299 he married again, by papal dispensation, his cousin who was only twenty and a daughter of the saintly King Louis of France. In March of the following year he took her to Walsingham for the first time and they both made offerings of gold clasps. This was at a time when he was very pressed for money and greatly in debt and not being very generous in other directions.

The king's last pilgrimage was once again in the snows at Candlemas in 1305. He died two years later at Burgh-on-Sands and there is a curious entry in the Lanercost Chronicle which says that his body was 'kept above ground in the Abbey of Walsingham until removed to Westminster for burial'. This may be true, in view of his great devotion to the place, but is probably a mistake for Waltham Abbey as is much more likely. In any case he was one of the most notable pilgrims in the history of the shrine, having visited the Holy House at least thirteen times and often making a prolonged stay. A chantry Chapel was erected to his memory in the Church of the Canons at Walsingham, who had every reason to be grateful to him.

So the fourteenth century began with Walsingham on the crest of a wave of popularity and privilege.

Edward II would appear to have left it till 1315 before he made his first regal pilgrimage to Walsingham when he stayed for two nights. Ten years later he was there for Candlemas, which seems to have been a favourite feast for royal visitors, and it is recorded that he 'made an offering at the High Altar to the image of the Blessed Virgin in a small chapel situated in the burying ground'. This implies that at that time the shrine was a building apart from the rest of the Priory.

Edward III was only fourteen years old when he was crowned and his father murdered in 1327. He came to Walsingham early in his reign, for the royal chancery was there, both in September and November 1328. In the following years he came frequently. At this time Isabella the Queen Dowager of France came on pilgrimage, and in the records of Lynn there is an entry of a payment for bread sent to her at the shrine. It is odd that after visiting Walsingham in 1343, having come straight from France, there is no record of the king making any other visit for the remaining thirty-four years of his reign.

The great scourge of the Black Death first appeared in England in 1348 at Weymouth and began to spread across the country like fire. It was particularly severe in Norfolk and the Eastern Counties. Whole villages were depopulated and left to fall into ruins. Not far from Walsingham in the middle of a field can be seen the ruined tower of Egmere Church, which is all that remains of a village which was wiped out by the plague. It is hard to imagine the horror and panic caused by this disaster and men turned to religion for comfort and protection. The monasteries were hardest hit, in many cases they never recovered and it was the greatest cause of their decline. The small numbers who survived found it impossible to maintain the life and some monastic communities, one fears, completely forsook the ideals for which they had been founded. It is probable that Prior Simon of Walsingham, who had led the opposition to the establishment of the Friary, died of the plague. It is not surprising to find it breaking out at the shrine because the upsurge of religious fervour must have sent even greater crowds along the pilgrim way. The toll of deaths in Norfolk is appalling: of 799 parishes 527 lost their parish priest. In Norwich alone 57,374 people died, and the total population is not thought to have been much more than 60,000. Perhaps it is not surprising that Edward III kept away from East Anglia when one remembers what was happening at that time and the dangers of mixing in a crowd.

In 1364 David Bruce, King of Scotland, came on pilgrimage with a score of his knights, but he had to secure letters of safe conduct to enter what was, more or less, enemy territory. This gives some indication of the value he placed upon his visit.

King Richard II and his beloved Queen Anne were pilgrims at the Shrine in 1383. Ten years later she died and the king never recovered from his loss.

The royal procession to Walsingham continued amidst the conflicts of English history, and Henry IV, V and VI all came on pilgrimage. Henry VI was thought mad by some, largely because of his intense piety. He was only interested in religion and his scholastic foundations, such as Eton College. As might be expected, he was a regular pilgrim to Walsingham and many people regarded him as a saint. After his death efforts were made to secure his canonisation and his figure appears amongst the saints on several rood screens in East Anglia. In recent years efforts have been revived at Rome to have him enrolled in the official Calendar of the Saints.

Edward IV and his queen made a pilgrimage in 1469 on their way north to quell the Yorkshire insurrection. The king was defeated and captured, but shortly afterwards he was released and when he returned to the capital his preservation was hailed by his friends as little short of a miracle. It is therefore a pity that in 1471, when himself the victor at the battle of Tewkesbury, he violated the laws of sanctuary and slew Edward, Prince of Wales, and would have gone on to further slaughter had not a priest bearing the Host in his hand driven him from the church.

The House of Plantagenet were good friends to Walsingham even in its last sovereign, the much maligned Richard III. It is now widely conceded that Richard was a victim of Tudor intrigue. A whispering campaign against him blamed him for deaths which may well have been contrived in an effort to disgrace him. In this smear technique, as in many other ways, the Tudors indeed heralded the coming of a new regime which was to see the end of the shrine. Yet at its beginning Henry VII was determined to show that anything Plantagenets could do Tudors could do better. This was certainly true in relation to Walsingham, for soon after he came to the throne, while things were still uncertain, he made a pilgrimage to the Holy House and it is recorded that he prayed long and devoutly before the image of the Blessed Virgin that he might be delivered from the wiles of his enemies. He himself was something of an expert in 'wiles', but he seems to have had a great and sincere devotion to Our Lady. After the defeat of Lambert Simnel he sent his standard to be kept at the shrine for a memorial of what he regarded as an answer to prayer made there. He made many pilgrimages and many gifts to Walsingham. On one occasion be brought with him as his votive offering a kneeling figure of himself made of silver and gilt. His will reveals a very great devotion to Our Lady in all the many bequests he made to her shrines in various parts of the country, but Walsingham seems to have been his favourite.

He certainly passed on this devotion to his son, Henry VIII, and it is ironic that it should have been in his reign that the shrine was destroyed, for in his early years he was a most devout pilgrim. He is recorded as having walked barefoot to the shrine from East Barsham Manor and offering on this occasion a valuable necklace. His obsessive desire for a son may well have been responsible for his intense preoccupation with the

shrine, and he made payments for Masses to be said there and
wax candles to be burned before the image which continued
to be done right up to the time that the shrine was destroyed
in 1538. There is a tradition that on his deathbed he constantly
invoked Our Lady of Walsingham, and this may well be true,
for his personal religion never kept pace with the ideas of the
reformation. His much abused first wife, Katherine, was also
a devout pilgrim, and after the victory of Flodden Field she
wrote to the king ' . . . and with this I make an end, praying
God to send you home shortly, for without this no joy can be
accomplished; and for the same I pray, and now go to Our Lady
of Walsingham that I promised so long ago to see.' Poor lady,
she had a hard path to travel and we may hope she received
comfort at England's Nazareth, for she needed it. In her will
she provided 'that some personage go to Our Lady of Walsingham in pilgrimage, and in going by the way dole 20 nobles'.

Simply to record these very grand pilgrimages cannot give any
idea of the work, excitement and pageantry which must have
surrounded this small Norfolk village while they were taking
place. Inns and hostelries were to be seen on every side and an
old account tells us: 'On entering Walsingham from the south,
close to the walls of the Priory stood "le Beere", formerly "le
Dowe".' Then in the Friday market-place were the 'White
Horse' and 'Crownyd Lyon'; in the adjoining street the 'Mone
and Sterr', the 'Cokk', the 'Sarassyns Hede', the 'Swan' and
the 'Bull', which had appropriated part of the buildings of
the 'Angel now wasted'; and then the 'Ram' offered hospitality.
In Stonegate there were the 'Chekker' and the 'Bolt and Tonn'.
In North Town-end there were the 'White Hart' and the
'Madynhede'; by the Prior's water-mill the 'Gryffon' and the
'Bell'; in Church Street the 'Crane', and by the churchyard
the 'George'. And there were no doubt many more!
    Even the number named is a large one for a small village,
but the accommodation was needed. The commercialisation
of places of pilgrimage is always spoken of with great disapproval, but it is hard to see how it can be altogether avoided
because, with crowds of people gathered together, there is
money to be made simply from supplying their ordinary needs,
and there will always be those with the commercial sense to

take advantage of this. Sometimes the advantage is too greedily
taken and in 1431 four of the inns were burned down, which
was thought to be an act of revenge on the part of pilgrims who
had been grossly overcharged by the innkeepers.

The list of royal pilgrims does not mean that humbler people
did not come to the shrine in great numbers throughout these
centuries, but they have not left the same records behind them.
In so many cases we only know of the visit of particular and not
very important people to the shrine because of some misfortune
which took place on their journey. Thus we know that John le
Chaumpeneys and his mother were going on pilgrimage to
Walsingham in 1261 because he became involved in a man-
slaughter which led to legal action. Otherwise we might never
have heard either of him or of his pilgrimage. Here and there
the names of persons come to light because they died on pilgrimage or met with an accident, but we would wish to know
much more about the identity of the great crowds who jogged
along the Walsingham Ways.

In 1787 an antiquarian called John Fenn, who lived at
East Dereham, published some manuscript letters which he had
acquired from a chemist in Diss and which he called 'Original
letters written during the reigns of Henry VI, Edward IV,
Richard III and Henry VII, by various persons of rank and
consequence, and by members of the Paston family'. These
are now known as the Paston Letters, and their survival has
been a wonderful gain to historians for they throw considerable
light on the day-to-day affairs of a family of what might be called
the smaller gentry. Paston is a tiny place on the coast near
Cromer, so that it is not surprising that the family took a great
interest in the Priory of Bromholm, but they were close enough
to Walsingham to feel a special link, and throughout the letters
the place and the shrine are continually mentioned: people
known to them who have gone on pilgrimage, rumours that the
king is to be there, all show that in such circles Walsingham
played a natural and important part. When John Paston was
ill his wife immediately went on pilgrimage to the Holy House,
while his mother-in-law sent an offering of wax equivalent to
his weight.

A character who appears often in the Paston Letters is Sir
William Yelverton, who became involved with the Pastons in

the prolonged disputes about the disposition of the property of Sir John Fastolf, of whom he was an executor. In the course of one of the letters Sir William wrote to John Paston he urged him to support Our Lady's house at Walsingham. One would like to know whether he was eliciting support for some particular project, such as the rebuilding of the covering Chapel which must have been going on about this time, or simply directing attention to his own favourite charity, as someone in his position might well do today. The connection with Sir John Fastolf brought him in touch with William of Worcester, who for many years acted as Sir John's secretary, and they were both embroiled with Paston over the unfortunate will. It is this William of Worcester who left an account of his travels through England in his *Itinerarium* and was at Walsingham in 1479 when he mentions 'the new work', which seems to have been the covering Chapel; he gives dimensions of this and the Holy House it contained. Other measurements which he notes and which can be checked appear to be accurate, so that one is the more inclined to accept his findings where there is an aura of mystery.

Another literary discovery which has increased our knowledge of ordinary life in the early fifteenth century was *The Book of Marjory Kempe* published finally in 1936. It was a book which was known to exist, but unrepresentative selections in other works had led to the belief that she was a purely mystical writer. However, when the manuscript was discovered it was found to be a very vivid autobiography of a most unusual character and to give an account both of her travels and mystical experiences. She was something of an hysteric and much given to noisy lamentation whenever she heard Our Lord's passion spoken of in sermons, which not only annoyed the preacher but her neighbours. In 1433 she records going to Walsingham 'to worship in honour to Our Lady', but as she lived at Lynn she may well have been a regular visitor. Obviously there was no preaching of the Cross while she was there, so that she did not get embroiled with the clergy and we are deprived of many sidelights about the pilgrimage we might otherwise have enjoyed. To read her book takes one very vividly into the religious world of her time and one has a picture of the sort of setting in which pilgrims performed their devotions. Marjory, because of her pecularities, was often taken for a Lollard and indeed dragged before the bishop to be examined for heresy, which she much enjoyed as it put her in the limelight. We can see from her experience that already seeds of dissension were growing within the Church and that pilgrimages were one of the main targets for criticism. Chaucer has been claimed as an anti-clerical, but it would seem that he tried to give a fair presentation of fourteenth-century life as he saw it. With a character such as the 'Summoner' he is merciless in his satire, yet for the 'Poor Parson of a Town' he has nothing but praise and respect.

These are the sort of people and this is the sort of life which surrounded the shrine at Walsingham, but the truth is that nothing very sensational happened during its years of growth. There were miracles of healing, but then in the Middle Ages if you recovered from anything it was a miracle. There was also the moving of the house, which got embedded in legend, and the rather extraordinary wonder performed at what came to be known as The Knight's Gate. A plaque erected by the small north wicket gate of the Priory told how in 1314 Sir Ralph Bontetourt, being pursued on horseback by his enemy and approaching this entrance to sanctuary through which, fully armed and mounted as he was, he had no chance of passing, invoked Our Lady and immediately found himself and his horse within the priory grounds. There are many possible natural explanations of this event, but at the time it obviously caused a great stir and was regarded as the most notable miracle connected with the shrine.

The only pilgrim who has really left any full account of his visit came to Walsingham only shortly before the shrine was suppressed. It was Desiderius Erasmus who was regarded during his lifetime as the most famous scholar in Europe. There can be no doubt that his scurrilous satire on the Church's doctrines and institutions had a great deal to do with arousing the forces of the Reformation. Like many other trouble-makers, Erasmus himself kept clear of the upheaval for which he had been in part responsible and never got swept up in the Reformation itself. He was not a very lovable or admirable character. He was invited as a distinguished scholar to visit England, where he was already in touch with such men as Colet and More, and he stayed at the University of Cambridge. He seems to have visited Walsingham twice, probably in 1509 and 1511, and as a result wrote fairly fully about the shrine in his *Colloquy on Pilgrimage* which was published in 1526. This was a subtle attack on superstition, written in an ingenuous and seemingly innocent style, in which he records visits made to Walsingham and Canterbury.

It must be remembered that Erasmus was a foreigner who did not speak English very well, and it is obvious that on several matters he did not understand what he was being told. He reveals himself as something of an intellectual snob, making fun of the poor Canons at Walsingham because they did not understand Greek, which ought not to have been surprising, and displaying his own piety in a supercilious way which is rather disagreeable. However, he does provide us with the only picture we have of the shrine in its maturity, although we know from contemporary records of Episcopal Visitations held at that time that the affairs of the Priory were somewhat in disorder, and it is a pity that his visits did not take place at a period when there was less material for the censoriousness. As a rather affected literary device he tells his story in the form of a conversation held with a friend on his return to Antwerp.

He alone gives us some clue as to the general set-up of the place. He describes the Canons' church as 'well ordered and handsome' but goes on to say 'the Virgin does not occupy it . . . She has her own church that she may be on her Son's right hand.' He then says that the building is unfinished with open doors and windows. This may be the 'new work', spoken of by William of Worcester, still going on, although we know the windows were being reglazed about this time, which would have given the covering Chapel a feeling of incompleteness. He then gives us his impression of the Holy House, the only record of this sort which we have: 'Within the church which I have called unfinished is a small chapel, made of boards, and admitting devotees on each side by a narrow little door. The light is small, indeed scarcely any but from the wax lights. A most grateful fragrance meets the nostrils . . . you would say it was the mansion of the saints, so much does it glitter on all sides with jewels, gold and silver.' In spite of his cynicism, Erasmus has left us with a very clear picture of the awe and reverence which surrounded this little house of England's Nazareth. He then goes on to poke fun at the relics which were easy meat for satire.

Ever since the Crusades Western Christendom had been flooded with spurious relics. The residents of the Middle East have always had a talent for providing what they think visitors may want. They very soon discovered that the Crusaders wanted relics and they provided them in plenty. They were brought back and received in good faith, however fantastic they may seem to us. Erasmus particularly makes fun of the relic of Our Lady's Milk, which he treats in a very gross manner. It is almost certain that this was white chalky earth scraped from the 'Grotto of Our Lady's Milk' in Bethlehem and a favourite souvenir brought back by pilgrims from the Holy Land. How far this was really claimed as the Virgin's milk we cannot know, but it is a mistake which would easily arise amongst simple people. The fact that offerings made at the relic at that time amount to £2 2s. 3d. as opposed to £250 1s. od. offered at the altar of the Virgin show that pilgrims were not perhaps as credulous as Erasmus supposed.

When he tells us with irony of a shed over the wells which the sacristan claimed had been brought from a great distance and had an old bear skin in the rafters which proved its age, it would seem that it is Erasmus himself who is being made fun of – regrettable, perhaps, but not unnatural when a pompous foreigner tries to make fools of his hosts.

Some indication of the wide popularity of the shrine is given by the great number of wills which have come to light making bequests of money and property to the Holy House of Our Lady, and there must be many more, particularly in the registry at Norwich, which have not yet been noted. To record long lists of these would be very tedious, but a book did once exist called *Annals of the Chapel of Walsingham* It is quoted by the fifteenth century chronicler, John Capgrave, who had seen it, and we may well regret its disappearance for it must have contained an account of many gifts and events about which we know nothing.

It is well established that the treasury of the shrine was extremely wealthy, for Roger Ascham, who visited Cologne in

1550, makes the observation that 'the three Kings be not so rich, I believe, as was the Ladye of Walsingham'. It has already been noted that Henry VII had a silver gilt statue of himself made as a votive offering, but as early as 1381 William de Ufford, Earl of Sussex, gives directions: 'I will that a picture of a horse and a man, armed with my arms, be made in silver and offered to the altar of Our Ladye of Walsingham.' There must have been many such gifts which accumulated at the shrine over the years and became one of its attractions. In 1367 Sir Thomas Uvedale, a notable benefactor who founded a chantry, bequeathed a silver gilt tablet with the Salutation of the Blessed Virgin, together with a painted image. Perhaps the most touching offering recorded was that of Sir R. Wingfield, English Ambassador to the Emperor, who wrote to Henry VIII for permission to resign his functions in order to go to Walsingham and make a gift of his very full white beard to Our Lady. But the steady source of wealth was from the ordinary pilgrims who generally left a small piece of money in the Holy House where one of the Canons was in attendance to collect it, and this amounted to a considerable sum.

These thousands upon thousands of unidentified pilgrims are the real story of the rise of Walsingham. They came to the shrine by various routes which still retain memories of the hosts passing along them. Bishop Kirk has traced various lines of churches dedicated to the Assumption which seem to lead towards Walsingham, and his suggestion is that these owe their titles to the fact that they were used by pilgrims to the Marian Shrine. Special chapels for the pilgrims to pray in were built at Hillborough, Southacre, Westacre, Lynn, Priors-Thorns, Stanhoe, Caston and many other places. The closest to Walsingham in this line was built about 1380 at Houghton-in-the-Dale, a mile and a half outside the village. There is evidence that at one time it was in charge of a hermit who lived beside the chapel. It was dedicated to St Catherine and has been later known as the Slipper Chapel, from the tradition that the pilgrims walked into Walsingham barefooted from this point. We know that, like Henry VIII, they walked barefooted from anywhere they happened to start from, and it seems more likely that it was originally known as the Slype Chapel, which means a covered passage. We do not seem to have much knowledge of how these buildings were used by the pilgrims. Presumably they paused to say prayers and were able to have Mass if they had a priest with them. Some of the chapels were well endowed and probably had a priest attached to them. Thus the famous John Colet, Dean of St Paul's, held the wealthy chaplaincy of the pilgrim chapel at Hillborough, dedicated to St Margaret, but he presumably delegated most of his duties in connection with it.

The principal road for pilgrims was that which passed by Newmarket, Brandon and Fakenham. The Cluniac Priory at Castleacre had a particularly large guest house to give them shelter on their way. Those coming from the north crossed the Wash near Long Sutton and went through Lynn, passing the priories of Flitcham, Rudham and Cokesford where they would have received hospitality. Another route came from the east, through Norwich and Attleborough where the Bec Hospital was founded with thirteen free beds for poor pilgrims each night. All these routes were known as The Walsingham Way. The mysterious track known as the Pedders Way, which can be followed right across the county to the coast at Holme, seems to have been earlier than the shrine at Walsingham and not connected with pilgrimage.

There was a connection with the continent, particularly the Lowlands, and such pilgrims would have come by sea and landed at Lynn. The cost of a pilgrimage to Walsingham from Ghent is put down as four livres. On landing at Lynn they went straight to give thanks for a safe journey at the Red Mount Chapel, which was built about 1485 as a pilgrim chapel. It is a very remarkable building, which appears outside to be a red brick octagonal tower but inside is an exquisite little cruci-form chapel of stone with a roof which resembles that of King's College Chapel, Cambridge. The image venerated within the chapel, and known as Our Lady of the Red Mount, was most likely a copy of that within the Holy House at Walsingham.

The shrine and the Priory developed side by side but were, of course, separate institutions. The Canons obviously had a lot of work in connection with the pilgrims, although there were other chantry priests who said Mass at the shrine. In King Henry VIII's book of payments there is an entry for: 'William Halys, King's priest, singing before Our Lady at Walsingham, half a years wages 100s.' There is also mention of another priest 'Sir Richard Warde, singing before Our Lady at Walsingham'. In the same book there are payments made for the King's candle to be kept burning there.

We know that the Canons had considerable bother about guarding the very large amount of treasure given to the shrine over the ages. In the Episcopal Visitations we find directions given for the door of the treasury to have two locks, one key to be kept by the Prior and another by a senior brother. We also know that the priory gates had to be kept locked at night to guard against thieves. All these things, together with the constant comings and goings, must have been a disturbance to the orderly living of the religious life.

It is not surprising that Visitations of the Priory reveal disorders, although we must remember that many of these are complaints made by disaffected members of the community and may not have been true. For example, it is hard to believe that Prior Lowthe, 1504–1514, kept an old fool whom he took in public processions wearing a surplice and insisted on his being given Holy Communion with the Community. He must have had a lot of enemies or been slightly mad for he was also accused of misappropriating the treasure and consorting with the wife of John Smith, who had been given a key to his lodging. The Visitor, who was the Bishop of Norwich, appears to have considered that there was some truth in all this, for Prior Lowthe was forced to resign, which was just as well, for it was also claimed that he had made wild threats against those who had acted as informers.

Another stormy period in the life of the Priory was during the priorate of John Snoring from 1374 to 1401. He appears to have been a very ambitious man and to have engaged in controversy with both the Bishop of Norwich and King Richard II in an attempt to get the status of the house raised to that of an Abbey. This would have released it from Episcopal Visitation, placed it directly under the Roman See, and raised his own status to that of a mitred Abbot. In pursuit of this the Prior had to go to Rome and seriously impoverished the Priory in the legal fees and bribes he paid. It was all to no avail and Archbishop Arundel came to Walsingham and carried out a visitation which ended with the removal of the Prior from office.

This was a fairly common type of controversy in the Middle Ages and contains in it all the seeds of worldliness and love of power which were eating out the heart of the Church.

It is easy to see how the defects in human nature can impose themselves even upon the noblest ideals and degrade them. This had certainly happened in the case of pilgrimage. There were those who were eager to make money out of it, there were those who found it convenient to get away from home, there were those who found it easier to wander about than settle to any work. As the forces of the reformation gathered momentum we have plenty of evidence that all these things were going on, but it is hard to believe that the simple faith which had made men and women long to visit England's Nazareth had completely died away and been replaced by corrupt and venal motives.

Late in 1536 there is a record of some Cornish soldiers who were coming from the north to visit Walsingham and in June 1537 there were men from Lincolnshire there on pilgrimage, but the first era of the history of the shrine was drawing to a close.

3
Destruction of the Shrine

IT IS VERY EASY to over-simplify the issues of the Reformation by regarding it simply as a reaction against grave superstition and abuse. So many elements are entangled that it sometimes becomes difficult to assess how far different forces were at work. All sorts of ideals and ideas were struggling to be born throughout Europe, and in so far as the Church was an integral part of the mediaeval structure, so it caught the main assault of the new learning which was gripping and changing men's minds. The Great Schism, during which for a long time there appeared to be two Popes, had seriously weakened the idea of the papacy in men's eyes and John Wycliffe, as far back as the fourteenth century, had started an attack on the Church as an institution. His 'poor preachers' had singled out clerical celibacy, transubstantiation, indulgences and pilgrimages for particular criticism. Already these things were in men's minds and the force of many of the arguments was demonstrated by obvious abuses in the name of religion which spoke for themselves.

In addition to this, new social structures were springing up and new economic factors making themselves felt, so that the whole of Europe was in a ferment. In the midst of this upheaval a strong character like Martin Luther was able to wield an enormous influence. He broke no new controversial ground, he simply hammered away at the weak points already indicated long ago by Wycliffe. As a theologian his study of St Augustine led him to the conclusion that too much emphasis had been placed upon 'good works', but he did not regard himself as an innovator and always claimed to be returning to a primitive excellence which had been lost. Having rejected the papacy as a centre of authority Luther developed the idea of the 'godly prince' to whom the plenitude of power was confided for the protection and direction of God's people. The tragedy is that Rome would make no attempt whatever to come to terms with these things and simply fortified herself for warfare and, even when conceding the need for reformation, set about it with as little contact with the reformers as possible.

The reformation in England took very much its own course, as it was a response to social and political pressures peculiar to this island. The English had for many centuries been regarded as heretics on the continent and they had a long history of resentment at the interference of the papacy. The troubles of Prior John Snoring at Walsingham would seem to stem largely from his appeal to Rome at a time when King Richard II was so sensitive to anti-papal feeling that he had revived the Statutes banning papal provisions and appeals to papal courts on certain important matters; so that it was not only the Tudors who felt that the ideal of monarchy was that its sovereignty should extend into all spheres of national life, including the church and the governance of the clergy. Yet the person and character of Henry VIII undoubtedly had a profound influence on the nature of the reformation in England. He was quite naturally much influenced by his exceedingly pious father, and being a precocious child he readily absorbed the cultural influence of the renaissance during his formative years. It has often been said that he was intended for the priesthood and that, had his brother lived, he would have been launched upon an ecclesiastical career. There is no evidence for this except that theology was amongst his major interests and with youthful enthusiasm he set himself up as a champion of orthodoxy against the reformers. In 1521 he published his defence of the seven sacraments against Luther, for which he was given by Pope Leo X the title of Defender of the Faith, of which he was inordinately proud. He regarded himself as a traditionalist and throughout his life he showed a great zeal in the outward practices of religion. He attended several Masses each day and we have seen evidence that he was an enthusiastic supporter of the cult at Walsingham.

Under such a king the reformation movement was unlikely to make much progress and it is doubtful whether it would have got started at all had it not been for a great personal conflict within the monarch between his sensual appetites and his conscience. There have been those who have dismissed the king's talk of his conscience as a hypocritical ruse for getting out of a situation he found inconvenient, but we very much mistake his character if we believe this. The psychopathic qualities which in old age turned him into something of a monster were not at all evident at the beginning of his reign and he was hailed with enthusiasm as being a fitting symbol of the new age. He appeared to be liberal, generous and open, and he charmed his subjects wherever he went. How far he was uneasy when he was given a dispensation to marry his brother's widow we do not know, but when it became evident that she was not going to give him a son, what had been a slight uneasiness became a mania. He had tried all the right celestial doors, his pilgrimage to Walsingham had been for this intention, and they seemed to be closed to him. He was a very over-sexed man and for some time the devout and slightly frigid Katherine had not been able to satisfy him. Yet when he consoled himself with any of the not unwilling ladies of the court his sensitive conscience tormented him with the thought that this was adding to the divine displeasure which was threatening to leave him without an heir. This to a Tudor with memories of what it had cost to secure the throne was an intolerable situation. He began to take steps to get his marriage dissolved and instituted an inquiry, held by Wolsey as papal legate with Archbishop Warham as assessor, on the possibility that Katherine's child Mary was not legitimate. Katherine made a sworn statement that her first marriage had never been consummated.

Everybody concerned was now in a very delicate situation and started playing for time, but Henry was already developing an overpowering impatience and a wild fury with anyone or anything which prevented him from getting his own way. Pope Clement VII was ready and anxious to be obliging about almost everything, but anything prejudicial to Katherine of Aragon involved him in the greatest embarrassment as he was virtually the prisoner of her nephew Charles V. Thus when Henry sent his secretary, William Knight, to Rome to sue for a decree of nullity coupled, ingenuously enough, with a plea for a dispensation to marry Anne Boleyn, needed because her elder sister had been Henry's mistress, it is not surprising that he was unable to get any very definite results. In July 1526 Clement at last made a move – which was to revoke the cause to Rome where Katherine would have rather more chance of being fairly represented. Henry was furious at this attempt to make him plead his cause outside his own realm, and Wolsey was ruthlessly made the scapegoat and died with the pathetic complaint: 'Had I but served God as diligently as I have served the King, he would not have given me over in my grey hairs!'

From this time Henry turned his attention to the possibility of repudiating papal authority altogether and gave his support to reforming elements in the country who would otherwise have been kept in check. A Cambridge don, called Thomas Cranmer, suggested that opinions should be sought from foreign universities outside the dominions of Charles V, and was himself sent to collect such opinions which in the event were not surprisingly all favourable to the king. Henry was clever enough to realise that he must associate as many of his people as possible with his design to transfer the headship of the Church of England from the Pope to himself. Cranmer was made Archbishop and, an Act forbidding appeals to Rome having been passed, Henry suggested that he and Katherine should appear before the Archbishop at Dunstable. There, in spite of Katherine's refusal to attend, her marriage was declared invalid.

Clement, stung into action by this, excommunicated Henry and declared his divorce and remarriage to be null and void. The first Act of Succession entailed the crown on Anne Boleyn's children, and imposed an oath which men of the stamp of Sir Thomas More and Bishop John Fisher simply could not take and so suffered execution in 1535. From this moment the process for the dissolution of the monasteries really began to gather momentum, and it was in this upheaval that the Priory at Walsingham and the shrine were destroyed.

The last Prior of Walsingham was Richard Vowell who was elected in 1514. It is easy to condemn him as a weak and time-serving man, but such evidence as we have seems to show that he made great efforts to save his monastery, and almost to the last he had hopes that it might be transformed into some sort of College. We know now that he was fighting a losing battle and that Thomas Cromwell was determined to close down all religious houses by fair means or foul. The concessions which Vowell made, often with great qualms of conscience, were not likely to affect the outcome. He was in much the same position as those who tried to negotiate with Hitler before the Second World War.

In 1534 the Prior and entire Community acknowledged the Royal Supremacy. We do not know what went on in the Chapter House, but obviously Prior Vowell was able to persuade the brethren that this was the only course to take although the terms of the document were bound to have caused some of them great scruples. It runs:

> Let all to whom the present writing may come know that we, the Prior and Community of the Priory of Walsingham, in the diocese of Norwich, with one mouth and voice, and with the unanimous consent and assent of all, by this deed, given under our common seal in our chapter-house, do, for ourselves and our successors, all and each, for ever, declare, attest and faithfully promise and undertake, that we, the said Prior and our Community and our successors, all and each, will ever render an entire, inviolate, sincere, and perpetual fidelity, submission, and reverence to the lord our King, Henry the Eighth, and to Queen Anne, his Consort, and to the issue of him by the said Anne lawfully begotten, as well as to be begot; and that we will make known, preach, and counsel the same to the people whenever an opportunity or an occasion shall be given. Item, that we hold as confirmed and ratified, and will always and for ever hold, that the aforesaid Henry our King is the Head of the Anglican Church.
>
> Item, that the Bishop of Rome who in his Bulls usurps the name of Pope and arrogates to himself the sovereignty of Chief Bishop, has not any greater jurisdiction conferred on him by God than any other extern Bishop.
>
> Item, that none of us, in any holy discourse to be held in private or in public, shall call the said Bishop of Rome by the name of Pope or Chief Bishop, but by the name of the

Bishop of Rome, or of the Roman Church; and that none of us shall pray for him as Pope, but as Bishop of Rome.

Item, that we will adhere to the said lord the King alone, and to his successors and will maintain his laws and decrees, renouncing for ever the laws, decrees, and canons of the Bishop of Rome which shall be contrary to the Divine Law and Holy Scripture.

Item, that not one of all of us shall, in any sermon, public or private, attempt to misconstrue any passage taken from Holy Scripture into a foreign sense; but each shall preach, in a catholic and orthodox manner, Christ and His words and actions, simply, openly, sincerely, and to the form and rule of the Holy Scriptures and of the truely catholic and orthodox doctors.

Item, that each of us, in his accustomed prayers and supplications, shall recommend to God and the prayers of the people, first of all the King as the Supreme Head of the Anglican Church, then Queen Anne with her offspring and then, lastly the Archbishop of Canterbury and of York with the other orders of clergy as shall seem fit.

Item, that we all and each aforesaid, Prior, Community and our successors, firmly bind ourselves by the pledge of our conscience and our oath; and that we will faithfully and for ever observe all and each of the promises aforesaid. In testimony whereof we have affixed our common seal to this writing, and each with his own hand, have sub-scribed our names. Given in our Chapter-house the 18th day of the month of September the year of the Lord 1534.

Their signatures follow headed by that of the Prior, but most of them must have signed that document with a heavy heart. It had obviously been drawn up by a lawyer, but it must have appeared very strange to older members of the community who had little knowledge of what was going on in the world. Prior Vowell had probably persuaded them that to sign this would be likely to save their house from any possible molestation by the authorities. However, even as they were signing it the information for the Valor Ecclesiasticus, which was a survey of the wealth of the English Church, was being compiled. This was a first step towards taking over monastic property and, as it showed Walsingham amongst the most wealthy houses, it was not in the least likely to be overlooked. Indeed, already there were being drawn up some Articles of Enquiry which were intended as a guide to the Commissioners who were to go into the matter. They are undated and anonymous, but they were obviously drawn up by someone who had read Erasmus's account of Walsingham and show quite clearly the harm his style of smear technique could do. The questions are interesting as they show a preoccupation with the treasure coupled with a heresy hunt against superstition. Slightly shortened, they run thus:

1. Whether there was any inventory of jewels, relics, ornaments and plate?
2. If there was no inventory is there a book recording jewels which have been given to Our Lady?
3. Whether any of these things have been alienated, sold or pledged – if so, to whom and for how much?
4. What were the main relics and how were they esteemed?
5. What have they to show that the relics are genuine?
6. In how many places were relics exposed and were people pestered to make offerings to them?
7. Why were the relics shown in several and not in one place?
8. What was the offering made to Our Lady and to the relics on an average?
9. If the relics have been laid aside, how long ago was this done and why?
10. What was the greatest miracle claimed to have been worked by Our Lady or by the relics and what proof was there of these things?
11. If the fact was well proved what proof is there that it could not have been worked by natural means?
12. If that was proved, why could it not have proceeded directly from God and why should it be attributed to Our Lady or, if so, why to the particular image of Our Lady in that house?
13. Whether the miracles were proclaimed from the pulpit?
14. What was the legend of the building of the Lady Chapel and when was the image first put there? What of the house

where the bear skin is and what of the Knight and other wonders claimed there and what proofs are there of these things? (One can see the influence of Erasmus here.)

15. Whether they know that miracles should not be lightly claimed unless there is clear proof?

16. Whether Our Lady performed as many miracles now as she did when there were greater offerings made to her?

17. What proof they took of miracles claimed by pilgrims and whether they were accepted on the parties' own report or whether witnesses and depositions were taken?

18. Whether Our Lady's milk was liquid?

19. Who was Sexton ten years ago, that he may be examined as to whether he renewed Our Lady's milk when it dried up or whether he had invented any relic for profit; whether the house over the wells were not made in time of remembrance or at least renewed? (Here again the questions reflect Erasmus's muddle.)

There is no record of any answers made to these questions, but they show the pressure which was being exerted to discredit the shrine. There is, however, a letter written to Cromwell by Richard Southwell:

It may please your good lordship to be advised that Sir Thomas Lestrange and Mr Hoges, according to the sequestration delegated to them, have been at Walsingham, and have there sequestrated all such money, plate, jewels and stuff as was there in the inventory. Among other things they did find a secret privy place within the house, where no canon or any other member of the house did ever enter, as they claim, in which there were instruments, pots, bellows, flies of such strange colours as the like none of us had ever seen with weights and other things to sort and refine gold and silver, nothing being wanting that belongs to the art of multiplying. Of which things they desired me to advise you by these letters also that from Saturday night to the following Sunday there was offered 33 shillings and 4 pence beside wax. Of this multiplying it may please you to have them examined and so advise them of your further pleasure.

This is dated 25 July 1536, and shows that with the sequestration of the valuables the intentions of the Commissioners are beginning to be revealed. The little laboratory is thought to have been the place where pilgrim tokens were made, but it is odd that the community claimed to know nothing about it, as this would have been a perfectly respectable explanation. It is possible that the room had been rented to someone in the village who was using it for making counterfeit coin. If this is so, it was very unfortunate that it should have come to light at this particular moment when every blemish in their administration was being carefully noted.

The year 1536 must have been a difficult year for the Priory because, in common with other religious houses in the diocese of Norwich, they suffered one of the standard visitations from royal officials who were collecting material to justify the complete dissolution of all monasteries. These visitations can hardly be taken very seriously, as they were made by men of dubious character who were acting as tools for an unscrupulous authority and had already made up their minds what they were going to find before they arrived. They do not seem to have had very much imagination, for they repeated the same accusations about fleshly sins over and over again in almost the same words. While such disorders were certainly going on in some religious houses, it is hard to believe the situation was exactly the same in all of them, unless one takes a very poor view of human nature. Potential robbers can hardly expect to be accepted as very reliable witnesses, and so we may well allow the poor monks and nuns the benefit of the doubt in the grosser charges brought against them. There is a letter from the Prior of Walsingham to Cromwell written in September 1536 which shows he was conscious of the trouble which was brewing for them, and was doing his best to counteract some false report which had been made in their name, although he does not make clear what this had been. There was obviously cause for serious alarm if this was being done and the Canons must have felt surrounded by enemies.

By this time, although the pilgrimages were still going on, one did not need to be very sophisticated to realise that their days were numbered. This would have been the moment when the ancient and much loved image could have been taken from the Holy House and another substituted. The fact that it was probably dressed in a veil and cope would have made it easier to effect the change with only a few realising what had happened. There have been stories handed down that this is what was done and there have been expectations that the image might one day be found walled up or hidden in the earth. At one time some digging took place in the cellar of the house where Nicholas Mileham, the Sub-Prior, is supposed to have been imprisoned and which is still known as the Martyrs House, but nothing was discovered. Against this theory is the fact that we know a careful inventory had been made and the King's Commissioners were only too conscious that something of this kind might take place. The penalties when they discovered such deception were very severe and must have provided a strong deterrent. Also it would have needed the Prior's knowledge and consent before such an action could have been taken, and from what we know of Richard Vowell he appears to have been more than anxious to keep on the right side of the law.

The year 1537 was a very unfortunate year for Walsingham because in the spring of this year it was claimed that a rebellion was being planned at the shrine. This was the time of the Pilgrimage of Grace in the northern counties when there was a very strong reaction on the part of the common people against the suppression of the smaller monasteries. The King and the Government became extremely nervous and employed spies and informers everywhere, and the sort of thing which happened at Walsingham was the result. It was reported to Cromwell that a man called Ralph Rogerson, talking to a native of Walsingham named George Gysburghe, had said: 'You see how these abbeys go down and our living goeth away with them; for within a while Binham shall be put down and also Walsingham and all other abbeys in the country.' This was a very moderate statement of the truth, but it was claimed that they then went on to discuss means of preventing further destruction and a plot was hatched to rebel. A Letheringsett man, called John Galant, seems to have betrayed the affair. He may have heard the original conversation but he also knew of a shooting match at Binham which was to be used as a cover for a seditious gathering. John Galant reported the affair to his master, Sir John Heydon, who was a great supporter of the government and a great alarmist who immediately took the most serious view of the whole thing. He wrote hastily to Southwell of 'a great

insurrection like to be among the King's subjects about Walsingham', and he says: 'Tonight or early in the morning I intend
to be at Walsingham to apprehend some of these rebels and
trust to hear from my lord how I should act.'

Sir John was obviously ready for heavy action, so that it
comes as rather an anticlimax to find Southwell reporting to
Cromwell: 'the conspirators do not pass twelve in numbers,
all very beggars and there is no likelihood of any commotion'.
The only big catch was the Sub-Prior, Nicholas Mileham, who
seems to have got himself involved in this very minor expression
of dissatisfaction, and there is a suspicion that the information
against him was laid by the Prior, Richard Vowell. There is
no evidence for this, but it cannot be entirely discountenanced
for the Prior was doing all in his power to save his house at this
time and ingratiate himself with Cromwell; and it is the sort of
situation in which he may well have felt justified in throwing
one person to the wolves if by so doing he could save the rest of
the Community. He would not be the first person to decide
that one man should die for the people.

Henry was at his most ruthless in dealing with the Pilgrimage
of Grace and the attendant disorders, and letters were sent to
Norfolk ordering punishment 'without sparing' for all those in
any way involved. It was suggested that the executions should
be held in different parts of the county to have the maximum
effect as a deterrent. On 30 May 1537, Nicholas Mileham
and George Guisborough were hung, drawn and quartered as
well as beheaded in a field at Walsingham. It is still known
locally as 'The Martyrs Field' and lies behind the former railway station.

Those who hoped that the shrine might be spared must have
been very depressed by this incident and in June there was
more trouble, for it would seem that during a pilgrimage of
four men from Lincolnshire a beggar at the door of the shrine
made such a nuisance of himself that they asked a priest to deal
with him. Whether this was one of the Canons is not made clear.
The beggar was so saucy that the priest called the constable and
had him put into the stocks. As a revenge he claimed that he had
heard the priest say to the men that 'if Norfolk and Suffolk
would have risen when Lincolnshire and Yorkshire did, that
they had been able to have gone through the realm'. In ordinary

times such an incident would have passed unnoticed, but after the recent troubles and executions it was taken by the authorities to be further evidence that the shrine was a hot-bed of discontent.

It is uncertain when the image was removed from the house, but it may have been soon after the executions and this fuss made by the beggar. In July 1538 the Prior reported to Cromwell that the Commissioners had taken the image away as also the gold and silver and treasures. He complained that under these conditions they were liable to be put to great expense by being unable to fulfil their obligations. This probably means that he was afraid that those families who had endowed Masses might demand the return of the endowment when they discovered that they were not being performed under the conditions upon which they were given, and it would appear that the saying of Mass in the Holy House had ceased.

The Canons must have realised by this time that the Prior's efforts to keep the house in being were going to be thwarted, and have been making plans for their futures. The blow fell in July when Sir Richard Gresham received instructions that 'the King's pleasure is that the priory of Walsingham be dissolved', and he at once notified the Prior of this. It must have been a bleak meeting in the Chapter House when he passed on the message to the brethren, and on 4 August they met in the same place before the royal commissioner, Sir William Petre, to execute the deed of surrender. Sir William afterwards became Secretary of State and received large grants out of the spoils from the monasteries. During the reign of Queen Mary he obtained a papal bull permitting him to keep them and his family became notable recusants.

The problem was how the former Canons were to be provided for. The Prior, calling himself simply 'Priest', wrote to Cromwell begging for the parsonage of Walsingham for himself and for some settlement to be made for the financial security of his brethren. Four days later Sir Richard Gresham wrote on his behalf, urging that he was a 'very discreet and learned man of good name and can set forth the Word of God very well, whereof the town hath great need'. He also refers to him as 'both impotent and lame'.

In the event Vowell did not have the chance of introducing the new Services to the people of Walsingham, but he was made Vicar of North Creake, which was a very valuable living. In spite of his decrepit physical condition he managed to get married and found a family. Most of the rest of the Community received benefices or pensions and these pensions continued to be paid throughout all the religious upheavals of the next three reigns. Even in the time of James I there were a few ex-religious still on pension and they were all faithfully paid until their deaths. Presumably when the Canons left Walsingham the church ceased to be used, and it is probable that special precautions were taken to destroy all things particularly associated with the cult.

It seems to have been Latimer's idea that there should be a grand burning of cult-images as a blow against superstition. The figure of Our Lady of Walsingham was an obvious choice if such a demonstration was to be made. This deliberate act of sacrilege is supposed to have taken place in the courtyard of Cromwell's house in Chelsea, but there is some confusion about the date of the bonfire. In Wriothesley's *Chronicle in England* he says: 'Also in this year (1538) in the month of July, the images of Our Lady of Walsingham and Ipswich were brought up to London with all the jewels that hung about them, at the King's Command, and divers other images both in England and Wales, that were used for common pilgrimages, so that the people should use no more idolatry to them, and they were burnt at Chelsea by my Lord Privy Seal.' Yet another account says: 'In September, by the special motion of Lord Cromwell, all the notable images unto which were made any special pilgrimages and offering were utterly taken away, as the images of Walsingham, Ipswich, Worcester, the Lady of Willesden with many others.' There may have been two burnings but Chelsea is probably the place where the image, to which so many English kings and their subjects had devoutly bowed the knee, was destroyed with a blasphemy which only very strong feelings could have dictated. It is the more surprising when we know that the king's own personal religion had not changed much and that he would have found such a spectacle very distasteful.

Those who were distressed by these things had learned to

keep their mouths shut. In January 1540 Sir Roger Townsend wrote to Cromwell about a poor woman of Wells, the little sea port near Walsingham, who had imagined a false miracle done by the image of Our Lady of Walsingham since the same was brought from thence to London. The tale had been traced back to this poor old soul who was put in the stocks at Walsingham on Market Day with a card reading 'a reporter of false tales' hung round her neck. She was then dragged round the town in a cart while youths threw snowballs at her, which shows that the month is correct, and she was then returned to the stocks till evening. He ends his letter 'How be it I cannot perceive, but the said image is not yet out of some of their heads'.

It must have remained in many heads with a great sense of nostalgia and one would like to know some of the thoughts which passed through the mind of ex-Prior Vowell as he sat by the fire in his comfortable rectory at North Creake. The most eloquent expression of the grief felt at the destruction of Walsingham is given in a poem which exists in a manuscript in the Bodleian Library at Oxford, and is attributed to Philip, Earl of Arundel:

> In the wrackes of Walsingham
> Whom should I chuse
> But the Queen of Walsingham
> to be guide to my muse?
> Then thou Prince of Walsingham
> graunt me to frame
> bitter plaintes to rewe they wronge,
> bitter wo for thy name.
>
> Bitter was it, oh to see
> the seely sheepe
> murdered by the raveninge wolves
> while the sheephards did sleep.
> Bitter was it, Oh to vewe
> the sacred vyne,
> whiles the gardiners plaied all close,
> rooted up by the swine.

Bitter, bitter, oh to behould
the grasse to growe
Where the walles of Walsingham
so statly did shewe.
Such were the workes of Walsingham
while shee did stand.
Such are the wrackes as now do shewe
of that holy land!
Levell, levell with the ground
the towers do lye.

Which with their golden glitteringe tops
pearsed once to the skye.
Where were gates, no gates are nowe;
the waies unknowen
where the press of peers did passe
while her fame was blowen.
Oules do scrike where the sweetest himnes
lately were songe;
Toades and serpentes hold their dennes
wher the Palmers did thronge.

Weepe, weepe, O Walsingham
whose dayes are nightes,
Blessings turned to blasphemies,
holy deedes to dispites.
Sinne is wher Our Ladie sate,
heaven turned is to hell,
Sathan sittes wher Our Lord did swaye,
Walsingham, ohfarew ell.

4
The Years Between

IF ONE HAS VISITED the buildings of a large school out of
term time one may have experienced something of what the
monasteries were like immediately after the dissolution: long
empty corridors, a silent unused chapel and a great feeling of
emptiness.

There was, however, an unseemly rush to get hold of monastic
property and most of it did not remain untenanted for long.

Walsingham would seem to have been left empty for a year
and probably a lot of movable things quietly disappeared during
that time. Much of the property went to Sir Thomas Gresham,
but on 7 November, 1539, Thomas Sidney, an ancestor
of Sir Philip Sidney, who already lived in Walsingham as
Master of the Leper Hospital, bought the buildings and the
site of the Priory for £90, which even in those days was a small
sum for such an estate. There is a story that he was supposed
to have been buying it on behalf of the town and for their use,
but having effected the sale he kept it for himself. The buildings
must have presented many problems in their adaptation for
family use and Thomas Sidney set about building a new house
incorporating some of the old building. This meant the demoli-
tion of much of the Priory and there seems to have been some
kind of sale of materials not required in the rebuilding. There
is a reference to 'windows, doors, stone called free-stone, glass,
iron and tiles' being disposed of in lots, and many ancient buildings in the vicinity probably have bits of the Priory built into
them. In the last century some mediaeval alabasters were

discovered in a barn at East Barsham which were thought to have come from Walsingham. One of St Anne still remains in the church at East Barsham. A few years ago, during the restoration of a house on the site of the former Leper Hospital in Bridewell Street, some carved panelling was found hidden within the walls. It is not easy to identify the saints represented, and because of the apparent trouble taken to hide it the suggestion has been made that it was part of the decoration in the Holy House. This is doubtful but it is likely to have come from some part of the Priory.

Some of the manuscripts survived, the most interesting of which is a Breviary now in Keble College library at Oxford. It has the Rule of St Augustine arranged to be read on each day of the week and may well have been used in the refectory pulpit which can still be seen at Walsingham. There is also in existence a small collection of prayers which belonged to Prior Vowell, a very fine volume of a twelfth-century bible and a collection of medical writings of the thirteenth and fourteenth centuries, but apart from these nothing else is known to have survived from what must have been a considerable library.

The Priory obviously had a house in Norwich, for a door from it remains in the Stranger's Hall Museum with an inscription in memory of Prior Lowthe, who, it will be remembered, was deposed for rather curious behaviour.

There was some glass in the parish church which was said to have come from the Prior's Lodging, but it was destroyed in the fire which burned most of the church in 1961.

This is not a very large number of remains to represent the vast possessions of one of the wealthiest monasteries in England.

The Sidneys held the property for a hundred years, but left little trace of themselves except for a fine monument in the parish church, much damaged but luckily not destroyed in the fire which burned up the font cover given by Jane Sidney. They are a good example of the families which greatly enriched themselves from the fall of the monasteries and for whom the Reformation became a vested interest.

In the reign of Charles I the property was bought by John Warner who was Bishop of Rochester from 1637 to 1666 and an ardent royalist. He went into exile during the Civil War but lived to take part in the coronation of Charles II. He enlarged the house, which was now called 'The Abbey' so that poor Prior Snoring's aspirations were fulfilled at last with no expense whatever.

The bishop's sister married into the Lee family of Shropshire, and as he had no children his estate passed to her son John, who had become Archdeacon of Rochester, which showed that his uncle already had his interests at heart. He took the name of Lee-Warner and founded a family which owned the estate at Walsingham for the next three hundred years. They were interesting people and maintained strong connections with the church, producing many generations of parsons. Once or twice the male line of the Lee-Warner family family died out but it was always continued from the female side. There was always a streak of eccentricity in them, in the best English tradition.

The Abbey was turned into a farm and sheep grazed over the site of the Canons' church and the place where so many pilgrims had knelt in prayer. The carefully kept domestic accounts show that at Michaelmas 1688 '1800 and 5 score sheep, ewes and rams' were bought. Other items recorded in 1695 which have a human and local interest are payments made 'for candles bought at Fakenham and for a Periwig'; 'for ye weeder for clensing Wighton river'; 'Cost of our servant Jane coming by water to Wells'.

There is an engraving by Buck, dated 1738, which shows that by that time nothing remained of the church but the great east window, as it does today, and that there was not much more of the monastic buildings than we can now see. It does show, however, that there was an elegant eighteenth-century house and that the gardens had been laid out with a formal elegance of hedges and shrubs.

Something of the eccentricity of the family comes to light in an account of a visit to Walsingham in 1798 and published in a book entitled *Gleanings in England* by Mr Pratt. The author records that as he approached Walsingham he noticed that most of the trees and shrubs had been cut down. The reason for this he discovered in conversation with a Mr Jacobs, who was landlord of a public house. The Squire, said Mr Jacobs, allowed the tenants and the village to take whatever they liked, and they repaid him by cutting down everything they could

find on his estate. The most he would say on coming across
someone stealing his timber was: 'Take care how you get down
that tree, or you may hurt yourself'. He did not get much chance
to see them often for he had turned night into day and arose
and had breakfast in the evening, his dinner in the small hours
and retired to bed again as the dawn was breaking. He was
obviously a pacifist of extreme convictions and Mr Jacob
recounted a story of his rescuing a fly from a spider's web, but
taking care not to damage the web or harm the spider. He then
left the fly lying on his silk handkerchief till it should recover
and remarked mildly: 'I suppose everything that has life
wishes to live as long as it can, friend Jacobs, and as so many
animals die that we may live, it is the least we can do to save
one or two when we can.' The estate was swarming with birds
as he would not have them touched but fed them with his
own hand, so that they even lighted on his head and shoulders
entirely unafraid. Many of his tenants never bothered to pay
their rent and he never reproved them. They used all his farm
implements as if they were their own and none of his men
bothered to question anyone removing anything, for the
offender would say: 'Let the Squire come and tell me so himself', and they knew that, if asked, the Squire would simply say,
'Let them have it.' He had even himself refused to remonstrate
when he discovered a group of men cutting down his favourite
chestnut tree.

Mr Pratt was anxious to meet this strange character and got
himself invited to dinner, which took place at 4 a.m. He found
him old fashioned in his dress, but very alert and well read and
extremely courteous.

Pratt gives a history of the shrine in his book which shows
that he had done a lot of reading about it, including Erasmus.
He begins by saying: 'In our days of darkness and superstition,
when priests and monks ruled not only the consciences but the
purses of the English laity, they who had not made a pilgrimage
and an offering at the shrine of the Blessed Virgin of this place
were looked upon as impious and irreligious.' Most of his
account was written in this rather ironic tone, but his most
interesting personal encounter was undoubtedly with a deaf
and lame old gardener at what had begun to be called 'the
wishing wells'. The old man said to him: 'If you are for a wish,

sir, now is your time; and they do say you may have just what you will; though, for my part, I have been wishing here these thirty years and have not got my wish yet.' He revealed that his wishes had been about his deafness and lameness which remained unaltered, and then he said: 'I have wished a hundred times the Squire would let this yard and wilderness be kept in the trim it used to be, and that he would get someone to trim the thieves that rob him of all they can lay hold of, but no such luck. Why, as sure as you are alive, sir, they come into the yard and garden in broad day, knowing master is safe in bed, and carry off what comes to hand, without taking any more notice of me than if I was a dead thing: and a dead thing I don't doubt they would soon make of me, if I was to say much to them. A pure good man – a right good master – and won't harm a worm: pity, an't, sir, he should let them go on thus. Well, it's no use to talk to him; he's fast asleep, I suppose, now, God bless him! – it's some comfort though, there is little or nothing left for the rogues to take, without they begin upon the garden trees here, which I dare say they will when they have cleared the abbey-yard of the fell'd and standing timber now in it.'

One cannot help feeling that Mr Pratt is somewhat exaggerating things to make a good story, but Squire Lee-Warner must have been an interesting character at a time when England was rich in such eccentrics, and many of his ideals were certainly Christian when enthusiasm of any sort was regarded with the gravest suspicion.

The upheaval of the Reformation, in which Walsingham with its shrine and religious houses was destroyed, led to a century of fierce controversy in which the Established Church of England tried to steer a middle course between the Papists and the Puritans. She had both these elements within herself and they led to unhappy tensions, but by the eighteenth century she had reached a state of quiescence in which theological disputes had become unpopular and the Church and State were firmly allied against all subversive forces. Sacramental religion fell into disuse and church buildings tended to become ruinous and neglected. It was at this time that the chancel of St Peter's, Great Walsingham, was allowed to fall down.

The Methodist revival caused a wide split in the church

whose leaders were violently opposed to any enthusiastic movement and made it impossible for Wesley's followers to practise
frequent Communion. Yet the subjective piety which they
valued, was responsible for the Evangelical revival which stayed
within the Established Church to bring new life and personal
devotion into what was sometimes opprobriously called Lati-
tudinarianism or the High and Dry School of churchmanship.
The things for which the shrine at Walsingham had stood
appeared almost to have vanished, for the emphasis in reformed
churches on justification by faith alone had obliterated any
idea of the invocation of the saints, whose remaining images
and shrines had been ruthlessly destroyed in the iconoclasm of
the seventeenth century. Yet a tradition of Catholic thought
and piety can be traced through the Caroline Divines and
continued in the Church of England so that John Keble always
maintained that the principles of the Catholic Revival he was
promoting were no new thing, but those which he had learned
at his mother's knee in a High Church home at the end of the
eighteenth century.

With many of his friends at Oxford, such as Newman, Froude,
Pusey, Williams and Palmer, Keble became increasingly conscious of the dangers threatening the church from the reforming
and liberal movements which were trying to bring some life
into the very dead Establishment. His University Sermon,
delivered on 14 July 1833, at St Mary's, Oxford, before the
Assize Judge, and entitled 'National Apostasy', has always
been regarded as the beginning of what came to be called the
Oxford Movement. Keble's sermon did not attract very much
attention at the time, and the threatened suppression of ten
Irish bishoprics which provoked it does not seem to us today to
have been a very mighty issue for the beginning of a spiritual
revival. But, with Newman and others Keble co-operated in
writing a series of Tracts which bore such tedious titles as
Adherence to the Apostolical Succession the safest course and *Thoughts
on the Benefits of the System of Fasting enjoined by our Church*. These,
although surprisingly popular amongst the clergy, would not
have caused any violent stir had not the Tractarians themselves
started hostile action against those whom they regarded as
Liberals in theology, and begun a heresy hunt.

Their belligerence provoked their victims to take violent

counter-action and look for any excuse to retaliate. They did not have to wait long, for in 1841 Tract No. 90 was published in which Newman took the most controversial passages from the 39 Articles and showed that they could, if anyone wished, be interpreted in a completely Catholic sense. The storm which this provoked ended by Newman becoming a Roman Catholic and led to several decades of fierce religious dispute.

It is odd that the Oxford Movement failed almost completely in what it set out to do, which was to establish a rigid doctrinal orthodoxy within the Church of England, but it was almost unbelievably successful in something which it never intended, a restoration of many of the externals of Catholicism which had been lost at the reformation. English protestants were seriously alarmed by the submission to the Church of Rome of many prominent Anglicans associated with the Oxford Movement, followed by the establishment of a Roman hierarchy in England under Cardinal Wiseman in 1850, which was popularly known as the 'Papal Aggression'. When they discovered that pre-reformation ceremonies were being performed in Anglican churches it led to wild battles about ritualism, and staunch protestants felt that they were justified in using violence against what they considered as a plot to Romanise the Church of England.

Hand in hand with the Catholic Movement, and in many ways preparing for it, went the Romantic Revival which was a reaction against classicism both in art and literature. The novels of Sir Walter Scott and others had stirred a passionate interest in the Middle Ages. Monastic ruins became so endowed with thrilling mystery that several people built ruins to give their estate the right archaic atmosphere. This fantasy of mediaevalism was brilliantly parodied by Jane Austen in her novel *Northanger Abbey*. Thus it is not surprising, when so much attention was concentrated on ancient monasticism, that religious orders began to be revived in the Church of England and aroused passionate interest. At first a few Sisterhoods were founded, but later the religious life for men was established, although males have remained fewer in numbers than the women who flocked to Convents so that soon there were more under religious vows than when the monasteries were suppressed. Of course, it must be remembered that the population was much greater. An extraordinary figure in this movement was Father Ignatius, whose efforts to revive the Benedictine Order in the Church of England were so exhibitionist and eccentric that he drew most of the fire of the opposition upon himself, while other founders, like Father Benson of Cowley, progressed relatively unnoticed and appeared in comparison fairly harmless.

The Lee-Warners tended to be old-fashioned high churchmen and in 1807 one of the family, James Lee-Warner, became Vicar of Walsingham. Members of the family continued to hold the living till 1870. The passionate interest in old monastic sites had its effect upon Walsingham and in 1853–4 the Rev. Henry James Lee-Warner, who was then Vicar, carried out a series of excavations at the west end of the priory church and the eastern part of its north wall. He published an account of these in 1856 and his friend and collaborator, Henry Harrod, published more information in his book, *Gleanings among the Castles and Convents of Norfolk*. By this time the site had become very definitely the garden of the house and so much terracing had been done that not only were the original levels hard to find, but many things had been tidied up and moved so that it was hard to establish their original position. This was particularly true of the site around the 'wishing wells' and the open bath. The present house was built by Henry Lee-Warner at the beginning of the nineteenth century still incorporating a certain amount of the old Priory. At the same time more was done to the gardens and he employed a certain John Haversfield who was described as 'one who has displayed much taste in laying out the grounds around these ruins'. All this made the work of the antiquarians more difficult.

With the excavations of James Lee-Warner and Henry Harrod an antiquarian interest in the Shrine of Walsingham revived, but the work of the Oxford Movement was also making itself felt. From the 1850s the Ritualistic Revival had begun, but the memory of elaborate liturgy and ceremonial had so completely disappeared from the national scene that few clergy had any idea how such things were done and developed pious customs of their own devising. Some of the Tractarians went abroad for inspiration and tried to reproduce what they saw in Roman Catholic churches on the continent. It is a pity that they did so at a time when the baroque was in its declining and most decadent period. Some, later known as the 'British Museum School', delved into ancient manuscripts and claimed to produce the ceremonial which was in use during the second year of the reign of King Edward VI, as being what the Prayer Book envisaged. Astonished English protestants were suddenly presented with the sight of church furniture and fittings which looked suspiciously like those in French and Italian churches which they had seen on their holidays abroad. The Book of Common Prayer was embellished with a setting of chasubles, incense and genuflections which were undoubtedly popish in origin. St Barnabas', Oxford, built like an Italian basilica, with a high altar skied up a steep flight of steps and under a balda-chino, must have astounded contemporaries, and even Bishop Wilberforce at the consecration, propped up at the north end of this altar and almost hidden by the pillars, did not reassure many people that this was a loyal following of the principles of the Reformation.

Riots broke out around churches where ritualistic practices were taking place and unpleasant scenes of wild intolerance followed. A great storm centre was the church of St Barnabas, Pimlico. People shouted 'No Popery' during the services and Mr Henry Drummond, MP, who lived in the parish, sent his butler to demonstrate, which he did so violently that he was arrested. The magistrates were entirely on his side and dismissed the case with some hostile references to Romish practices. The Vicar had letters threatening his life and even parcels of dung sent to him through the post. It would seem that vaunted English tolerance had reached its limits. A curate at this notorious church was George Ratcliffe Woodward, and he was a relation of the Lee-Warners. The Walsingham estate had passed to a cousin called Woodward in 1804 and he changed his name to Lee-Warner. In 1882 they persuaded George Ratcliffe Woodward to become Vicar of Walsingham

James Lee-Warner and his wife Ellen had become ardent Puseyites and they had devoted themselves to the restoration of the parish church, for which they employed Street as their architect. This was the period of great church building and restoration which, under the influence of the Camden Society, which had started in Cambridge as early as 1837, had gothic ideals which strove to make parish churches as much like cathedrals as possible. At Walsingham the Sidney Tomb was moved out of the chancel and into the Guilds Chapel, stained glass put into the windows, the floor levels altered and covered with encaustic tiling, and gothic woodwork and stalls for a surpliced choir were all introduced without regard to expense. Indeed, so much money was spent on the restoration of the church that the family fortunes never really recovered. Having got their parish church arranged as all Tractarians longed to see them, the Lee-Warners produced Fr Woodward to introduce the right sort of religion to go with it.

In one way Fr Woodward was a disappointment for he got married, and the Lee-Warners were very much in favour of clerical celibacy. From that time they would never again speak of him as 'Father', but always 'Mr Woodward', which is probably why he only stayed six years. He was a very fine musician and composed church music which is still sung. He was also responsible for the *Cowley Carol Book* which bears his name as its compiler. Obviously in a country parish he had to go very carefully, and the wild scenes at St Barnabas, Pimlico, had probably taught him to proceed rather more slowly than he would have wished with ritual introductions, but six candles were placed and lit upon the altar and Eucharistic vestments introduced. In the Intercession Paper of the Confraternity of the Blessed Sacrament, a devotional society whose name reveals its character, in August 1883 there is a petition 'That God's blessing may be upon the work at Walsingham'. The church at Houghton St Giles was in advance of Walsingham as far as churchmanship was concerned. The Priest in Charge, who later became a Cowley Father, had already started to reserve the Blessed Sacrament, and kept a diary which is preserved in the church safe in which he records such triumphs of high churchmanship as carrying Communion to the sick through the village street wearing a biretta.

Fr Woodward employed his musical talents in the parish of Walsingham and from this time they sang plainsong. A local paper recorded that he had started 'a Sung Eucharo' (sic). He instituted daily sung Evensong which went on many years after he left the parish. It was held in the Guilds Chapel with the squire accompanying the singing with a cello. This was Henry Lee-Warner, the son of James and Ellen and a somewhat eccentric bachelor. He was very musical, which is probably why a villager who had a grudge against him blew up the organ in the parish church as a revenge.

The early Tractarians had been very reserved about devotion to the Mother of the Lord and were genuinely shocked by some of the Marian piety they saw on the continent and the somewhat exotic counter-reformation writings on the subject. John Keble had been brought up with a simple love of Mary, but he was persuaded by the prudent Coleridge and Dyson to leave out of his 'Lyra Innocentum' the verse:

> Therefore, as kneeling day by day
> We to our Father duteous pray,
> So unforbidden may we speak
> An Ave to Christ's Mother meek,
> (As children with 'good morrow' come
> To elders in some happy home.)

which they regarded as going too far and very likely to cause grave offence.

The second generation of the Oxford Movement, which produced the ritualists, had no such inhibitions. Statues of the Virgin decked with flowers and candles began to appear in 'high' Anglican churches, despite the disapproval of bishops and archdeacons who took what legal steps they could for their removal. Many of the clergy of the Catholic revival were men of noble family and great wealth which, together with the parson's freehold, placed them in an impregnable position. When the tradesmen of Burford met to protest about the 'goings on' of their Tractarian Vicar they said to him: 'What will you do if we report you to the bishop?' and he calmly replied: 'I shall deal at the Stores', which promptly squashed the revolt, because he was the richest man in the place and so a customer they could not afford to lose. Fr Bennett, who was Vicar of St Barnabas, Pimlico, in its stormiest period, retired to Frome in Somerset where he rebuilt the church, largely from his own fortune putting a flight of steps from the town with big Stations of the

Cross at regular intervals, which was not exactly in line with earlier Tractarian restraint.

Another priest, who spent his entire patrimony on building churches, was Arthur Douglas Wagner. His father was Vicar of Brighton and placed his son in charge of a newly built daughter church of St Paul, where he instituted very advanced ritualistic services and started on a plan of church building all over Brighton, which produced such amazing structures as the church of St Bartholomew, built, it is said, to the dimensions of Noah's Ark. His father, who was an old-fashioned high churchman, was as surprised as anyone and is said to have preached a sermon at St Paul's from the text: 'Lord, have mercy on my son; for he is a lunatick and sore vexed.'

Fr Wagner built a church in the country at Buxted where he had founded a rest home. It was dedicated to St Mary and inside there was a Lady Chapel screened off from the church and made to the dimensions of the ancient Holy House at Walsingham. It was popularly called 'the Walsingham Chapel'. We shall probably never know why he did this for there is no other record of his having taken any interest in Walsingham, but it had a profound effect, for a future Vicar of Walsingham often visited Buxted and first heard the name there. A possible explanation is that Wagner was a great friend of Dr Neale of East Grinstead, who was a keen antiquarian and would almost certainly have followed the excavations at Walsingham in 1856 with great interest. It may well have been his influence which caused Fr Wagner to make this gesture towards the ancient Shrine of Mary in England. Fr Wagner had a great devotion to Our Lady and built a church in Brighton dedicated to the mystery of the Annunication. There is a (probably apocryphal) story that as a very old man he saw the statue of Queen Victoria which the Brighton Corporation put in the Old Steine Gardens to commemorate her Diamond Jubilee, and thought that his life's work had been crowned by the public erection of a statue of the Blessed Virgin Mary in Brighton.

Another sign of interest in Walsingham came through the wealthy and eccentric Charlotte Boyd, who was a lady passionately interested in the revival of the Benedictine life in the Church of England, an enthusiasm she probably got from Fr Ignatius of Llanthony. She conceived the very romantic idea of buying back all old monastic property in England and restoring it to the Church. She founded a society with this object. While staying with a Canon of Norwich she went over to Walsingham and saw Mr Lee-Warner to discover whether he would be prepared to sell the Abbey, as she was most anxious to find a home for some nuns founded by Fr Ignatius and living at that time in unsatisfactory conditions at Feltham. She did finally settle them at Malling Abbey in Kent, but in the course of time they moved to Wales to be near the monks of Caldy, and another community took their place and are still there today.

Mr Lee-Warner had no wish whatever to part with his family home, but Miss Boyd had seen during her visit the rather ruinous Slipper Chapel which was being used as a farm building, which shocked her very much. She persuaded him at least to let her buy this and restore it to use as a place of worship. Her idea was to build a small hermitage and people it with one or two Benedictine monks. There seems no evidence that she was interested in a revival of the cultus of Our Lady of Walsingham, for it was the Benedictine life that she was most enthusiastic to promote. A subsequent visit to the continent was too much for her romantic spirit and she became a Roman Catholic and was received as a Benedictine oblate at the Abbey of Maria Lach. From this time she seems to have gone about coifed as a nun, and there are photographs of her so dressed. This change in her own status altered her plans for the Slipper Chapel which stood ready, with a small house beside it, for occupation.

The two nearest Roman Catholic parishes were at King's Lynn and Bungay, and as there were no Roman Catholics around Walsingham it had never been decided into which area it came. Bungay was a parish which had been founded and served for many years by the English Congregation of Benedictines from Downside, and so seemed providentially designed to fulfil the monastic dreams of Miss Boyd. She had counted without the parish priest at King's Lynn, who had taken steps to revive a devotion to Our Lady of Walsingham in his church with full papal approval and had built a chapel containing a copy of the image in the Holy House at Loreto. He was most unwilling to have the Benedictines from Bungay planting themselves in Walsingham itself, and so he obtained a ruling that Walsingham was in his parish.

Charlotte Boyd had not been brought up a high church Anglican for nothing and was determined to have things as she wanted them, so she made the house and chapel over to the monks of Downside as their personal property. The parish priest at King's Lynn had not been brought up a Roman Catholic for nothing and was certainly not going to allow himself to be thwarted by a convert lady, and so he got an order from Rome forbidding Mass or any public service to be held in the Slipper Chapel. This papal prohibition lasted until 1934, by which time all the original parties to the dispute were dead and it was easy to bury the hatchet. Downside made over the property to the Diocese of Northampton and the chapel was opened for worship and as a Shrine of Our Lady of Walsingham for Roman Catholics. There was a strong rumour that Charlotte Boyd returned to the Church of England before her death, but there does not seem to be any evidence for this. She may not have had much interest in the revival of the cult of Our Lady of Walsingham as such, but she certainly was led to play a part in this, and about that time at least one party of Roman Catholics did come over from King's Lynn and make an official pilgrimage, which may well have been the first since the small group of men returned to Lincolnshire in 1537.

The parish of Walsingham went on in a quiet but definite 'high church' way. The pattern of worship had become an eight o'clock Holy Communion every Sunday, followed by Mattins or Sung Eucharist on alternate Sundays, and a celebration of Holy Communion on two weekdays and all Prayer Book Saints' Days. It was indeed an example of what the Oxford Movement had accomplished all over the country and there were many surrounding churches, such as East Dereham and Blakeney, where Tractarian Vicars had established the same sort of thing. The two parish priests of Walsingham who followed Fr Woodward were both in the Catholic tradition but they did not make any sensational changes. The Rev. Edgar Lee Reeves was Vicar from 1904 to 1921 and during his time a small figure of the Blessed Virgin was provided for the church by the League of Our Lady, which had been founded to encourage devotion to Mary within the Church of England. Fr Reeves had been a colleague of the Rev. F. E. Baverstock who was an official of the League. When Fr Reeves decided to leave in 1921 it proved difficult to find anyone to replace him. The stipend was very small and there were three churches to serve and a large parsonage house to be maintained. After many people had been approached Fr Reeves wrote to Fr Baverstock, who was Vicar of Holy Cross, St Pancras, and asked him if he knew of anyone suitable. Fr Baverstock suggested a young man who had been his curate and who he knew had a particular devotion to Our Lady. After some hesitation the young man accepted the living and the second era of Walsingham's shrine began, for his name was Alfred Hope Patten.

5
Alfred Hope Patten,
the raising up of a restorer

ALFRED HOPE PATTEN was born on 17 November 1885, and if one is to understand what he did at Walsingham and why he did it, his background and upbringing must be considered. He was always very reticent about his early years and this probably arose from the fact that his father had been 'in trade', as it was known in those days, and that he himself had little or no formal education. He was born at Sidmouth in Devon, the place of birth being given as the 'Town Brewery' and his father's occupation as 'brewer'. His names were registered as Alfred Hope and it has never been established what prompted his parents to call him Hope, as it was not a family name. When he grew up he much disliked the name Alfred, which was the same as his father's, and even suggested that he was intended to have been called Hugh, having been born on the Feast of St Hugh of Lincoln, but that the clergyman at his baptism made a mistake. If he really believed this it was an example of wishful thinking, for it was as Hope that he was registered in the Registration Sub-district of Ottery St Mary before he was brought to the font on 3 February 1886.

There is some mystery in what his parents were doing in Devon at that time, but from the memories of his cousins it is possible to get some idea of what happened in the family. The Pattens were an old family and lived at Hare Street House, Great Hormead, Hertford. It was sold by Hope Patten's parents to Mgr Robert Hugh Benson, and there are photographs of it in his brother's biography of him. It appears a large and attractive house and very much a 'gentleman's residence'. It was bequeathed by Robert Hugh Benson to the Roman Catholic Archdiocese of Westminster. There was a brewery in the family, but it is difficult to know what part his father took in its management which entitled him to call himself a brewer. Hope seems to have been over sensitive about this, for his contemporaries would have thought of Alfred Patten as a 'gentleman brewer'.

Alfred Patten married Mary Sadler, whose brother was a Church of England priest of moderate churchmanship, but a gentle and lovable man who had a very happy and affectionate relationship with his nephew, while not sharing his views. Hope Patten had many relatives on his mother's side, but his father had only one brother who died young and had no children. His parents lived with his grandfather at Hare Street House and the impression is that the family fortunes were becoming somewhat depleted, which is why his father took to brewing. However, before Hope was born his father had an accident which resulted in his becoming a permanent invalid and had a profound effect on the way in which he brought up, and his relationship with, his only son. He tried to get out of a railway train before it stopped and fell on his head, and although the family were rather mysterious about it, the presumption is that he suffered brain damage which affected him permanently.

It was to convalesce from this illness that he and his wife went to Sidmouth, where Hope was born. It was obviously through his connection with the brewery trade that they were living at the town brewery and it may well be that he was making an effort to get back into harness, but there is no record of his ever having held any permanent position in the brewery there. He and his wife returned with their baby son to Hertfordshire and lived with his father until he died and they were forced to sell the house. They then began a series of moves. The memory of one of his cousins is that every time they moved it was to a smaller house, and the impression was that their finances became more straitened, although they were always able to make themselves comfortable.

Hope had early memories of Hare Street House where he must have lived until he was over ten years old. The house lay on the old pilgrims' way and in later life he claimed to have been conscious as a small boy lying in bed at night of a press of people moving past. This may have been so as he showed signs of having a degree of psychic insight at an early age. His childhood must have been slightly unnatural, an only child with a doting mother, who was ready to satisfy his every whim, and an invalid father with whom he had little or no real contact. In early life he had few friends and was much on his own, which seems to have developed in him gifts of imagination and fantasy which remained with him all his life.

He was entered for Christ's Hospital, then in London, and admitted in November 1896. His father claimed, on the petition of entry, to have been unemployed for five years and dependent upon relatives for the support of his family. After his accident he would seem to have been entirely dependent upon his father. This was the only experience of boarding school which Hope ever had, and he did not care for it at all. He was removed in September 1898 on the grounds that he was not strong enough for school life. He himself said later that the reason was that his father had objected to his sleeping in a dormitory with other boys. If this was so, it is an indication of the rather hot-house atmosphere in which he was being reared. All through the rest of his life, when he disliked something his health broke down, and the experience of school was probably an early manifestation of this psychosomatic trait.

While he was away at Christ's Hospital, it would seem that his grandfather died, Hare Street House was sold and his parents moved to Redhill where he attended a day school when he ceased to be a Blue Coat boy. After various moves they finally settled, soon after the beginning of the twentieth century, at Hove in Sussex and, after living for a short time in a rented house in Brunswick Square, bought a smaller one in Wilbury Villas. This is along the New Church Road and very close to a road called Walsingham Road, so that the name must have been often before Hope's eyes as he grew up.

His father was definitely low church and his mother had the same sort of religion as her clerical brother, so that there was no high church influence in his home. When they moved to Hove he came into the centre of what had come to be called the Anglo-Catholic movement, and was sometimes referred to in jest as the 'London, Brighton and South Coast Religion'. This introspective, solitary and rather romantic boy took to it as a duck takes to water. Compton Mackenzie, in *Sinister Street* and *The Altar Steps*, has chronicled the impact of Anglo-Catholicism on an impressionable youth and he might well be describing the experience of the young Hope Patten when he first came in contact with the churches of Brighton. To understand it we need to know a little more of what had happened to one section of the Church of England at the end of the nineteenth and beginning of the twentieth centuries.

The attempt to put down ritualism by an act of parliament was a ludicrous mistake and a manifestation of the fear of Romanism which still lurked in English breasts. When the Public Worship Regulation Act was passed in 1874 an eye-witness said that the House of Commons had been worked up to such a state that 'if it had been proposed to cut off the hands of all the offending clergymen, they would have carried it'. The only visible result was that a few priests, like the famous Father Tooth, were sent to jail for wearing Eucharistic vestments. This so shocked fair-minded Englishmen that the bill soon became, and remained, completely ineffective. Yet it had far-reaching results because, apart from the fantasy of thinking that the worship of God could be regulated by Act of Parliament, it made martyrs, and that has always proved the best way of strengthening any movement, whatever it may be.

From this time the High Churchmen of more than one school had an enduring grievance. It was an added insult that Lord Penzance, an elderly 'dug-out' Divorce Court judge, was chosen to preside over the legal prosecutions for ritualism. This real sense of injustice had the effect of driving the extreme wing of Anglo-Catholics further along the road they were following with a militancy which had all the excitement of a crusade. From this time Anglo-Catholics began shock tactics, arriving in parishes and turning everything upside down, with the sincere belief that one had only to show people 'correct' Catholic ceremonial for them to be converted instantly. One new Vicar arriving in a tiny country parish read, on his first Sunday, the 39 Articles, and then closed the book and said: 'Dreadful, dreadful, there will be Holy Mass next Sunday at 11 a.m.' Of course there were mighty parochial reactions, but many of these men were devoted pastors and they stayed on and, in course of time, the things they introduced were accepted by the parish, so that if anyone tried to change them today, there would be a similar outcry.

Most of the bishops were very unhappy about the new Act, but they were more or less powerless to do anything about ritualism themselves since the parson's freehold protected the innovators from all but verbal rebuke and completely ineffective suspension. The Tractarian movement had a curious 'love-hate' relationship with the episcopate, for they loved and venerated the office of a bishop, but soon found themselves engaged in violent conflict with the holders. This relationship also became true of their attitude towards the Book of Common Prayer which in early years of the revival had been loved and venerated and regarded as the treasury of true Catholic doctrine. The new generation of Anglo-Catholics delighted in abandoning the Prayer Book in favour of the Roman Missal, which they called vaguely 'the rites of the Western Church'. Fr Wason, who had a stormy passage in the Cornish villages of Cury and Gunwalloe, once held up a copy of the Prayer Book when in the pulpit and said: 'This is a Book of Comic Prayer and this is where it is going', throwing it down on the ground. This forsaking of the Book of Common Prayer was probably one of the greatest mistakes of the later development of the Catholic Revival, because with the adoption of modern Roman Catholic baroque ceremonial it became more and more separated from the Church of England as a whole. Anglo-Catholics tended to become a 'people apart' and their churches almost unrecognisable as Anglican. However, this position had its excitement for the young who loved the feeling of rebellion against authority, and in many churches young curates pushed on their vicars in a ritualistic direction as hard as they could.

There were two schools of ritualism in the Church of England which at various times turned to rend each other. There were those, represented by the Rev. Percy Dearmer who published *The Parson's Handbook* in 1899, who wished to reintroduce the ceremonial of the immediate pre-reformation period strictly adapted to the Prayer Book, but there was a growing reaction amongst Anglo-Catholics at what was regarded as a return to a dead past. They wanted the Church of England to be as it might have developed had the Reformation never taken place. The churches in Brighton, with their baroque fittings, were very much under the influence of the latter school of thought. It was in their incense-laden interiors that the teenage Hope Patten first encountered Anglo-Catholicism, and he knew immediately that this was for him.

He embraced Catholicism with an enthusiasm which he never lost till the end of his life and with an extraordinary power of communicating his ardour to other people. He went round all the Wagner churches but finally settled at St Michael's, where a very handsome extension had just been built alongside the original Bodley church. He became an altar server and for the first time formed intimate friendships with boys of the same age who had the same interests. The solitary boy, who had not been able to stand boarding school, became a somewhat possessive friend who demanded companionship; this too was a lasting trait, for as he grew older he could never go anywhere alone and always had to have someone with him, preferably someone he could dominate. Photographs of him as a baby show a very strong and determined mouth and as he grew up, his parents, even had they wished to do so, were entirely unable to check his will to do something if he wished it. His father remained a shadowy figure, and Hope once bemoaned to a friend that he had never known what it was to have the support and companionship of a father. His mother tried to go along with him in his passion for Catholicism, but the impression in the family was that she did it to please Hope rather than from any strong convictions, and she did not attend St Michael's church with any regularity.

Since he left Christ's Hospital he had been to a private day school in Redhill and a succession of private tutors, but at any suggestion of examinations his health broke down immediately. He was very intelligent and a voracious reader of things that interested him, upon which he made copious notes; but the discipline of learning did not appeal to him and it proved almost impossible to teach him pedestrian things like Latin grammar. To the end of his life no one was ever able to explain to him the agreement of cases. He had a large notice over the Guilds Chapel at Walsingham which read 'Verbum caro factus (sic) est'. This unfortunately was not taken down before it had been photographed and immortalised in a postcard of the church. Someone obviously tried to explain the mistake to him for shortly afterwards a notice of a pilgrimage was headed 'Caro factum (sic) est'. His lack of formal education may have had something to do with his inability to spell correctly, but this is a well-known defect which often exists in very intelligent people who have had plenty of tuition. He was quite capable of writing 'eny' and never mastered the spelling of proper names, however well he knew the people. Later in life he disguised this by making his rather good and firm hand-writing quite unreadable, but all these defects gave him an inferiority complex towards scholars from which he never recovered. Those minor limitations make the real genius which he had in many directions the more remarkable.

It has been said that one of the gravest defects of the Oxford Movement was that its followers fell in love with the middle ages in a completely uncritical way. This is well exemplified in the case of Hope Patten. From the moment he discovered Catholicism he longed completely to undo the Reformation in all its works and bring England back to what he would have called the 'ages of faith'. Anything to do with mediaevalism fascinated him: monasteries, relics and shrines became a passion and in the secondhand bookshops of Brighton, hidden in the picturesque Lanes, he began buying and absorbing all the anti-quarian literature that he could. Montelambert's *Monks of the West* and Wall's *Shrines of British Saints* were eagerly devoured in his own room, which was decorated with rubbings of mediaeval brasses that he had made during his explorations of Sussex churches. Heraldry became a passion and at one time he took to writing to famous and titled people asking for their autographs, cutting the crests off their envelopes and writing paper and sticking them in a book. He began to paint with a certain talent, but he could never bother to master the less exciting techniques of draughtsmanship and perspective, which rather limited his achievements. He was an inspired copyist in many fields, but had an impatience to get things done which prevented him from doing the unattractive donkey work; this is the more extraordinary as he became a perfectionist.

He had a love of acting and theatricals and to this Catholic ceremonial made an immediate appeal. Yet those who knew him at that time are insistent that he was never a 'Spike'. This was a word which had come to mean a person who was enthusiastic about the externals of religion without accepting its disciplines. He began to develop his spiritual life with the same zest as he embraced ecclesiastical ceremonial. He went to Mass and Holy Communion almost every day, read ascetical works and spent regular times in prayer. Although he went to church at St Michael's, he had connections with other churches. His confessor was first of all Fr Smallpiece of St Bartholomew's and later Fr Roe, the Vicar of St Paul's. He went every Thursday evening to Benediction at the Church of the Annunciation. He observed days of fasting with great scrupulosity and in defiance of his frail health. There is a good deal of evidence that throughout his life his indispositions were largely neurotic, because he never let them interfere with anything that he really wanted to do.

He had grown into a very good-looking boy and could be an amusing companion, full of high spirits. One of his girl cousins remembers him on long bicycle rides racing ahead singing: 'I fear no foe with thee beside me' at the top of his voice. He was happy and at ease with his girl cousins, but in general he was frightened of women. He was obviously attractive to the opposite sex and he was capable of admiring some of them, but if they tried to get closer he would freeze up immediately and could be ruthless in doing so.

The particular friend he made through his connection with St Michael's was another server called Wilfred Leeds; they promptly found an identity of interests and became inseparable. They developed the rather flamboyant habit, when serving, of prostrating themselves flat upon the ground, and for this reason were known to some members of the congregation as 'the twin soles'. Hope was definitely the leader in this partnership and insisted on their meeting every day, often at his own home, which Father Leeds remembers as being comfortable but with something of the restrained hush of a sick room hanging over it.

Since the sale of Hare Street House and the Brewery his parents had modest private means and Hope never wanted for anything, but he never seemed to have a private allowance and never understood about money at all. It was not until he was in his first curacy that he learned to sign a cheque.

A great moment in his life was when he went abroad for a week in Belgium at the age of sixteen. For the first time he saw continental Catholicism in action and it fulfilled all his dreams. 'This', he thought, 'is what England would be like if there had been no Reformation.' Particularly he was fascinated by the Shrines of Our Lady and the May devotions which were going on at the time of his visit. He had already developed a devotion to Mary, but he came back from the continent with a new vision of how it ought to be expressed by Christians. He also managed to get hold of a relic of some sort, and this resulted in a lifelong devotion. When later at Walsingham objections were made to the great part played by veneration of relics, he would say loftily, 'I have always possessed relics since I was sixteen years old', as if that were sufficient explanation.

Monasticism was a very strong interest and he was greatly drawn to the religious life and read everything he could lay his hands on about it. He often cycled over to the Carthusian Monastery at Cowfold, and Wilfred Leeds remembers going with him to a meeting held in Brighton by Fr Ignatius, at which this astonishing monk appeared in a wonderful fur cape which he claimed was part of the ancient Benedictine habit. Hope was anxious to have some practical experience of a life under discipline, and so he drew up a rule for himself and Wilfred Leeds to live as a kind of third order of St Benedict. This was far too strict for them to be able to do for long as it required, among other things, the recitation of the day hours as well as the night office, provided by Dr Neale for the nuns of East Grinstead, and this recited at 2 a.m. by a boy supposed to be a semi-invalid. Parental disapproval very soon put a stop to this, but it is significant that, in this community of two, Hope was the Superior. This provoked Fr Leeds to say, later in life, that while he was by no means sure that Hope had a vocation to be a monk, he was quite certain he had the call to be an Abbot.

This may sound like 'playing at religion', but many genuine vocations have begun in this rather unsure way.

In pursuit of the real thing he set off in 1906 with Wilfred Leeds to visit the Anglican Benedictine monks who were at that time settled in a house at Painsthorpe, Yorkshire, lent to them by Lord Halifax. The two young men cycled from Brighton, going via Rochester, Bury St Edmunds, Ely, Norwich, Lincoln, York and Beverley. In Lincolnshire they stayed with his Sadler clergyman uncle near Sleaford and it was on the way there from Norwich that Hope later recalled seeing 'Walsingham' on a signpost, pausing in indecision and then thinking, 'the time is not yet', and riding on. Fr Leeds has no recollection of this whatever. He says: 'Unless he kept it a secret (and I think it unlikely) the thought seems to have come as a later explanation for an omission of which neither of us was aware at the time.'

They arrived at Painsthorpe for the Feast of the Assumption and he met for the first time Abbot Aelred Carlyle, who was to have a profound influence upon him. Everyone who knew Carlyle witnesses to his immense charm and his capacity for catching up others in his enthusiasms. His astonishing life has been chronicled by Mr Peter Anson in *Abbot Extraordinary* in which he records how inspired Carlyle had been by some words of Fr Maturin, s.s.j.e.: 'Paint your picture in strong colours, keep it ever before you, and strive to live up to it; if you do this conscientiously, you will not find yourself very much out in the end.' It is possible that he may have passed this on to the youthful Hope Patten, for nothing could better express how, in spite of many limitations, he managed to create the restored shrine at Walsingham as something which will endure.

Hope was enchanted by the experience at Painsthorpe. Here were some of his dreams come to life, and from this time he seriously considered a vocation to the monastic life and kept in constant touch with Carlyle. Staying in the guest house at the same time as the young men were Lord Halifax and his son, the future Viceroy of India, as well as Bishop Hine of Zanzibar, and they all rose for the night office at 1.30 a.m. It is no wonder that he persuaded Wilfred Leeds to stay on longer than intended till they had to return home by train, having spent all their money.

When Abbot Carlyle moved his community to Caldy Island in South Wales the two friends visited him there and Hope listened entranced while the Abbot told of his plans and the magnificent buildings he proposed to erect. There is no doubt that many things Hope Patten did when he rebuilt the shrine, such as the use of ancient stones from abbeys and priories to make the altars, were ideas that he got from Caldy. It is surprising that he did not throw in his lot with Carlyle. He was already over twenty and had not made any decision what to do with his life. It was not unnatural that members of the family would ask rather pointed questions about his future, and he would say in a lofty way which brooked no discussion: 'I cannot make up my mind *what* to decide on.'

It is interesting that, even with his youth and the immense fascination Caldy and its Abbot had for him, he was not unaware of some of the defects of character which led Carlyle to run his community into crippling debt and himself disappear to Canada leaving a slightly sinister reputation behind him. Hope Patten once explained that the reason he never joined the Caldy community was that he told the Abbot in confession that he had made up his mind to do so, and then discovered that he had passed on the information to several other people. This so shocked Hope, who all his life had the most scrupulous integrity about anything connected with the confessional, that he promptly changed his mind and privately considered Carlyle irresponsible, as he indeed proved to be. They did, however, remain good friends and on more than one occasion the Abbot stayed with the Pattens at Hove. Once when he had come to conduct a Quiet Day at St Martin's, Brighton, he was very mysterious and hinted to Hope that very soon the Church of England was coming to an end. Not long after this the news broke that most of the Caldy community had seceded to Rome. While it was a great blow to many who had high hopes of this Benedictine revival, it did not have quite the catastrophic effect that the extraordinary Abbot had foretold, and the Church of England went on her way, as she has so often done, 'bloody but unbowed'.

Hope was greatly distressed about this secession, yet he never wavered himself. He had already become a curious mixture of apparent utter Westernism with a rooted adherence to the

Church of England, which he believed to be the Catholic Church in this land. To him it was Roman Catholics in England who were interlopers and their claim that he was copying them was too ridiculous to take seriously, as was any possibility that his priesthood might be invalid. Sometimes one felt that he did not think of the Pope as a Roman Catholic and the complaint recently heard in the shrine: 'They've even stolen our Little Flower' would have been incomprehensible to him. Probably one of the secrets of his success was the complete assurance he had about everything which he believed and which nothing could shake.

It would seem that the idea of a monastic vocation was uppermost in his mind and in this he found a kindred spirit in Fr Gateley, a curate at St Martin's, Brighton, and they were soon engaged in definite plans. Gateley knew the Vicar of St Margaret's, Aberdeen, in Scotland, and it was decided that they should join him with one other aspirant and try and form a brotherhood. It is of interest that the basis of this experiment was to be the Rule of St Augustine, in view of the fact that it was a house of Augustinian Canons which Hope Patten later tried so hard to revive at Walsingham.

So at last he had decided what he was going to do, and left for Scotland with Gateley to start on his life's work. There is in existence a notebook in which he had recorded the lessons learned from the Aberdeen experiment, which did not last very long. He records that one of the causes of failure was that there were three different ideas about the type of house which was being formed. This leads him to the conclusion that before making a similar attempt there must be a Rule decided upon, some idea of a constitution and customs, freedom from external ties, such as parish work, and a recognised leader holding the position of Superior. Reading between these lines one can imagine what had proved to be some of the tensions at Aberdeen. According to Hope Patten they had persuaded the Cowley Fathers to send them a Novice Master to train them and, while waiting for this to happen, he went off to Edinburgh to meet an aspirant. While he was there he got a telegram from Fr Williamson, Vicar of St Margaret's, Aberdeen, telling him that the whole thing had come to an end and that he was not to return. Gateley went off to Caldy and Hope Patten went miserably back to Brighton. Wilfred Leeds, who saw him on his return, described him as 'woebegone', and it must indeed have been a sad humiliation after all the effort of making up his mind, to have it finish so ingloriously.

He was now in his mid-twenties and had not yet settled on any career and, indeed, had no qualifications of any sort. After the Aberdeen experience he gave up the idea of the religious life and settled down to the possibility of the secular priesthood. The disappointment led to one of his debilitating breakdowns and it was decided by his doctor that he must go to Switzerland for three months. He asked Wilfred Leeds to go with him and he was delighted to do so. On reaching Switzerland Hope quickly recovered and was full of zest, and soon they were travelling all over the place visiting monasteries, churches and shrines with an energy which would have taxed all but the most healthy. By strange chance they encountered one of the curates of the Church of the Annunciation, Brighton, who told them that the new Bishop of Chichester was making such demands upon his clergy in an attempt to regulate ritualism that by the time they got home there would be no Catholic churches left in the town. There was in fact a wave of secessions amongst the Brighton clergy who took many of the laity with them. At the Annunciation the Vicar and two curates, including Fr Shebeare whom they had met in Switzerland, all made their submission to Rome, having had a final farewell Benediction and sung 'God be with you till we meet again'. Hope seemed unmoved by all this and at the same time stayed completely devoted to all that was Latin.

On returning from the continent he and Wilfred Leeds began to discuss seriously how they were to get themselves ordained. One of the fruits of the Oxford Movement had been the establishment of Theological Colleges, but bishops had little say in where candidates were trained and often only came into the picture when they were ready for ordination. They decided that they would go to Lincoln Theological College, but Hope's attempt to pass the examination on which entrance depended was not only a failure but left him physically ill, so that he was forced to withdraw as the place could not be left open. It was another humiliation, but he managed to get a place at Lichfield

1: All that remains of the great church of the Augustinian Priory.

2: The Pilgrimage Church from the gardens.

3: The interior of the restored Holy House.

4: The Holy Well of Saxon origin which was discovered in 1931.

Theological College in the preparatory class in which some with late vocations worked until they had passed their entrance exam. The faithful Wilfred Leeds joined him there in the autumn of 1911.

Lichfield was not a definitely high church college and there were men there of all types of churchmanship. Hope made a great impression and was well liked, although his uncompromising Catholicism was much in evidence. He was slightly ragged and it was here that he was first called 'Pope Hatten', an obvious joke which continued to be made throughout his life. There is something slightly monastic about a theological college with its regular services and hours for work, and it was this which made the greatest appeal to the disappointed novice. And yet for all his powers of romantic fantasy there was always a streak of common sense in Hope Patten which came to terms with reality. Almost fifty years later, writing to a young man who was beginning at Lichfield, he said: 'If you have as happy a time there as I did you will be very happy indeed. Of course one has to make up one's mind not to let the liturgical and rather cold side of the religion disturb one – and to throw oneself completely into the ecclesiastical atmosphere one finds. There is much to appreciate in the cold and B.C.P. form of worship, and you need not let it worry you. The term soon passes.'

The only dark side of the landscape for Hope was the exams. After a few attempts he passed the entrance exam and started on the normal two-year course demanded of non-graduates. It is recognised that the examination system, while providing a test of ability for the majority of people, is completely useless in some cases, and Hope was one of these. Not only did the sight of an examination paper empty his mind completely, but it made him physically ill. On one occasion before his final exams he became so ill that he had demanded to be sent home, and was finally dispatched to Hove in a special railway carriage accompanied by a doctor and nurse. He was convinced that he would never recover at Lichfield and his body produced alarming symptoms which completely disappeared when he got home.

As a result of these constant breaks in his training he arrived at the end of his two years without having been able to pass the usual examinations, but he had made a good impression and was commended to the Bishop of London as a special case. Arthur Foley Winnington-Ingram, who was then Bishop of London, was one of the few prelates at that time who would have been prepared to waive the rules. He became bishop as a young man at the turn of the century after the violent ritualistic troubles which followed the Public Worship Regulation Act, and his good nature and pastoral sense brought an uneasy peace to the diocese. He made fierce noises about lawless clergymen from time to time to keep the other bishops happy, but in private he would pat the offenders on the knee and say: 'Go on doing just as you are, dear boy, but don't tell anyone I said so.' At the end of his long episcopate it was said that it would take two Bishops of London to reduce the diocese to order and that one of them would lose his life in the attempt! Certainly Anglo-Catholicism made astonishing advances in London during his time as Bishop.

The thought of his deacon's exam had put Hope to bed, but the bishop sent one of his examining chaplains, Archdeacon Phillimore, to his bedside to give him an oral examination. The Archdeacon realised that he was a special case and was impressed by the man he saw. He asked him only perfunctory questions but was satisfied with the answers given. He recommended that Hope Patten be ordained and this acted like a tonic for his health immediately improved, and on St Thomas's Day 1913 in St Paul's Cathedral he received the diaconate from the hands of Bishop Winnington-Ingram with a title to the parish of Holy Cross, St Pancras. This was one of the early churches of the Catholic revival and was at that time considered amongst the most 'advanced' in London under the Rev. F. E. Baverstock, one of two brothers who became priests through the influence of the famous Fr Stanton of St Alban's, Holborn. Holy Cross was the first church in London to have perpetual reservation of the Holy Sacrament, although this was in a locked chapel made out of the north porch.

The new curate arrived at the clergy house in a frock coat and top hat, and from this time forward he was always very meticulous about clerical dress. He went about the parish in a well-cut soutane cassock with a round furry curé hat, and in church and in the clergy house wore a biretta planted on the back of his head in the fashion popular amongst the high church clergy of that time.

Fr Francis Baverstock had three curates at that time, of whom Hope Patten was one, but the others found him strangely innocent and naïve. They had to show him how to fill in a cheque, and he was obviously quite unused to managing money, and the presumption was that he had always simply asked and been given it by his parents. He borrowed money from one of the other curates, which he repaid, but gave the impression that he no longer wished to approach his parents for money, having had so much from them in the past. As a result of his primness his companions subjected him to a certain amount of ragging and horseplay, which he did not much care for. From the first moment of his ordination he had a very high regard for the dignity of the priesthood and he was very particular about his decorum. This was very impressive as he grew older, but one can well see that it was irritating to his contemporaries.

Fr Baverstock had a reputation for being difficult and had had a long succession of curates. He was something of a slave-driver and demanded a complete report on every moment of his assistant's day. This cannot have been congenial to Hope who had, until this moment, always been very much his own master and had his own way in everything. It is surprising that the two parted on good terms and remained lifelong friends.

It was not an easy parish in which to work, being full of depressing tenement houses, while some of the streets were mostly brothels, but Hope threw himself into parish life and showed, from the first, a great sense of pastoral responsibility and an amazing power over certain people.

One morning at breakfast in the clergy house Fr Baverstock showed him a small carved image of Our Lady and told him it was being sent to Walsingham in Norfolk, where his own former Vicar at St Michael's, Camden Town, was now the incumbent. He already knew of Hope's special devotion to Our Lady, which was why he showed him this figure and remarked on its appropriate destination.

When Hope was ordained priest the following year in Advent 1914 the Great War had already started and he said his First Mass at Holy Cross on 22 December, distributing a card which depicts a priest saying Mass before a theophany and printed in the Rue St Sulpice in Paris, where the thunders of the great conflict between England, France and Germany were making themselves more evident than in London.

One change which took place after his priesting was that he moved out of the clergy house into a flat in a newly raised block in the parish. His reason for going was that he claimed that the clergy house was haunted. The occult had always been one of his consuming interests and in Brighton he had got to know one of the high priests of the cult, the Rev. Montague Summers, who always wore clerical dress although he never became more than a deacon in the Church of England. Later in life he came to see many ghosts and persuaded those around him to see them, so that it is interesting to find him already the centre of psychic disturbance. One of his fellow curates remembers having to accompany him upstairs to his room in a state of terror which he experienced with him.

There may well have been other reasons for his move, as he did not altogether relish the hearty banter of his colleagues and the clergy houses of those days were somewhat rugged in the way of comfort. Hope may have had a vocation to the monastic choir, but he certainly never appeared to have one to the refectory. One of his fellow curates accused him to wanting 'religion de luxe', which was rather unfair, but the daintiness of his flat was in great contrast to the austerity of the clergy house. Also Fr Baverstock was given to fits of moodiness when he would sit at meals without saying a word, and this must have been very trying to someone as sensitive and easily upset as Hope. He himself was a master at expressing silent disapproval and he may have learned something of this in his first curacy.

After one year as a priest he left the parish and moved to St Alban's, Teddington, where he was a curate to Fr Cazalet. He parted on good terms with his first Vicar and the move seems to have been dictated by his desire to have his parents to live with him. St Alban's is a splendid church and Hope was a great success in this parish. His Vicar was very easy going and prepared to let his curate have his own way in most things. He was a lovable and rather inefficient man with a very defective memory. He would start out to take a funeral and before he got to the front gate of the vicarage would see that the hedge wanted cutting or the lawn mowing, and would start to do it while the mourners waited impatiently in the church.

Hope was never one to shirk taking the lead and he organised the first High Mass ever to be celebrated at St Alban's on Lady Day of 1915 when the sub-deacon, who had been a music-hall artist before ordination, did such curious things that even he was provoked to helpless laughter. He also organised the Catechism and started boys' clubs and a servers' guild. He began saying the 'Hail Mary' publicly in church, which caused some consternation, but he did everything with such a note of authority that opposition quailed. His pastoral gifts began to show themselves in a very marked way and there are still people who remember with gratitude his help at difficult moments in their lives; and during those war years there were many for everybody.

St Alban's had a devoted band of women who worked in the sacristy, cleaning the silver and mending vestments, and Hope took a great interest in them and very soon had them making things to his design. It was one of his great gifts to be able to inspire people to use their talents to put his fertile ideas into practice, and for the rest of his life he was always able to get artists and craftsmen to make his dreams come alive. He himself still drew and painted and while at Teddington did a drawing, which was published as a postcard, of one of the altars with himself saying Mass, which is rather like his own First Mass card, but without the theophany.

All this time the war was going on, but he does not seem to have been much affected by it. All through his life he w as able to concentrate on one thing with such an intensity that he was apparently insensible to anything else, however grave, which was not connected with it. On his birthday, the Feast of St Hugh, he always had a High Mass at 6.30 a.m. followed by breakfast for the servers and a party in the evening, despite wartime austerity. He is remembered for his youthful gaiety and humour, but he was never able to laugh at himself. He had his parents living with him, for they had sold the house at Hove, and while he was at Teddington his father died. It would not seem that poor Alfred Patten ever understood about his son's religion, but he made no opposition and allowed himself to be given the Last Sacraments without demur. He was a sad shadowy figure and Hope once lamented that he never really knew his father.

The end of the war and the death of his father had unsettled Hope and he decided to have a change. He had been working at Teddington for four years and it may well be that he felt that if he did not break up the household he would be tied to his mother for the rest of her life. In any case he decided to go as curate to his old friend and confessor, Fr Roe, who was now Vicar of St Mary's, Buxted, Fr Wagner's country paradise for Anglo-Catholics. The church at Buxted and the Walsingham chapel he already knew from his boyhood expeditions, but it was when he was curate there that he read anything he could discover about the history of the shrine. Nothing could have been more completely in tune with all his interests and devotional inclinations. The processions of kings and queens, the Austin Canons, tales of the supernatural with the romantic cult of the Mother of God at its centre. Wilfred Leeds has pointed out that Hope's interest in Walsingham came via a passionate love of the saints and their shrines and a fascination with the Middle Ages and chivalry. He was an avid reader of historical fiction and this all prepared him to see Walsingham in its most romantic light.

He only stayed at Buxted for a year. There was no trouble and he remained a devoted friend of Fr Roe to the end of his life and had a monumental brass in his memory placed in the Shrine Church. It is quite probable that he did not much care for the country and wanted to get back to a town parish. The Misses Hastings, who lived at Buxted and who later became great friends and fervent admirers of Hope, always said of this period that they could only remember a rather shy, good-looking young curate who was often late beginning Mass. This may have been the influence of the rather vague Fr Cazalet, for when he got to Walsingham he was extremely scrupulous about services beginning exactly as the church clock struck.

He accepted the job of priest-in-charge at the Church of the Good Shepherd, Carshalton, which was then nothing more than a tin hut. A handsome church, designed by Martin Travers, was planned while he was there, but the money was raised and it was built after he left. The Vicar, Fr Corbould, wanted to rename it the Church of St Francis de Sales, but the parishioners preferred its old title.

Fr Corbould was a great 'Papalist', an ecclesiastical position which has had a long tradition in the Church of England, but which has always appeared wildly illogical to those who do not hold it. It involves complete obedience to the Holy See in all things, but reserves private judgement on the matter of Anglican Orders. How far Hope Patten had come to this position before he arrived at Carshalton is uncertain. Many of his friends were papalists and it had been largely the position of the monks of Caldy, but his association with Fr Corbould certainly confirmed him in this view. Although devoted to the Church of England in one way, there was another in which he would refer to it as 'two potty little provinces of no importance compared with the whole of Western Christendom'. He accepted the Roman dogmatic line upon most things as completely binding.

He did not stay at Carshalton for much more than a year, but he made an impression and when he moved he took several people with him. He was beginning to show a charm and an ease with people when he felt sure of himself which was very winning. One person who lived there at the time has never forgotten his first visit when he swept her cat into his arms, saying: 'Oh, you adorable person!' and, of course, won her heart for ever.

He had thoughts of taking a parish of his own and was sent to see a living which was vacant in South London. He recalled coming out of the church and looking over the densely populated area and saying to Our Lady: 'I want the care of one of your churches.' Then without warning came the offer of the living of Walsingham. This may have seemed like an answer to the prayer he had offered, but it took him three months to make up his mind. He was not a countryman and his experience in Buxted had made him dread being buried in a remote place. The stipend of Walsingham was given in Crockford's Clerical Directory, 1921–22, as gross £224, net £197, and this was the main reason why the living had been rejected by over twenty people before the offer arrived on Hope Patten's breakfast table. He knew nothing about the value of money and never really learned, but even he felt that, with a large house to maintain, these figures gave one reason to pause.

He paid a visit to Walsingham and, while appreciating the large mediaeval church, it seemed to him very cold and bare after the baroque Brighton churches of his youth and the advanced parishes he had served as a curate. He talked about it to all manner of people and some gave one kind of advice which was contradicted by others, so that he became more confused rather than clearer in his own mind. At last he decided that he would consult the Superior of Cowley and leave the matter in his hands, and he journeyed to Oxford without an appointment. There is no evidence that he had had much to do with the Cowley Fathers, as they represented a rather restrained form of Catholicism which he did not find attractive, but they were indubitably monks and at this crisis in his life, with Caldy alienated from the Church of England, it was as close as he could get to consulting a monastic oracle. It was not the only time in his life that he adopted this dramatic way of dealing with a crisis, because at a very serious moment in the development of the shrine he suddenly appeared unexpectedly on the doorstep of a religious house and said: 'Mother, I want sisters for Walsingham' – and he got them.

He was received at the Mission House in Marston Street with that muted politeness which characterised the spirit of restraint and reserve which Fr Benson had inculcated into his Society of Mission Priests, a society which, to the astonishment of many Roman Catholics, managed to combine the special virtues of both their active and contemplative orders in one packet. He enquired for the Superior and was told that he was out of the house taking a retreat, and that it was impossible to see him. He was, however, invited to have some tea with the community which he gladly accepted, but felt that this inability to see the Superior could be taken as a negative answer to the question he had come to ask. While in the refectory he saw a Father come in for tea who he felt sure was the Superior, and on asking was told that he had been called back from the retreat to deal with some urgent business. He managed to get a word with him but the Superior, Fr Bull, s.s.j.e., said that it was quite impossible to make time to have a proper talk with him, and this again he took as a sign he was not to accept the living of Walsingham.

As he was about to leave the house, a Father ran after him and said that the Superior had sent a message to say that he would walk with him to the station and talk as they went. And so they set off up the High Street while Hope Patten poured out his problem and his doubts. He must have spoken of the possibility of reviving the pilgrimages for some years later, when rather angry and hard pressed, he said in private and with an uncharacteristic lack of humility: 'Do you think that I would ever have accepted this potty little parish if it had not been for the chance of restoring the shrine?' When he had finished, Fr Bull said without hesitation: 'I am quite clear that it is your duty to accept this parish.' The oracle had spoken and Hope Patten went home and sent a wire to Col. Lee-Warner accepting his offer.

6

Early years as Vicar of Walsingham

THERE IS A CUSTOM at the induction of a new incumbent to a living that he should ring the church bell as a sign of his taking over the parish. This is listened to with great attention by the congregation for they think that the number of times he rings it is an indication of the number of years he will stay as their Vicar. When Hope Patten was inducted by Bishop Pollock in 1921 to the benefice of Great and Little Walsingham with Houghton St Giles, he rang the Angelus on the bell, much to the mystification of the bishop and the congregation, who thought he was only going to stay three years and then changed his mind.

The parish church of Little Walsingham had originally been dedicated to All Hallows, but under the influence of its high church Vicars it had come to be called St Mary and All Saints. Hope immediately and with the quiet authority to which his new parishioners were to become accustomed announced that the church was now St Mary's, and the patronal feast would be the Assumption instead of All Saints' Day. On his first Sunday he made them sing a hymn in honour of Our Lady. He was a great one for beginning as he meant to go on. Some of the older people, particularly those who had been devoted to Fr Reeves, disliked the changes, particularly when he removed most of the fittings from the Guilds Chapel, which had only recently been restored to use. But most of the village people were intrigued beyond measure with this new young Vicar, very good-looking and full of energy.

He arrived in Walsingham with something of an entourage, as he brought two young men to live with him at the Vicarage and persuaded two ladies from Carshalton, the Misses Lloyd, to buy a house and move to Norfolk. The young men were both considering ordination. Oliver Richards was a good musician and an organist and he took over training the choir, and in a year or two produced a standard quite remarkably high for a parish church. He lived at Walsingham Vicarage for several years; but the other young man, Thomas Tapping, did not stay long. He decided to be a teacher and many years later came back to Walsingham as headmaster of the Sanctuary School. The Misses Lloyd fitted into village life very well and were able to take a lead in church affairs. Once, when asked how he had managed to teach the villagers things like crossing themselves and genuflecting, Hope Patten said that he thought they had just picked it up from the Misses Lloyd, who sat up in the front, and everyone copied what they did.

There can be little doubt that when Hope Patten came to Walsingham the idea of reviving the pilgrimage was very much in his mind, but he quickly realised that this would be impossible without the active goodwill of the village, and so he set out to convert them with an energy which caught them up almost against their will. At that time people still had a great loyalty to their church, which has been somewhat lost today, so that although they might not agree with the changes they continued to attend and grew to accept them. One sometimes wonders if Hope Patten could have done today what he accomplished in the 1920s, before people adopted the plan of punishing the Vicar by abandoning God. If people wrote protesting about something which had been introduced, Hope would read the letter from the pulpit and answer it in public, and if he did not convince the writer he convinced a lot of other people. His preaching was remembered at Teddington as being forthright and at times outstanding. At Walsingham he gained in stature in every way, and he seemed to speak with a compelling authority and simplicity which made a deep impression on those who heard him. A parishioner, remembering those early days, said emphatically: 'It was the sermons that got us.'

He threw himself into the work of the parish with great enthusiasm. He was in and out of the people's houses constantly and was a very welcome visitor, making them feel that he was interested in them. So great was his power of attraction in those early years that, when later his time was almost completely taken up with the rebuilding of the shrine and his parishioners saw little of him, he still retained their affection and his power over them.

He gathered round him a group of young men who were servers and kept open house for them and their girl friends at the Vicarage. This was a large and handsome house built by the Rev. James Lee-Warner in the last century, when parsons were expected to take their place amongst the local gentry, and the stables provided accommodation for several horses. Hope had his parents' furniture, as his mother was living with relations, and he attempted 'gracious living' on an income which would scarcely had sufficed for a far smaller establishment. On Sunday evenings he would entertain the servers to supper and loved to sit at the head of a crowded table, like a baron in his great hall. Afterwards biosterous games would be played with much noise and laughter. The village was agog with tales of the rags which took place at the Vicarage. It was all so unlike the behaviour of the shy and rather retiring clergy to whom they were accustomed. And yet he formed a permanent link with these boys, many of whom remain in the village today with their children and their grandchildren, wholly devoted to their church and to the memory of 'Father', as he came to be called throughout the parish by everyone – chapel as well as church.

He cycled around the parish in these early days with his cassock tucked up around his waist and showing a pair of rather old-fashioned knickerbockers. He was sometimes driven around in a little pony trap by a parishioner called Lewis, who earned for the rest of his life the nickname of 'Jockey' because of this. Older people indulgently called Hope 'the boy' behind his back, but in spite of his youth there was already a reserve in him which made people pause before they took any liberties.

There was never much overt opposition to the changes in the Church Services. His mixture of charm and determination seemed to disarm those who might in other circumstances have made a fuss. George Back, who was organist for many years, remembered him saying: 'Play loudly this morning, George, because we are going to have incense and there will be a row.'

But apparently all went off quietly, for Back added: 'You should have seen their eyes popping out of their heads as they saw them come from behind the organ swinging that old pot, but they never said a thing.'

In fact nothing was 'introduced', for Hope would always say: 'As is our custom we shall . . .' There were those who were amused that if he did not wish to preach, he was quite capable of saying: 'As is our custom, there will be no sermon on the third Sunday after Trinity.'

As far as the Liturgy was concerned he did not at once make many changes except by putting the 'Gloria in Excelsis' at the beginning. He retained the Prayer for the Church Militant, the Consecration Prayer and the Prayer of Thanksgiving, and always claimed to be basing his teaching and practice on the Book of Common Prayer. Throughout the forty years he was parish priest he often said: 'We are very Prayer Book at Walsingham' – and not with his tongue far into his cheek. The general practice in the churches he had served, and which was quite common in advanced Anglo-Catholic churches at that time, was to use the form of the Prayer Book inserting Propers from the Roman Missal and the Roman Canon of the Mass, said silently. There was a long tradition of this practice for it would seem that at the time of the Reformation many priests conformed outwardly to the new book while continuing to say the old Canon silently. Even in the reign of James I one is still able to find records of puritans complaining that their parish priest is really muttering the old Mass to himself, which probably means that some were saying the Canon in this way. There is the remarkable example of Bishop Goodman of Gloucester, so heartily disliked by Archbishop Laud, who was such a convinced papalist that he even went so far as to enquire from Rome if he might be received as a Roman layman while remaining an Anglican bishop. He recited the Roman Breviary and ordained from the Latin Ordinal, but one fears that his continuing in the Church of England was not entirely unconnected with the emoluments of his See.

At the beginning of the Oxford Movement priests like Dr Pusey, who made very few ritualistic innovations, did begin to insert the Roman Canon as a private devotion when celebrating the Holy Communion. This was the tradition which had been

handed on to, and somewhat embellished by, the second generation of Tractarians. The general policy was to get in as much of
the Roman Mass as possible while appearing to use the Book
of Common Prayer. During the 1920s a strange reversal of this
took place and Hope Patten was one of its enthusiastic supporters. The main object seemed to be to use as much of the Prayer
Book as possible and to make it appear like the Roman Mass.
A great influence in this was Fr Humphrey Whitby and his
church of St Mary's, Graham Street (slyly pronounced to
rhyme with Farm Street). This was where the church of the
Jesuit Fathers was situated, but the L.C.C. have spoiled this
joke by renaming the street in which St Mary's is situated,
Bourne Street. Fr Whitby once claimed that he had provided
against any objection any Anglican bishop might make against
the services at St Mary's. It could only have been a bishop of
his own imagination, for if there is one thing that would make
an Anglican bishop angrier than not having Mattins on Sunday,
it would be to have it on Saturday evening, as they did at
Graham Street. His rearrangement of the Mass was sometimes
called 'The Interim Rite' from the idea that it should be used
for an interim period and get Anglicans used to the Roman
Order before reunion made adoption of the Roman rite
throughout the Church of England a reality. These were the
days of Lord Halifax's sub-rosa conversations with Cardinal
Mercier at Malines when the sudden dizzy prospect of such a
thing taking place opened before the eyes of Anglo-Catholics.
It also presupposed that Rome would never in any circumstances alter the form of her Mass.

In fairness to Hope Patten and others who acted on this
principle, there was no way in which they could know that the
august Lady of the Tiber was capable of such a brisk somer-
sault as she has made in recent years. Little by little Hope began
to say more and more of the Prayer Book parts of the Mass
silently, and, as someone remarked: 'You only knew it was
there when he came up for air and sang 'Our only mediator and
advocate' instead of 'throughout all ages world without end'.
He then had the Canon rearranged and printed with headings
in Latin from the Roman Missal but containing almost entirely
words from the Prayer Book prayers of the Church Militant,
Consecration and Oblation. This he had bound into the Missals

at Walsingham and used it himself for many years, although it is probable that few visitors who attended Mass during that time realised that he was not using a straight translation of the Roman Mass. During the last years of his life he changed again and did indeed say the Roman Canon, but it made no external difference to his way of saying Mass. He professed himself to have been converted by a book written by Hugh Ross Williamson about the Roman Canon and called *The Great Prayer*. Today, in view of the changes which have taken place in the Roman Church, it would need a lot of re-editing if it was to be regarded seriously. The idea of admitting change in his ideas was never very acceptable to Hope, and so to most people he simply explained the alteration he had made by saying that his eyes were now so bad that he could no longer read anything but very large print, and the Roman Canon was the biggest he could find.

He recited Morning and Evening Prayer from the Prayer Book and was rather truculently proud of this before his papalist friends. They suggested that he would have liked to have said the Breviary, but was prevented from doing so by his lack of Latin. Indeed, he was unable to join the priests' 'Sodality of the Precious Blood', of which he would very much have liked to be a member, because recitation of the Breviary was one of its rules. Yet once again he changed at the end of his life and instituted the Breviary in English to be recited in public by his Augustinian Canons. When an enquiry about this was made by the bishop, who had had a complaint, Hope Patten simply replied that the book, published in America, was entitled *The Anglican Breviary, with additional rubrics and devotions for its recitation in accordance with the Book of Common Prayer* as if that gave it full authority. The bishop wisely said no more.

Authority had always been a weak point in the Anglican armoury and Hope Patten was no different from many other priests who felt they could not obey bishops when they demanded something which was against the mind of the Catholic Church as a whole. For Anglican bishops to do this they regarded as using Catholic order for anti-Catholic purposes. Soon after he began reservation of the Blessed Sacrament at Walsingham Hope Patten had a slight altercation with Bishop Pollock, who was making a half-hearted attempt to stop it throughout the diocese. After the bishop's Visitation Charge, Hope asked to see him and said: 'Ever since I can remember I have never lived in a parish where the Blessed Sacrament was not reserved. Since I have been a priest I have always worked in a parish where the Blessed Sacrament was reserved, and now I am a parish priest I would not work in one where it is not reserved, so you can do what you like about it.' This head-on attack accomplished its purpose, for the bishop left him alone, at least for some time. Yet Hope would have been unable to see that, although it was not strictly true that he had always lived in a parish with reservation, even had it been so, it was not really a valid argument for opposing the authority of the diocesan in this matter. On the other hand, unless priests like himself had taken a stand against the bishops, it is probable that the Catholic Movement would never have become rooted in the Church of England.

Hope Patten created at Walsingham a picture of what he thought the Church of England ought to be like, and in a strange way refused to believe that it was not. He always behaved as if he thought every church in the country had a Shrine of the Sacred Heart in the month of June and showed mild surprise when reality proved it otherwise. Yet as a parish priest his pastoral sense prevented him from being logical in imposing all things Roman and he had a flourishing branch of the very Anglican Mothers' Union and always presided over a British Legion Armistice Day parade. Someone remembers seeing him, after his eyesight began to fail, peering at the special service and reading: 'They shall grow not old' as if he had never seen it before in his life. A priest who loved and venerated him saw the unreality quite clearly when he consulted him about his own difficulties as an Anglican. He wrote: 'I well remember how one Saturday evening, along the sunk road returning from St Mary's, I discussed with Father the meaning of the Catholic Church. As he explained it, it was lucid and wonderful, but when related to the existing situation outside Walsingham, and in particular in the protestant-dominated parishes where I laboured, it bore no relation to reality.' And yet if he had not had this single eye which would only see things as he wished them to be, he would not have been able to create what he did.

His great artistic gifts were poured out upon the embellishment of the parish church and its services. He had a talent for
creating atmosphere, and things that he put in had an established look, so that the first impression made upon visitors was
that this sort of religion had been going on for centuries. Things
were introduced or altered without consultation with anyone.
If it were a statue of St Anthony of Padua or a picture of the
Sacred Heart, it was always 'as our custom is'; and such was his
force of character that it was accepted without question. There
were those who thought that he put too many things into the
church, but his eyes were on France and Belgium and he wished
to reproduce the atmosphere of the continent, and he did so.
The amazing thing is that he managed to get the villagers to
follow suit and behave like continentals in their religion. They
came to Confession in surprising numbers, and before Festivals
and on Saturday evenings the church would be full of those
waiting to be shriven; 7.30 a.m. on Sunday mornings was
reserved for men's confessions, and they came. He made great
demands and these villagers, in a part of England always regarded as traditionally puritan, rose to them. When he started
reservation he expected them to keep a watch before the Tabernacle all day, – a practice that continued for several years. He
encouraged them to come to the weekday services and got a
response which never failed to astonish those who came to
Walsingham for the first time. Devotions, such as Stations of the
Cross in Lent, became a tradition of the village and continued
to be observed, so that even after his death people who had more
or less lapsed from coming to Mass would still appear at Stations. There is no doubt that, whatever he accomplished later,
the work of those first few years as parish priest of Walsingham
was the most outstanding and compares with the greatest
evangelistic work recorded of the heroes of the Catholic revival.
A year before his death, talking to a priest who had known
Walsingham at that time, he said rather nostalgically: 'Those
were the days; there was something of inspiration in them which
faded away to some extent when the shrine began to be a
success.'

Yet things were not all plain sailing and he soon found himself
in strained relations with the occupants of the Abbey. The

eccentric 'cello-playing bachelor, Henry Lee-Warner, died in 1916 leaving the estate in a most precarious position. His parents, James and Ellen, had overtaxed their fortune in the restoration of the parish church. Instead of husbanding his resources, he launched on a great plan of acquiring land whenever it became available, even if it were at the top of the market. He was forced to borrow money from Gurney's Bank, and by the time he died and his nephew inherited the estate, he owed the bank £57,000. This was a crippling debt which his heir could not cope with, and so after negotiation the estate passed into the hands of Sir Eustace Gurney.

The Gurneys were an ancient Norfolk family and amongst the earliest members of the Society of Friends, Elizabeth Fry having been born a Gurney. Although most members of the family returned to the Established Church, they bore marks of their Quaker ancestry in a deep social conscience and a religious earnestness. Eustace Gurney had married Agatha Lee-Warner in 1904 and she had been brought up at Walsingham, and since her father, John Lee-Warner, had died when she was young, she had spent a lot of time with her relatives at the Abbey. In 1922 she came back to live there with her husband who had been knighted while Lord Mayor of Norwich. Sir Eustace was a devout protestant, so that it was not likely that he would appreciate what was taking place in his village, and he found it more congenial to worship at Great Snoring, not far from Walsingham. His brother, Samuel Gurney, had become a prominent Anglo-Catholic, a great benefactor of the Caldy monks, and was one of the founders of the Society of SS Peter and Paul, which encouraged baroque Catholicism in the Church of England by a series of beautifully produced publications for which he was largely responsible. Agatha had been brought up in the Walsingham Lee-Warner high church tradition and she was never unsympathetic to the religion of the parish church. She was great friends with her brother-in-law, Sam, and remembered staying in his flat in London and finding Fr Ronald Knox, then an Anglican, hearing confessions in her bedroom.

In theory this new lady of the manor should have been a great stroke of luck for Hope Patten, but it did not turn out in that way. Both Sir Eustace and his wife were very strong personalities and very conscious of being the patrons of the living, and in their scheme of things the parson had a very definite place, but it was not the place that Hope Patten was either likely to appreciate or be prepared to occupy. They were conscious of his charm, but it was not long before they came up against his inflexible will and relations became strained. Hope always said that he had to choose whether to stay in with the village or in with the Abbey and its owners, and he felt the village to be the more important. It was not quite as simple as that and no doubt someone with a less autocratic nature could have handled the situation with more tact, but Hope had always had his own way and was charm personified to women as long as they did not oppose him. There were several areas of conflict. The Guilds Chapel in the parish church had always been regarded by the Lee-Warners as the family pew, and Agatha continued to regard it as such and always sat there when she attended Mass. It is not many squires who have found their pew suddenly transformed into the centre of a pilgrimage cult, and it was not appreciated. Sir Eustace had a justifiable grievance in that there was no Mattins on Sunday in his own parish church which he could attend, and when he pointed this out to the parish priest he was told rather coldly that it was recited every Sunday at 10.30, but he knew perfectly well that even if he attended it was not what he meant by Mattins.

Sir Eustace also was a man used to having his own way and as squire he had ways of imposing sanctions. The parsonage house at Houghton had been built by the Lee-Warners for the use of the parish, but had never been handed over. When there was no curate it was let and the rent increased the Vicar's meagre stipend. Sir Eustace directed that the rent should be paid over to him at the next quarter day, as the house belonged to him by law. He also discovered that the living of Great Walsingham had no official income and that the custom had been for the Lee-Warners to pay £90 a year to the incumbent of Little Walsingham. There was no legal obligation for this to be paid and Sir Eustace refused to do so. Hope Patten felt that an attempt was being made to starve him out and he had no intention of giving way. Nor had he any intention of changing his mode of life and, having no sense about money, he simply went on entertaining extravagantly and became deeply involved in debt. Agatha continued to attend the church, but there was little warmth or friendship on either side. It was a great tragedy, for she was an intelligent and affectionate character and could have been a valuable ally in the development of the shrine. Sir Eustace died in 1927, but Lady Agatha lived ten years longer than Hope Patten and would sometimes pretend that she could not remember the name of the last vicar.

In his early days at Walsingham Hope Patten had a very strenuous Sunday. He would say Mass in St Mary's at 8 a.m. and then cycle to Houghton for a Mass there at 9.30 and back to St Mary's for Sung Mass and Sermon at 11 a.m. He kept a very rigid fast before all Masses to the end of his life. He was back at St Mary's for Catechism at 2.45. He gave the children most exhaustive instructions, including how to behave when confronted with a ghost and how to deal with an unbaptised person dying in a railway train. Yet he caught their imaginations and passed on to them a real sense of supernatural religion. Children could often be seen in church praying before the Tabernacle and lighting candles at the shrine at a time when other Anglican churches were trying to entice them in with special corners filled with pictures by Margaret Tarrant. After Catechism he would cycle again to Houghton for Evensong and be back for the same thing at St Mary's at 6.30.

It has been said, and even appeared in print in a book of reminiscences by a Roman Catholic, that he drove a lot of village people to join the chapel. This is completely untrue – in fact it was the other way round and several Methodists joined the church in those early days. One of them has said how impossible it was to stay out of the church at that time for, once Fr Patten came, everything seemed to revolve around it and was dominated by the figure of the vicar moving constantly between the vicarage and the church wearing a black cloak and giving the impression of constant activity.

Samuel Gurney had heard stories of people being driven away and he wrote to a relative, Canon John Blake-Humfrey, who had retired to a charming house opposite the church, and who he felt would be in a position to know the truth about this. Canon Blake-Humfrey was an old-fashioned high churchman, but he and his wife had been completely converted by

Hope Patten and he allowed himself in his old age to be taught to say Mass according to the rubrics of the Roman rite. He replied:

My dear Sam,

I am in a position to know very well both the inward and outward church life here at Walsingham, and its very great influence over all conditions of people – young and old – under the guidance and teaching of Fr Patten. Since his advent, Church doctrine, life and 'go' have grown enormously in the parish, and his teaching, both amongst the young and old, has sunk in and 'holds' them in their lives. What makes people 'catch on' with him (humanly speaking) is his loving sympathetic manner; in spite of interruption, or being stopped, he is always ready to give a listening ear, always ready to give up his time to people. I have never known anyone so approachable, so winsome. Hence through God's Grace his power of attraction, his influence and faculty of imparting his Creed and Gospel.

The whole spiritual atmosphere of Walsingham and church life here is of the very highest order. I cannot speak of it too highly. To sum up: the congregations at all the services are always large and have vastly increased and are increasing.

The attendances at Holy Communion are wonderful both by the old and the young. Old men and women, and women, girls and boys: they all come.

I should say that the influence of Church Life in Walsingham is very great, extending to the whole Parish and in consequence the Moral Tone is high. We certainly have

a Model Priest in Fr Patten
a Model Church
Model Services in Church
Model Congregations
Model outside influences bearing fruit.

This is something to be optimistic about.

Yours affectionately,
UNCLE JOHN.

This is a remarkable letter and Sam Gurney kept it because he felt that one day it might be valuable as evidence of what really happened. It is a sad fact in Church life that a priest who does a great work is often plagued by detractors, and Hope was no exception.

Some have thought it strange that Sam Gurney, who had in his long and gentle life such wide ecclesiastical interests, should have had no official connection with the shrine at Walsingham, which was in many ways a product of his own particular interests in the Church of England. He became and remained a friend of Hope Patten, but he was fully conscious of the tensions which existed between him and his own relations at the Abbey and he was reluctant to embarrass them by a public demonstration of sympathy with something which he knew caused them distress. It is a perfect example of the courtesy which made him so beloved by all who knew him and the explanation of why he was able to have and keep friends in all Christian denominations.

What Hope Patten did at Walsingham owed a great deal to the influence of the Society of SS Peter and Paul, of which Sam Gurney was one of the founders, and to the Anglo-Catholic Congresses which began in 1920. There was not only a brilliance but a sense of impish fun in those like Ronald Knox, Maurice Child and N. P. Williams, who were all active in the affairs of the Society. The persecution of ritualists had been so deadly earnest that it had been very difficult to see the funny side. Fr Stanton might remark to an indignant Archdeacon, who was glaring at the votive candle-stand in front of Our Lady at St Alban's, Holborn: 'If you put in half a crown she'll probably wink at you'; but there were not many who felt so relaxed about the assaults of authority. Such protestant objections as that Butler of Wantage had 'practised celibacy in the open streets' laid them open to ridicule, and by 1910 when things were easier members of the Society of SS Peter and Paul began a series of deliberate teases which made their victims very angry, but raised the morale of those who had felt a persecuted minority. They called themselves 'Publishers to the Church of England' which gave great offence in official quarters and was a parody of the R.C. 'Publishers to the Holy See', which did not please them either. Their goods were given such names as 'The Lambeth Incense' and 'The Ridley Votive Candle Stand'. The printed cards to hang in church porches

had forthright statements about the Holy Sacrament and Our
Lady which were attributed to the bishop of this or that:
omitting to mention that they were the holders of the See
several hundred years ago. A Missal and Tracts beautifully
printed, for Sam Gurney was a director of the Medici Art
Society and had great knowledge and taste in this direction,
reproduced all Roman ceremonies in the context of the Book
of Common Prayer, and presented them with a bland assumption that this was what the Church of England was like. The
Alcuin Club, the society for encouraging the old Sarum ritual,
had produced a book of illustrations of Gothic Altars. The
Society of SS Peter and Paul promptly produced a book of
drawings of a baroque High Mass to counteract what they
regarded as a dead mediaevalism.

They had a lot of fun themselves but they had more influence
than one might have expected. Not only were young men, like
Hope Patten, fired with a love of the baroque, but Anglo-
Catholics all over the country, who had felt a persecuted
minority, began to take heart. In 1920 a Congress was planned
on quite a small scale, but as support poured in the organisers
realised that not only had they caught the public imagination
but that support for Anglo-Catholicism was much stronger
than they had supposed. Congresses were held in 1920, 1923,
1927, 1930 and 1933 (which was observed as the centenary
of the beginning of the Oxford Movement). The Albert Hall
was packed with people night after night, famous speakers were
produced who, until that moment, the general public had no
idea were sympathetic to the cause. For some time the Catholic
Movement had been spreading quietly in the Mission field
outside the ritualistic turmoils of the establishment. A parody
of the Mission hymn 'From Greenland's icy mountains' contained the lines:

> With dark bewildered faces
> The heathen ask us why
> The Church in foreign places
> Should be so very high?

Delighted Anglo-Catholics saw on the platform at the Albert
Hall Anglican bishops, coming from such romantic places as
Zanzibar, Nassau and Korea, dressed and behaving like

Roman prelates. The whole decor was baroque and clergy from the provinces went back greatly encouraged to do battle for birettas and lace albs. This is a very unfair simplification of the matter because the moving speech by Bishop Frank Weston, urging Catholics to go out and find Christ in the unfortunate and underprivileged, still echoes today and many of the papers read were of permanent value. There were moments of moving enthusiasm and the things for which priests had suffered persecution and contumely were flaunted openly. It was a kind of Anglo-Catholic triumphalism, and what Hope Patten did at Walsingham had this background and inspiration, and the shrine which he restored gave the fullest possible expression to Anglo-Catholic Congress ideals.

Soon after Hope was settled at Walsingham some of the local clergy came to see him and enquire what exactly he was trying to do, and he suggested that he should hold a conference for them and invite distinguished speakers to explain Anglo-Catholicism. This began a series of clerical house parties held in Walsingham Vicarage for the inside of a week and intellectuals, such as Fr Alban Baverstock and Fr Monahan, later Bishop of Monmouth, read papers, while Hope acted as the 'Devil's Advocate' and put all the popular objections to Catholicism. Several churches in the district, such as South Creake, owe the beginnings of their tradition of Catholicism to these conferences. Hope entertained them at the Vicarage as his guests, which did not help the gap between his housekeeping expenses and his income. He liked the local clergy to come to him but, while he was always polite, he did not take much part in the affairs of his own rural deanery. The extraordinary Harold Davison, Rector of Stiffkey, was a member of it and one cannot imagine him and Hope finding each other very congenial company. Within his first year he had organised a small local congress and held a Solemn High Mass, the priests vesting in the Oddfellows' Hall in the High Street and going in solemn procession to the church. He was never one to hide the light of Catholic ceremonial under a bushel.

When Queen Alexandra died he erected in the parish church at Walsingham a catafalque of vast proportions, topped at each corner with black ostrich feathers and all the correct heraldry, which must have been far grander than that at the actual funeral. This was made by the village builder, Tom Purdy, who was a devoted churchman and sang in the choir. Already he was finding himself being called upon by the new vicar to carry out ambitious projects, before which he quailed and was only driven forward by the relentless will of their author. 'Purdy must be told' became a perpetual antiphon on Hope's lips when anything needed to be done, and for nearly forty years Tom Purdy did his best to do whatever it was in all sorts of circumstances.

One of Hope's most remarkable gifts was his power to use and enthuse other people. A girl in the village, called Lily Dagless, was a painter and under Hope's direction she painted a screen in St Mary's with figures of English saints which was quite comparable with the best mediaeval work. For some years she was of great assistance in the parish and managed a Church Shop, but she was one of the very few villagers who became Roman Catholic. Without the driving force of Hope behind her she never again reached the same standard of inspiration.

Many years later, when the shrine church was being built, he gave a young man who lived in the village and showed certain talent, stone and implements and under his direction the youth made the most ingenious and artistic piscinae and holy water stoups. There is no evidence that either before or since has he done any stone carving, but under the influence of Hope Patten, who would not have known one end of a chisel from the other, he was able to create real works of art.

Perhaps Hope's most astonishing find in the village was a boy called Derrick Lingwood, who was a son of the local baker and who had become a server at the church. One day in 1925, when cycling back from Houghton, he shyly confessed that he would like to be a priest. Hope listened sympathetically and was encouraging, but made no immediate proposal. He obviously let the thing simmer in his mind, for some time later he said to the boy that if he were serious about the priesthood they might come to some arrangement whereby they could help each other. He suggested that Derrick should come to live in the Vicarage and he would do his best to direct his studies. In return, as he came from a business family, he would be able to help with Hope's financial affairs. He did not reveal what chaos they were in, but with an unerring instinct he had picked on a boy who proved to be little less than a financial genius. It was a time when Hope Patten needed financial stability, for his ideas and plans for the shrine he had come to Walsingham hoping to revive were growing bigger and bigger.

7
The Pilgrimage Revival

HOPE PATTEN ALWAYS CLAIMED that from his youth he had experienced a strange feeling that one day he would be responsible for restoring an ancient shrine. It was nothing specific nor was it connected with Our Lady, but a kind of reverie which grew out of his reading about the past. His imagination worked with a great intensity and there is no doubt that he was slightly psychic, so that when he was physically exhausted he passed very easily into delirium and had curious experiences. Fr Leeds, speaking of their boyhood, says: 'A lot of this was genuine, but he would love to play up a bit and it was sometimes difficult to know whether or not he was pulling our legs a little.'

However busy the parish kept him during his first year at Walsingham, he did not forget that the deciding factor which determined him to accept the living had been the possibility of restoring the shrine. One of his new parishioners, occupying the house which is now the pilgrim hospice, was an old man called Bennett, who was a tremendous enthusiast about the past and had written in 1912 a pamphlet called 'An English Churchman's Guide to Walsingham'. In the foreword headed 'The writer's point of view' he says: 'I lament and deplore as much as anyone can the destruction of the grand old Priory, and am thankful that the decay of the town set in from the moment the last prior betrayed his trust, and for this reason, no new houses have been required since and not many old ones have been rebuilt. The result is that, though scattered, few of the stones of the Priory have found their way to any great distance, and when the fulness of time for its reconstruction as a Religious House comes (as please God I hope it may), I haven't the least doubt someone will arise able to sort them out.' The 'fulness of time' had indeed come, although it was not quite what the good Mr Bennett envisaged.

It has often been said that Hope Patten caused a search to be made at the British Museum and discovered the ancient priory seal. In fact there is a copy of the seal reproduced on Mr Bennet's guide-book, so that such a search, if it were made, would seem to have been unnecessary. He did, however, read everything available upon the subject including the very full account of the shrine given in Waterton's *Pietas Mariana Britannica*, published in 1879. His copy of this monumental work about devotion to Mary in Britain is scored and under-lined so that one can see the main things which caught his attention. Walsingham, even today, has not got very much night life, and during the long winter evenings Hope would read avidly anything remotely connected with Walsingham and pilgrimage, making innumerable notes. Someone who came to live at the Vicarage remembers him night after night in his study with one small lamp focused on his book, his complete detach-ment from the present creating a rather eerie atmosphere. Later in life his eyes were a constant trouble to him and had probably been badly overstrained.

His problem at this time was where to begin, and it seemed to him that it was necessary to have a suitable image as a centre for the cult. The one in the church provided by the League of Our Lady, which he had first seen in the Clergy House of Holy Cross, St Pancras, he felt just would not do, and it was only too obvious that it attracted little attention. Later he placed it, during festivals, on the window ledge behind the high altar, where backed with carved rays and wearing a crown and veil, it looked like something in a Bavarian church.

The idea of using the figure depicted on the priory seal seems to have been Hope's inspiration, for when the Roman Catholics revived devotion to Our Lady of Walsingham at King's Lynn in the last century, they set up a figure of Our Lady of Loreto. Hope seems to have collected money to have an image carved, for in 1965 a retired Anglican bishop from India visited Walsingham for the first time since 1922 and said: 'I remember the Vicar was collecting for a statue of Our Lady he wanted to put in the church and I gave him five bob towards it, and I thought I would come and see what had happened about it.' After going round the Shrine and its precincts he agreed that it had been five shillings well spent.

The order for carving a statue of this design was placed with the Art and Book Shop opposite Westminster Cathedral and they employed a Carmelite nun, Sister Catherine, whose convent was in St Charles Square, North Kensington. Whether she had a studio apart from the convent is uncertain, but Hope was accustomed to say that the image had been carved in Chelsea, close to the spot where the original figure had been destroyed. This nun later left her convent and took up carving as a profession, but one suspects that the story about her doing it in Chelsea may have arisen from Hope's love of coincidence which, when it did not exactly happen, he was prepared to help a little. He probably said 'close to Chelsea', and that would not be an unreasonable description of Kensington. He was always slightly mysterious about the origins of the image, and in a *Short Guide to St Mary's Church* he simply says it was 'remade from ancient sources'. He was also sensitive about its age and in *The Little Guide to the Sanctuary of O.L.W.* there is a note which reads: 'This image is a little under a year "older" than the statue of Our Lady of Loreto which was set up on 8 September 1922, having been remade after the destructive fire of 22–23 February 1921, in which the ancient figure was totally destroyed.'

Once when he was on holiday the sisters thought it would be a nice surprise for him if they washed the statue, which was covered in soot from the candles. It was certainly a surprise, but not a nice one, and he was almost speechless with rage. It was reported that he was seen standing on the altar with a candle, trying to restore some of the venerable grime.

During July 1922 he had arranged a conference at the Vicarage for local priests and this seemed an excellent opportunity to have the new statue blessed and installed. He chose a pillar in the sixteenth-century Guilds Chapel which already had an altar in front of the fine Sidney tomb. The stalls around two sides of this chapel were regarded as the family pew by the residents of the Abbey. The idea to place it in this position was brilliant because it made a shrine which was a little apart from the rest of the church and the right size for small and intimate gatherings, without being too restricted.

With his flair for the arrangement of ceremonies Hope made 6 July an occasion. The image was placed on a litter at the font and he had collected some of the village girls in white dresses and veils to carry it. Other girls carried branches of syringa in escort, which was the sort of dramatic touch which he was so good at creating. The blessing was performed by Fr Alban Baverstock, who was there for the conference, and the sermon preached by Fr Archdale King who later, after one or two false starts, settled down as a Roman Catholic and became an expert on Eastern liturgies. Hope had the bells rung as the image was carried up to the Guilds Chapel, and it was indeed a momentous occasion for this was the first deliberate attempt to set up such a shrine in Walsingham since the image was removed from the Holy House in 1538. The spirits of many ancient pilgrims must have joined in the *Te Deum*.

From this day the rosary was recited every evening before the image and a book of intercessions was started. They were read out at this time and the devotion held daily at 6 p.m. came to be called Shrine Prayers. It has taken place without fail every evening since that day. Almost at once there began to be remarkable answers to prayer. There is a certain percentage in this sort of thing which can justifiably be put down to coincidence, but anything beyond may reasonably be regarded as the working of some supernatural power. The percentage of prayers answered at Walsingham seemed very high, and Hope was convinced that these 'favours', as he called them, came through the intercession of the Blessed Virgin. He kept a careful record of outstanding 'favours' and encouraged people to put up small plaques recording their thanks, as is done at continental shrines.

There can be no doubt that, once the shrine was established, his visits to France and Belgium had a new zest, for he wanted to see what was done in other places. He had a very quick eye to see what could be adapted for use at Walsingham. If ever there was any question about something he had introduced, he would at once reply: 'But at the shrine of so and so it is quite usual.' At one time after the shrine church was built he began having Evening Prayer at 12.30 a.m. and Morning Prayer at 5.30 p.m., which was not a particularly helpful arrangement to ordinary Anglican visitors. When criticised about this he said: 'But at Loreto Mattins is always said at 5 p.m.', as though that completely dealt with the question.

He had a good deal of opportunity for seeing things on the continent as he not only went on holiday, but he would work himself to a standstill and then have to go away for several months. This is not surprising, given the frailty of his health and the enormous amount he accomplished in those early years. In his case there was a terrific expenditure of nervous energy in everything he undertook. He would go on, unsparing of himself, and end in complete prostration. In the early years he had to leave the parish in the hands of anyone he could find. At one time Fr Sandys Wason stepped in. He had been ejected by the parishioners of Cury and Gunwalloe where, amongst many things he had done which caused offence, his nailing an alms dish as a halo for Our Lady had enraged the family who had given it to the church. Compton Mackenzie has chronicled much of his stormy saga as a parish priest in *The Heavenly Ladder*, but he did not become a Roman Catholic as did the priest in that novel. He considered himself still vicar of the two small Cornish villages from which he had been driven by a small minority of enemies backed up by the bishop. He was a most lovable man, but lived in a world of his own and was always planning the most unrealistic and rather fantastic schemes, such as a 'League of Loyal Altar Boys' who would undertake to ring the bell without cessation if the Gloria was not said in its correct position at the beginning of Mass. Even the parishioners of Walsingham, who had begun to get used to peculiarities, thought him an odd fish.

On another occasion a rather Low Church clergyman came to take duty who demanded his breakfast before Mass. The villagers who were looking after him had already learned enough from Hope to say that their Vicar never broke his fast before Mass, and they refused to give him anything. He did not come again.

In 1922 Hope suffered a nasty shock when his old friend Wilfred Leeds, who had been ordained at the same time as himself, announced that he was going to marry his Vicar's daughter.

Hope considered that the Church of England had no right to abrogate what was a canonical requirement for priests in the Western Church. The fact that the majority of Anglican clergy were married did not alter his opinion one whit. At a Mission Service in St Mary's, when he was answering questions sent in, he was asked: 'Is it lawful for priests to marry?' and he simply said 'No. It is forbidden', and passed on to the next question. He was very upset at what he regarded as Wilfred Leeds's defection and for some time there was a great coolness between them.

To be fair to Hope Patten, there were many Anglo-Catholic priests at that time who would have behaved in the same way. The famous Fr Briscoe of Bagborough used to write to friends he had cut off on their marriage after a year or so and say: 'I think I can now regard you as out of quarantine.' Wilfred Leeds came 'out of quarantine' fairly quickly, as he went to do duty at South Creake and Hope Patten met and liked his wife and invited him to come and work at Walsingham and live in the disputed curate's house at Houghton. The arrangement worked very well and at various times Hope Patten disappeared from the parish for several months and Fr Leeds was left in sole charge. He stayed as the curate of Walsingham till 1932. He regarded himself very much as a victim of the new shrine, for when the Holy House was rebuilt the money with which he was paid was needed elsewhere, and he had to find another job. He became Vicar of All Souls', Clapton Park, where he stayed for many years. His relationship with Hope Patten remained cordial, but he complained that when revisiting Walsingham it became more and more like getting an interview with royalty to see him, although he was always charming when they finally got together.

The Vicar's long disappearances abroad intrigued the village. He was always so mysterious about his movements. He loved mystery and liked to create it around himself, so that few people would be allowed to know where he was. Then he would suddenly reappear with new things for the church and new ideas, both gathered in his travels. The following Sunday they would be told: 'As is our custom . . .', and another Walsingham tradition was born.

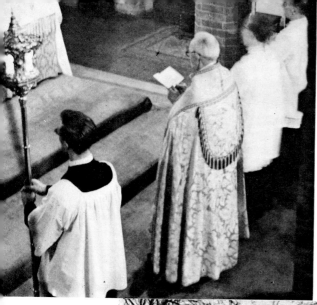

5: Fr Patten before the high altar of the Pilgrimage Church. Taken a few moments before death.

6: The parish Church, Little Walsingham. The vicar, Fr Patten, walks through the snow.

7: The annual national pilgrimage. Part of the procession passes along the High Street of Little Walsingham.

An amusing sidelight on these foreign travels has been provided in a story by a Roman Catholic layman who likes good stories. One day in Assisi, when he was praying in the Lower Church before the shrine, a man came up to him stealthily and whispered in his ear that he felt sure that, like himself, he was an English priest in mufti and would he hear his confession. He replied with amusement that the nearest English priest he knew of was in Florence. Later the same evening, when having coffee with some friends, he was introduced to 'Mr Hope Patten, the Vicar of Walsingham', and recognised the mysterious stranger in the Church. The friars, who had been much impressed by his piety, were astounded when told that he was an Anglican priest, as he had even insisted on getting into a hole in the rocks, known as 'the bed of St Francis', a devotion only performed by the very devout.

It was on this visit in 1924 that Hope obtained the Relic of St Vincent, the veneration of which became such a feature of early pilgrimages to Walsingham. He always said of the relic that it had been provided for Walsingham by the Bishop of Assisi. This seemed very improbable as the Bishop never appeared to have shown any knowledge or interest in the shrine before or after this extraordinary gift. The true story was that Hope had seen the Feretory containing the relic in an antique shop, but it had no letter of authentication and he let the owner know that, although he was interested, it was of no use to him without this certificate. The antique merchant, being a good man of business, took it at once to the bishop who very obligingly issued the necessary document under his seal. Hope brought home the relic in triumph, put it in a place of honour in the church, and started a Guild of St Vincent for servers.

The church at Walsingham began to have a very special atmosphere. Many people who knew it well have witnessed to the fact that there was an extraordinary feeling of holiness about it in those days, which in a strange way seemed to disappear after the image was removed in 1931. After that date and until it burned down, it retained a great charm, but the life had somehow gone out of it. Hope always said that it was full of evil spirits when he first came, and he claimed to have had some very unpleasant experiences there when alone. The moment he began the Asperges, he said, the spirits almost visibly retreated,

E

and he felt them retreating before him. The sceptic would find it a very bizarre mental picture to imagine evil spirits scuttling down the aisle in front of the Holy Water bucket. Yet there is no doubt that within a year of his arrival it had become a building which drew people to it in an extraordinary way. It was a sight not often seen in England that at Walsingham when the church bells rang on Sunday morning the doors would open all down the village street and whole families make their way towards the church.

Already he was gathering a small group of particularly devout parishioners and it was they who came night by night to pray at the newly erected shrine. In 1923 he bound them together in a local Guild which was the forerunner of the wider Society of Our Lady of Walsingham. A new picture postcard of the church was issued which was entitled 'The Pilgrim Church of St Mary, Walsingham', and that is what he was determined to make it. On his first coming to Walsingham, although he had moved a good deal in Anglo-Catholic circles, he had not made much of an impression and was not well known. In fact the very great power and personality he exhibited when he became Vicar of the parish was a surprise to many people who had known him as a youth. He needed contacts with people outside Walsingham to get the shrine introduced to a wider public.

It seemed to him that the best way to do this would be to try to interest religious societies, particularly those with a special devotion to Mary. With this in mind he got in touch with the secretary of the League of Our Lady, who was a young man called William Milner. This was one of the most fortunate approaches he ever made. Milner came from a wealthy family in Yorkshire and had almost the same mystical love for the Middle Ages as Hope Patten himself. He was artistic and had trained as an architect, although he never did much work. His indolence was largely due to his enormous size, for he was a giant of a man, and so much of his energy seemed taken up by supporting his terrific frame that he always appeared lethargic. Someone once remarked that the Catholic religion was the only discipline he ever exerted in his life, and while this is not wholly true, one sometimes wondered if he would ever have dragged himself early from his bed if it had not been to go to Mass. He had a very deep and natural piety.

Milner always remembered his first meeting with Hope when he came to London in 1923 to talk about the shrine to the League of Our Lady, dressed in a frock coat which was his 'town rig' in those days, and full of infectious enthusiasm. This was their first meeting and the two men felt an immediate affinity. It was the beginning of an intimate and affectionate friendship which, although severely strained at one point, remained constant till they both died. One practical result of this was that, when Milner discovered Hope's chaotic financial condition, he settled his debts and was for the rest of his life extremely generous whenever there was need. He also became one of the great benefactors of the shrine and indeed gave the land on which the Holy House was rebuilt.

The immediate outcome of Hope's visit to London was that the League of Our Lady decided to organise the first official pilgrimage to the Shrine of Our Lady of Walsingham. Hope returned to Norfolk and began making preparations for the reception of the first pilgrims. They were to leave London on a Tuesday and return on Thursday. This became the pattern of the early pilgrimages because the priory ruins were open to the public on Wednesdays and pilgrims were able to visit and pray at some of the original sites. Hope worked up a lot of excitement in the village about the event. Rooms were prepared and food ordered at the Black Lion Hotel, while the choir and servers at the church practised carefully in order to show these London folk that they knew how things should be done.

What went wrong has never been exactly established, but it seems that, as a result of a good deal of publicity, various people wrote making enquiries about this new place of pilgrimage and everyone who wrote was put down as intending to go. If William Milner was in charge of the arrangements it was not surprising, because efficiency was not the most outstanding attribute of that very lovable character. He himself was taken ill at the last moment and could not go, so that no one at the London end knew quite what was happening. It must have been a bitter blow for Hope when he went to the station with some of his helpers and the only people to get off the train were a very large priest and two very small ladies.

A lesser man would have admitted defeat, but Hope had an astounding tenacity when he set out to do something. He made a quick decision. The food was prepared, the charcoal was hot in the censer, everything must go forward as arranged and the villagers themselves must make the pilgrimage. Those who had come to the station with him went round the village collecting all who could spare the time. It was like the Gospel parable of the man who made a great feast. Thus the first organised pilgrimage was made by the inhabitants of Walsingham themselves. Nothing could have been more appropriate or more valuable, because it gave the village people an insight into what pilgrimage really meant, and from this time many became, and have remained, active in welcoming and caring for pilgrims.

The League of Our Lady began to organise two pilgrimages each year, one in May and one in August, and after the original fiasco, steps were taken to prevent the same thing happening again and they soon gathered momentum. As they took place in the middle of the week, they were inevitably composed largely of the leisured and were predominantly female, although the more advanced Anglo-Catholic priests came with them and began to be enthusiastic about the shrine. A definite pattern more or less evolved itself. The pilgrims would leave King's Cross and arrive at Fakenham, using a railway line which was abandoned even before Lord Beeching wielded his drastic axe, which cut Walsingham off from trains as effectively as Henry VIII had from Rome. They were then taken over to Walsingham in every sort of conveyance and shown their lodgings. After this they paid a visit to the shrine in the Guilds Chapel, and attended Vespers of Our Lady beautifully sung by the village choir, trained under Oliver Richards. The musical were astonished at the remarkably high standard of plainsong. Then came supper at the Black Lion, after which Confessions were heard, for Hope was insistent that this was a very important part of pilgrimage. Next morning the priests said Mass at the various altars in the church and the lay pilgrims received Communion. After breakfast there were Stations of the Cross and a Sung Mass, followed by a walk of some two miles to the church of St Giles, Houghton, and over the River Stiffkey to the Slipper Chapel for more prayers. They may have been the leisured classes, but they were made to work very hard. After

luncheon at the Black Lion a visit was paid to the Priory, everyone paying sixpence at the gate. Here more prayers were said
and water was drunk from the wells at the east end of the
ruined church. The water from these wells was ultimately
condemned as unfit to drink by the local health authority,
although no one seems to have suffered from it. Tea was held
on the Vicarage lawn, and it was here that Hope was particularly
remembered by early pilgrims, moving as host amongst his
guests with the great ease and charm which he could display
when he felt relaxed and secure. At these gatherings more than
any other he managed to light up several people who became
lifelong enthusiasts about Walsingham and worked hard for
it. Then came supper, followed by Vespers and Benediction,
and next morning after Mass the pilgrims departed.

A new element entered into this routine when Bishop
O'Rorke became Rector of Blakeney, a nearby parish, and took
to coming over on the Wednesday evenings of such pilgrimages
to pontificate at Vespers and preside over a procession round the
churchyard. People began to come over from the surrounding
villages to witness these 'goings on', which attracted a lot of
attention and made people of the neighbourhood think that
the religion at Walsingham was something on its own, and
certainly nothing to do with the Church of England.

Bishop O'Rorke was a doughty warrior in the cause of Anglo-
Catholicism. It has been said that in 1913, when he was appointed Bishop of Accra, the authorities mistook him for someone
else and had no idea that he held such extreme views, but this
is probably untrue, and has been told of other bishops. The
Diocese of Accra was largely supported by Low Church Mis-
sionary Societies and so had a strong protestant element
amongst those working in the diocese. They did not appreciate
the new bishop and felt that as they were paying the piper they
were entitled to call the tune. Bishop O'Rorke had not got
Irish blood in him for nothing, and gathered them all together
and asked if they intended to do things as he wanted them done.
Thinking that they were in a strong position, they were un-
co-operative, and so he simply put them all on to a boat and
sent them back to England. It was at this time that Anglo-
Catholics rallied round to fill the gaps and the Anglican Benedictines sent members of their community to work in Accra.

When he retired from Africa, Bishop O'Rorke became a rector in Norfolk, but helped a little as an assistant to the Bishop of Norwich, which gave him some standing in the diocese. There were those who said that Hope Patten had got himself a tame bishop and O'Rorke certainly allowed himself to be dressed up and given the tallest mitre in Christendom, but he was far too strong a character to allow himself to be dominated. What he did for the shrine at Walsingham he did from conviction.

One of the controversies of those times, which appears very odd today in the light of liturgical developments, was at what point in the Mass the ablutions should be taken. The Prayer Book directed them to be done after the Blessing, but the Roman Rite, beloved by Hope Patten and his friends, had the ceremony immediately after Communion. With a certain arrogance they coined the verb to 'tarp' (take ablutions in the right place). Bishop O'Rorke had very strong views against tarping. His reasons were quite unlike most of those who took the ablutions at the end, because he thought that to do so justified Benediction. The matter became a serious issue when he pontificated at Walsingham, for Hope would cheerfully have gone to the stake in defence of tarping and he tried every weapon of argument in his armoury, but nothing would shake the old bishop. Often at some solemn function he would finally tarp as an act of charity, but keeping Hope on tenterhooks till the last moment.

It undoubtedly made an enormous difference to the image of Walsingham to have a bishop in attendance at pilgrimages and gave the whole thing an appearance of acceptance by the diocese which it certainly did not have at that time. Bishop Pollock was somewhat embarrassed by this and rather tentatively suggested to O'Rorke, with whom he was on good terms, that it would help him if he did not appear at Walsingham in this way. The reply he received was that Almighty God had magnified Mary and the ex-Bishop of Accra was determined to continue to follow His example. His ashes lie buried in the shrine church with an effigy faithfully reproducing the mitre which in his lifetime looked as if it would pull him over backwards.

Another early pilgrim who became a great supporter of the shrine was the Rev. Henry Joy Fynes-Clinton. Hope had known him first when he was a curate at St Martin's, Brighton, but at the same time that Hope came to Walsingham, Fynes-Clinton was made Rector of St Magnus-the-Martyr in the City of London. He was given this living as a recognition of his work as general secretary of the Anglican and Eastern Churches Association, in the course of which he had spent a lot of time in Russia and had many contacts with the Orthodox Church. It was once said of him that he had the mind of an Eastern with the religion of a Western, for he held very strong papalist views and proceeded to make St Magnus as much like a baroque Roman Catholic church as possible. This involved him in very complicated law suits, but he had a love of litigation and thoroughly enjoyed them. He was a wealthy man and took each case through every court of appeal. When on one count he finally lost over having put six renaissance candlesticks on the altar, he replaced them with ordinary cheap wooden ones and made the complainants remove them themselves and sign a paper saying they had done so. He then replaced the original candlesticks and it was discovered that the case must start from the beginning again, and the objectors lost heart.

He became tremendously keen about Walsingham and had much in common with Hope Patten, particularly in a love of heraldry, about which he was very knowledgeable. The two would be closeted together for hours working out schemes and undoubtedly Hope Patten was enormously influenced by Fynes-Clinton in many ways. He was such a lovable character with an old-world courtesy which was irresistible, that it was difficult for anyone to be unpleasant to him, however much they might disapprove of his views. He had a monument in his church to Miles Coverdale, and to a protestant who had come to see it he said with a winning smile: 'We have just had a service in the language out of which he translated the bible.'

To some people Fynes-Clinton appeared a Don Quixote in a biretta for he was constantly tilting at ecclesiastical windmills, signing manifestos and having Masses of Reparation; but he had a great love of souls and a deep concern for Christian unity, which he could only envisage in relation to the See of Peter. It should be recorded that he was responsible for all the lunchtime activity in the city churches, for when he began to hold Mass at 1.15 p.m. at St Magnus, no other church had thought of having services at that time. Also he had contacts with Roman Catholics when such a thing was regarded as disloyal and it was he who sponsored Abbé Couturier's visits to England and his relations with Anglican religious communities.

He erected a Shrine of Our Lady of Walsingham in St Magnus and was active in arranging pilgrimages, particularly with the Catholic League, a papalist society of which he was director. On one of their first pilgrimages the train kept stopping with a jolt and the guard insisted that someone was pulling the communication cord. It was discovered that a gallant lady with an ear-trumpet, called Miss Few, inevitably known as 'the faithful Few', had hooked an enormous banner on to it, so that when the train went round a bend the pole slid along the floor and pulled the cord. At one point they were all thrown on their backs when standing to say the *Salve Regina*.

By this time there were about four pilgrimages a year, but more and more people were wanting to stay in the village and Hope felt that there must be a pilgrim hospice. A large house in Holt Road called 'The Beeches' came into the market with an old barn, a large garden and several cottages, and this seemed a property which could be developed. There is evidence that even as early as this he had ideas about building a chapel of some sort apart from the church. His love of mystery and reluctance to reveal his hand was unfortunate because the owners of the Abbey could have prevented the sale, and being unsympathetic to his project they felt strongly that they had been tricked.

He kept a very poker face when he was asked about rumours that he was interested, but he had already asked William Milner to lend him the necessary money on a business basis. This Milner consented to do, and so he took George Back, the local grocer who played the organ at the church, into his confidence and asked him to go to the sale and do the bidding. The Auctioneer was reluctant to begin and said he was expecting an interested party, but after a while he gave up waiting and the sale proceeded. That evening Hope wrote to William Milner:

By now you will have got my wire to say the property is yours. It was reserved and so a higher price was paid than we at first anticipated. Each of the three lots had a high reserve on it, and were not sold, but they were finally all three put together and were sold to you for £1,750.

I hope you are pleased. Now we shall look forward to the Hostel of Our Lady Star of the Sea, the Cell of St Benet and St Francis Borgia's Hostel for aged priests, etc., etc., etc.

By the way, George Back the grocer did the bidding for you – I don't know if you think he ought to have anything for his trouble; he is a 'great' person in his way.

It struck me suddenly – last night in the chapel – if you get the property you must arrange it *in your will* at once. This sounds as if I have an assassin's design on you – but it would be dreadful if anything happened and it goes back to pro-testant hands – or got to the R.C.s. *That was frightening me all last night.* I will be writing to you in a few days and sending the deeds unless Loynes does so. I think Our Lady is pleased. The first lesson at Matins this morning said:

For the land, whither thou goest in to possess it, is not as the land of Egypt, from whence ye came out . . . but . . . it is a land of hills and valleys and drinketh water of the rain of heaven . . . the eyes of the Lord thy God are always upon it . . . etc.

I took it as a good omen – for there I hope souls will rise high in the hills of spiritual things and dig deep into the valleys of mortifications – and be filled with the rain (i.e. Holy Spirit) from heaven.

It is an interesting letter as it shows all the schemes which were at that time fermenting in his brain. When he came to it, even Hope realised that St Francis Borgia would not be a very suitable patron for an Anglican establishment for retired priests.

Having obtained a suitable house as a pilgrim hospice, Hope Patten then directed his attention towards persuading some Sisters to come and run it. He already knew Mother Sarah of the Community of St Peter's Chains at Horbury, and he wrote to her suggesting that they should come and help in the revival of pilgrimage and the converting of the parish. He received a very ready response and it was agreed that three Sisters should come and, as 'The Beeches' was not yet available, they were settled into a cottage attached to the Vicarage. The village was getting used to excitements, but nuns were an entirely new experience and the people were a little reserved when they first arrived, and did not quite know what to make of it all. There were three of them, Sister Veronica, Sister Margarite and Sister Grace Mary, and they very soon broke down the barriers with the love and care they showed for everyone. They sang their Offices in the Guilds Chapel and their reedy little voices praising God soon became a familiar sound and added yet more to the atmosphere of the church.

When 'The Beeches' became free the Sisters moved in and it was renamed 'The Hospice of Our Lady Star of the Sea'. It was very primitive at first, but had a lot of charm and pilgrims who stayed there always wanted to come again. It was a pretty mediaeval-looking sight to see the nuns moving about the garden with white doves fluttering around them and clamouring to be fed. Inside there was a good deal that was mediaeval and some modern inconveniences. There was only one bathroom and the W.C. was beyond it, so that if one wanted a bath without company it was necessary to ensure that it was vacant. In the garden there came to be other more gruesome 'chapels of ease' and every night a sewage cart creaked around the village. The cellar was inevitably turned into a chapel and Hope wrote: 'The crypt chapel is quite a feature of the house, with its two altars and dim catacomb-like atmosphere and light.' But cold and damp won the day and it was not in use for long. At the big pilgrimages trestle tables were set up on the garden lawn and from now on the Sisters did all the catering, with invaluable help from women of the village.

In 1925 Hope Patten expanded the little local guild he had formed to found the Society of Our Lady of Walsingham and members were invested with a blue scapular. A very beautifully bound and illuminated book was made in which names were entered and it was kept at the foot of the image. In a short time the book was full and a card index in an office had to be substituted, but the book still exists as a witness of Hope's imagination and the perfectionist way he began to do anything to which he set his hand. The idea of the Society was to bind together all those devoted to the shrine and form a body of those who were prepared to support it. Already, through the activity of Fr Fynes-Clinton, the 'Walsingham Clergy Fund' had been started in London to supply an assistant priest and to supplement the inadequate stipend of the living. The secretary, Miss Doyle-Smythe worked with great devotion to raise money and plead the cause of the impoverished vicar. For many years the Sisters helped with a weekly cheque towards the housekeeping expenses of the Vicarage, and so the difficulties about finance were gradually resolved. In time Derrick Lingwood became Pilgrimage Secretary as well as taking over Hope Patten's private affairs. It was amazing that Hope so completely surrendered all this side of things to a teenage boy with complete confidence. He never enquired on the personal side how much money he had, but simply asked whether or not he could afford something and abode by Derrick's decision. The Pilgrimage accounts were kept in an old exercise book and involved fairly small sums. When Derrick Lingwood left Walsingham there was an annual income of £6,000 and assets of about £50,000.

It was not till 1927 that, in connection with the Society, Hope started the Priest Associates. He began by asking all priests who were members of the Society to reserve their Saturday Mass for the intention of Walsingham and to send him a postcard saying that they were doing so. Later he enrolled priests who promised to say one Mass on any day of the month and undertook in return that they would be prayed for at the shrine on the same day. He began to get a surprising amount of support. Amongst the first to join as a Priest Associate, and the very first to die as a member, was George Ratcliffe Woodward who had come as Vicar to Walsingham in 1882.

Another outcome of the Society was the production of a quarterly paper for members which was started in January 1926 and called *Our Lady's Mirror*. From this time it is fairly easy to chronicle, through its pages, things that were happening at Walsingham and the plans which were fermenting in the mind of the imaginative Vicar. It was printed on art paper and profusely illustrated with photographs of Walsingham, pilgrimages and rather exotic places of worship on the continent. The headpiece, which remained throughout its thirty years of production, was drawn by Lily Dagless and shows

Our Lady of Walsingham flanked by the patron saints of Houghton and Great Walsingham.

Most of the editing was done by Hope Patten, and he was responsible for the news section which in the early numbers contains many amusing misprints. It is recorded that protestants made a 'disgraceful and sacrilegious brawn (sic)' in the parish church. The mind boggles at the thought of what might have gone into such a mixture. The constant misspelling of proper names shows that such errors were not entirely the printer's fault.

The *Mirror* became enormously popular and supporters of Walsingham much looked forward to its arrival. They were kept in a good deal of suspense, for most numbers began with an apology for the lateness of its production. It contained many interesting things and is a very clear demonstration of Hope Patten's rather specialised interests in shrines and hagiography. In 1936, under the title *A Chronicle*, there began a series which contained in dated sequence every reference that Hope had discovered about Walsingham and the Shrine during his omnivorous reading. This is set against other contemporary events which had attracted his attention, such as: 'In 1182, a hundred and twenty-one years after the foundation of the Walsingham Shrine, St Francis of Assisi was born and the famous Samson was elected Abbot of Bury St Edmunds.' The war unfortunately brought the series to an end at 1471 and although the last number in 1939 says 'To be continued', it never was.

The *Mirror* adhered as rigidly to the 'party line' as any communist publication and every now and then there is a 'call to arms'. In 1928 it is recorded that the congregation of St Mary's, Leicester, are being 'shamefully persecuted by their bishop for their devotion and honour to the Most Holy Sacrament' and the comment is: 'Like unbelieving people of old, our Prelates seem to be deliberately preparing to persecute and force all who "call upon this name" to dishonour, which is the same thing as to refuse honour, to Our Lord Jesus Christ.'

Hope Patten does not appear at his best in the pages of the *Mirror*. He was sometimes petulant when people had not responded to appeals as he wished, and there is the frequent implication that people cannot really call themselves 'Catholics' if they do not support Walsingham. Also he was apt to make sly little 'digs', such as that the Oxford pilgrims had brought a banner 'which they did not leave behind them', and these were not appreciated by those concerned. He was very lofty in his references to Roman Catholics of whom he writes as 'our fellow Catholics who are not living in visible communion with Canterbury'. It is a good joke, but not very tactful. There was at times in Hope a strange lack of sensitivity as to what one could say in print without giving offence, which was odd in a person so courteous and polite.

It was sometimes a little difficult to know what members were expected to do. In 1932 there is a very severe note pointing out that the paper is private and that some Priest Associates 'have not been treating this leaflet with the discretion that we would wish'. It goes on to say: 'We must, therefore, ask all those who receive this paper not to circulate it amongst their friends.' This paragraph is followed by an even more pointed one asking any priest who has become an Associate and finds he is not in complete accord with the principles and devotion accorded to the Mystery of the Holy Incarnation and the Blessed Mother of God, to be good enough to inform Fr Patten and to resign from the Association. Yet only a few years later priests are urged to place copies of this 'private paper' for sale in their Tract Cases.

The *Mirror* certainly provides substance for the charge, which was often made, that Hope Patten continually pestered people for money. There are often lists given of 'Things wanted for the Shrine'. In fact, with his complete inability to understand about cash, the things had often been already bought and he was looking round for someone to pay the bill. A pilgrim of many years' standing once said that, whenever he heard the lines of the popular song:

> If your wish is in your dream,
> No request is too extreme.

he always thought of Hope. With the single purpose he had before him he did sometimes give the impression that the shrine ought to come first. 'What!' he would say in a spirit of fun, which nevertheless betrayed a point of view: 'you are having a new organ in your church when we haven't got a proper organ in the Shrine!' Fr Leeds was infuriated by a comment in the

Church Times which said that pilgrims were being pestered to make offerings following their visits to Walsingham. He regarded it as malicious, for he was working there at the time and could certify that there was nothing more than an unobtrusive invitation to make an offering by way of thanksgiving for blessings received. Of course there were appeals for money as the shrine developed, but Derrick Lingwood took the responsibility for these. He had been given the job of bursar and simply had to see that bills were paid. All the evidence is that to the end of his life Hope remained supremely indifferent to money and always went forward as if things would be miraculously paid for. They were, but the miracle was worked by a very young bursar who spent sleepless nights about it.

Also in the *Mirror* one finds evidence of Hope's constant breakdowns in health. In the second number it is recorded that 'On account of health the parish priest of Walsingham is away, and no letters addressed to the Vicarage are being forwarded. He does not anticipate seeing his correspondence till December.' In 1930 the Vicarage is offered 'To let furnished' from June to November. These long sojourns abroad were another headache for the young Derrick Lingwood, who held the purse strings but did not have much coming into the purse. It was here that friends like William Milner, Fynes-Clinton and others showed their affection and generosity towards Hope. Also in 1929 a devoted friend and admirer, Georgina Keith Falconer, who lived in grace and favour apartments at Hampton Court, died and left him some money and also the services of her old housekeeper, Hannah, who came to live at the Vicarage. This made things a little easier for him.

It was in 1929 that he started the May Revels which became for a few years a great feature of the district. The May Queen was crowned in the Vicarage garden, after a procession of trades through the village, and there was dancing round the maypole and other sports. The day ended with a masked ball in the Oddfellows' Hall and the Queen was conducted home in a sedan chair with a torchlight procession. The whole event bore the unmistakable mark of Hope's imaginative genius.

The shrine had undoubtedly won a good deal of support and received a certain amount of publicity, some of it deliberately sought. This had the effect of bringing it to the notice of those who would be likely to disapprove of it violently. To them, and indeed to many more moderate Anglicans, it seemed an outrage. Since 1890 the spearhead of resistance against romanising tendencies in the Church of England had been the 'Protestant Truth Society' whose secretary, Mr John Kensit, organised a series of dramatic and rather lamentable demonstrations in which they disturbed the worship of other Christians in churches of which they disapproved. John Kensit himself did not last long, for he was silly enough to stage a protest in Liverpool, where there are a lot of very tough Irish Roman Catholics, and somebody threw a brick with remarkably accurate aim and despatched Mr Kensit to the fires of purgatory, the efficacy of which he had been so doubtful about in life. His memory is perpetuated by a misericord of a demon carved in his likeness on the choir stalls of the church of St Cuthbert, Philbeach Gardens. His militant spirit went marching on in his family and in his Society, which obtained large subscriptions from retired protestant army officers living in Cheltenham and Tunbridge Wells, who expected to read in the newspapers from time to time that their money was being well spent in exposing and harrying ritualists in various places. It is not surprising that they thought Walsingham a suitable target, and the 'brawn' made in the parish church was one of the results.

It is interesting that the protestant demonstrators were unable to get any support whatever from the inhabitants of Walsingham, for even the Chapel people gave them the cold shoulder. On one occasion when they were holding a meeting in the High Street the butcher, who was a Methodist, appeared at his door with a knife and shouted: 'Don't say that about our Vicar!' with such ferocity that it broke up the proceedings and they beat a hasty retreat. But they came back with coach-loads of protesters who made such a nuisance of themselves during pilgrimages that in August 1932, a marquee was pitched in the garden of the hospice and the services held in private grounds to which only those with tickets had the right of access. This, as the *Mirror* recorded, ensured 'freedom from outside annoyance', which was a slight understatement, for during the 'brawn' in the parish church the Kensitites had gone around the confessionals shouting: 'What are you doing with that woman in there?' This made pilgrims very angry and there were unseemly scuffles and perhaps some unnecessary force used in their ejection.

Miss Diana Dors has pointed out, with great perspicacity, that 'All publicity is good publicity' and certainly these protestant attacks brought more people to the shrine and helped to arouse public interest in general.

Not all the opposition came from what has been called 'the protestant underworld', and in 1926 Hensley Henson, who was Bishop of Durham, wrote an article on pilgrimage for the *Evening Standard* in which he attacked Walsingham. He had been staying in Norfolk and visited Walsingham on 17 August, which is a date when he would have been likely to find it looking very unrestrained. It is difficult to understand why he should have thought it worthy of breaking a lance upon, but he had a deep-rooted dislike of Anglo-Catholics which sprang from the fact that they had organised a protest at his election to the See of Hereford in 1918 on the grounds that he was a Modernist. From this time he lost no opportunity for 'getting one back', and Walsingham seemed an excellent target. He wrote:

> Walsingham is, I suppose, as complete an example of triumphant Anglo-Catholicism as the country can present. The Parish Church might easily be taken for a Roman Catholic church: there was certainly nothing Anglican about it except the fabric. . . . Perhaps it is inevitable that the revival of pilgrimages should be included in the general policy of 'undoing the Reformation' which the Anglo-Catholics have adopted, and are pursuing with such remarkable vigour, pertinacity and success, for the abolition of pilgrimages and the demolition of the Shrines to which pilgrims resorted were conspicuous features of the religious revolution which the Reformers effected.

He ends:

> It would probably be an error to attach much importance to the revived pilgrimages, which are rather 'pageants' than religious acts. The pitiable rubbish of the Walsingham processional hymn could only be intelligible as part of a 'pageant'. As an act of religion it would be profane.

The processional hymn was not without its critics even amongst devotees of the shrine, and after one pilgrimage a member of the clergy said: 'Good heavens, Patten! Who on earth wrote that balderdash?' Poor William Milner, who was present and was the author, looked very embarrassed and uncomfortable!

Hope Patten republished the Bishop's article in the *Mirror* with his own comments, which were much in the same tone as the Bishop had adopted. He ends:

> Read his paper, and then say your Our Father and Hail Mary for the writer and the enlightenment of the Protestants in the fold of the church in this land.

In controversy between Christians the final coal of fire is always a request for prayers for the opponent. A parish priest in Portsmouth once put in his magazine: Your prayers are asked for the bishop of this diocese and all other aged incompetents.

It is interesting that when Hensley Henson retired from Durham during the war he took charge of a country parish in Suffolk and his published letters reveal that he revisited Walsingham several times. At first none of his acid was alkalised and he writes of 'this revolting illegality', but the pla e seemed to hold a fascination for him and he returned again ar d again, while the references in his letters, although far from f. 'endly, become noticeably milder. He had suddenly for the firs time come up against the realities of parochial life in his small p rish in Suffolk and discovered that all his cleverness and mordant wit did not bring people to church. He had a very sharp intelligence with a genuine pastoral zeal and he wonders rather sadly what it is about Walsingham which obviously appeals to ordinary people.

But bigger storm clouds gathered when Bishop Pollock began to get restive about this neo-Lourdes which was arising in his diocese. He was bombarded with letters from enraged protestants, but when some 'backwoodsman' peer shouted out 'What about Walsingham?' when he was speaking in the House of Lords on obedience, in relation to the Prayer Book, he felt the time had come to take some kind of action.

8

Conflicts and Opposition

THE RIGHT REV. BERTRAM POLLOCK played a very important, if rather unwilling, part in the reconstruction of the Shrine of Our Lady of Walsingham. To those who went on pilgrimage there a legend arose that he was some kind of ogre lurking in the background, trying to stop devotion to Our Lady and make Hope Patten's life a misery. Nothing could be further from the truth and Hope gave no grounds for this idea. Writing in 1947 he said:

> Bishop Bertram Pollock had been, and remained to the end, always a very kind and considerate friend to the parish priest and their relations were always, even when sometimes they were certainly very strained, both gracious and even affectionate. The revival owes much to the Bishop of Norwich for his patience and Christian toleration. May he have his reward.

Bertram Pollock was consecrated as Bishop of Norwich in 1910, the year in which Hope went to Lichfield Theological College, and he had been, since ordination, first an assistant master at Marlborough and then Master of Wellington. It has been said that whoever is chosen Bishop of Norwich must be very much 'persona grata' with the royal family, as Sandringham House is in the diocese. Pollock had caned several royal rumps and was highly thought of by King George V. He remained to the end of his life very much a courtier. It is unfortunate that his autobiography, written when he was an old man, was published posthumously, for he was somewhat in his dotage and it does not do him justice. In its pages he appears to be a most arrant snob, but he was in fact a rather humble and very sentimental man. He formed affectionate friendships with his boys and they were devoted to him. The high water mark of his sentimentality came when his young secretary, called Violet, died and he had a marble statue of her carved and put into the cathedral, with a little poem in which she was apostrophised as 'Sweetest Vi' – one of the vergers is supposed to have asked: 'What does "Sweetest Six" mean?' A copy of the statue in plaster stood at the head of the stairs in the episcopal palace looking appealing as one went up to bed, but after the bishop had married a young woman who had healed his broken heart, poor Vi was relegated to the attic. She did not fare much better in the cathedral, for she has been moved dangerously close to the north door and the inscription has been turned towards the wall.

When an old man marries a girl young enough to be his daughter it tends to be regarded somewhat frivolously, but Hope Patten, and those who thought as he did about clerical celibacy, could hardly be expected to enjoy the joke. The new Mrs Pollock was a lady of decided views and it was rumoured that she had more influence in the diocese than might have been expected outside the pages of Trollope. A young ordinand arriving at the palace was asked his name, and when he gave it she is supposed to have said: 'Ah yes: we didn't think we were going to ordain you.'

It is interesting that the bishop's attitude towards Walsingham hardened after his marriage and many thought, perhaps unjustly, that his wife was responsible. Hope, in writing to friends about the difficulties he was having, said several times: 'I am told that the lady is at the bottom of it.'

After their early brush about reservation there was little trouble for several years. The bishop was fully conscious of the remarkable work Hope was doing in the parish of Walsingham and, while he could not approve of everything he did, he was prepared to admit that from a pastoral point of view there were few parishes in his diocese where the results were more encouraging. The Anglican Communion has only managed to hold together at all by bishops knowing when to turn a blind eye. The system simply does not work with a bishop of too rigid views, be they 'high' or 'low'.

In 1927–28 a controversy arose which brought Hope and the bishop together as curious bedfellows. It was the effort to throw out the measure for the reform of the Prayer Book which brought these two unlikely champions to fight for the same cause, but for totally different reasons.

It is today hard to imagine the heat which was generated on this issue and the amount of printer's ink expended in a last abortive attempt to retain the fading vision of uniformity in worship. A Royal Commission had been set up in 1904 as a result of the persistent ritual controversies, and it reported in 1906 recommending a revision of the Prayer Book. This proposal was before Convocation for almost twenty years and its final decision was that the 1662 book, which plays the part of 'the old man of the sea' to the Church of England's 'Sinbad', should be retained, and a new book drawn up the use of which should be permissive. It was left to the bishops to put such a book together, and this was presented before Convocation in February 1927.

It would not be unfair to say that their Lordships then, as now, were not primarily interested in liturgy, but in finding some formula which they could persuade clergy to use. The great cry of the day was 'Ordered Liberty'. The book ran into opposition from the extreme wings of the Catholic and Protestant parties within the Church of England. The latter felt that any departure from 1662 was a sacrifice of the principles of the Reformation, and the former were unhappy about the Canon of the new order for Holy Communion, particularly the position of the 'Epiclesis' (the invocation of the Holy Spirit). It had been put after the Words of Institution, and they regarded it as near blasphemy to call down the Holy Ghost upon the already consecrated Elements. Also they could hear the crack of the whip in a rubric put in about Reservation of the Sacrament which was obviously designed to bring them to heel.

The Bishop of Norwich was one of only four bishops who voted against the book, but it was passed by both Convocation and Church Assembly with large majorities. He represented a small and central minority who were violently conservative and were prepared to make use of the arguments and protests of both sides to prevent any change going through. The Bishop of Gloucester, Arthur Headlam, wrote in the *Times*: 'The statement of the Bishop of Norwich that the rejection of the Prayer Book will further the cause of reunion only shows how much his absorption in his own point of view has cut him off from his fellow clergy.' He revealed that 'a determined minority, defeated both in votes and in argument, are trying to influence members of parliament by an organised campaign of letter writing'. He showed the mind of the bishops as a whole when he warned that the rejection of the book 'would not promote order in the church or restrain the excesses of Anglo-Catholicism'.

Bertram Pollock was amongst those who felt an organised crusade was justified and he considered Hope Patten to be the most influential Anglo-Catholic in his diocese, and soon the two were in regular correspondence on the subject.

Hope, in spite of his absorption in his parish and in the restoration of the shrine, did from time to time turn his attention to current controversies in the church and appear in full battle array. In 1930 the statement by the Lambeth bishops on birth control disturbed him to such an extent that he tried to rouse his old ally, Bishop Pollock, but this time with little success. He also wrote to the secretary of the Confraternity of Unity, suggesting that they should print a card to hang in church porches 'stating the enormity of the sin'. Such a card was indeed printed in connection with another campaign in which he was involved to prevent the establishment of the Church of South India, and someone has recalled with great difficulty managing to penetrate to a remote church in the heart of the Norfolk Broads and finding a notice saying 'Members of the Church of South India may not receive Communion in this Church'. It seemed very unlikely that a lady in a sari would be able to negotiate the path to the church, even if she were to make a determined effort to do so.

The letters Bishop Pollock wrote to Hope Patten about the Prayer Book crisis are on deep black-edged paper, for he was still suffering from the loss of 'Sweetest Vi'. On 3 August 1927, he recommends that Anglo-Catholics should declare in large numbers that they do not intend to observe the rules of the new book. This is amusing in view of some of his later and less harmonious correspondence with Hope on the subject of obedience. On 5 August he suggested that Anglo-Catholics and what he calls 'the Protestant underworld' should publish their agreement on three points: '(1) Wrong time – general instability and inconsistency. (2) Church Ass's authority at any rate too little established. (3) No prospect of peace and contentment.' On 21 August he commended the intransigent attitude of the English Church Union communicated to him by Hope and wrote: 'You know my practical turn of mind. Is there anything that I, an outsider, can usefully do in the matter?' A long letter on 11 September said: 'It will be a great pleasure to see you again one day as developments come along.' There was a postscript: 'You speak of the lion's mouth – I suppose your letter was running in my head this morning when I pictured myself as the victim in one of the psalms of the day, Psalm 57.4 (My soul is among lions).' On 26 September he wrote to say he would use his influence to get a manifesto, being prepared by the Vicar of St Andrew's, Leicester, published, and suggested getting as many signatures as possible. On 6 October he suggested that the Fellowship of Catholic Priests should seek an interview with the archbishop which would be reported in the press. On 20 October he concedes that such an action might appear a threatening attitude, but argues that facts which would tend to hinder the passing of the book should be made known now rather than when it is too late. On 24 October he enclosed a cutting from the *Sunday Times*, which said that the new book had a chance of getting through if assurances could be obtained from the Episcopal Bench and the Anglo-Catholics that it would be regarded as a settlement and not a jumping off ground for further 'Romanism'.

On 15 December the proposed book was rejected by the House of Commons with a fine display of protestant frenzy. The bishops lost respect by trying to get it through the next year with most of the concessions to Anglo-Catholics removed, only to have it defeated by a larger majority.

The Bishop of Norwich did not let matters rest after the first rejection and wrote to Hope on 24 February, 1928, asking what his position was towards the re-revised book. He said: 'I have no doubt at all that the step which you took after, or

because of, our talk together in the summer played a considerable part in the rejection of the book last winter.' On 27 February in a long letter he said: 'On one thing you and I and many
wise men are agreed, namely that this is not the right time. The
authorities have consistently derided my policy described in
the enclosed, but it might prevail in the end.' His view was
that the non-contentious parts of the book might be authorised
for use. He said, with rather naïve optimism: 'I really believe
that this is not a negative policy, but that it would draw people
together, including some who do not go to church.'

He and Hope never achieved such intimacy again, and it was
not long before they were engaged in a great battle of wits
against each other. It was extraordinary to find Hope such an
enthusiastic champion of the Prayer Book of 1662, in view of
the fact that Walsingham was becoming the epitome of the
Roman rite and a Mecca for all those who would gladly have
seen anything peculiarly Anglican swallowed up. It was an
example of a certain ambivalence which he always retained and
which irritated his papalist friends. His great devotion to King
Charles the Martyr was always regarded by some as a lowering
of the 'Walsingham standard' – a phrase which had come to be
used by those advertising for curates and indicating the type
of churchman they required.

It was ironical that his alliance with the bishop over the Prayer
Book controversy was the very thing which drew that prelate's
attention to what was going on at Walsingham and caused him
to come and see for himself. He must have given Hope some
warning of his intention to make a personal visitation of the
parish church, because the faithful were all told that they must
pray hard for a right outcome from this event.

There are those who have contended that Hope had already
made up his mind to build a shrine apart from the parish
church and that he used the bishop's intervention as an excuse
to justify this. There is plenty of evidence that for some time he
had been contemplating a chapel in the hospice garden, mainly
for the Sisters, since the cellar had soon proved so unsuitable.
At one time he got so far as having some footings done in the
hospice garden for a building which was to cost £200, but
it came to nothing. It is more than probable that the thought

of placing the image in this chapel had been amongst the many plans he had fermenting in his mind at that time, as he must have foreseen that there would be likely to be trouble about it in the parish church sooner or later. One of his great characteristics was looking ahead and foreseeing the possible obstructions which might be put in the way of his objectives. It was both a strength and a weakness. Already he was concerned about the survival of the shrine and convinced that, should he die suddenly, it would be suppressed. This later became an obsession and was responsible for many of the things he did which were unwise and even culpable. He made others believe that the patron of the living was only waiting for his demise to change the type of churchmanship in the parish. This was proved entirely untrue in the event and the greatest care was taken to find someone who would continue the tradition.

Bishop Pollock arrived at the vicarage early one morning and Hope, with his most ingenuous smile, said: 'How nice to see you, my Lord.' 'Not nice at all', replied the bishop, 'I have come to see the church', and off they went.

There is a great element of comedy in the whole of this visit, and looking at it from a distance one can appreciate this, but both the parties must have been deeply disturbed at the time.

The first thing that caught the Bishop's eye was the Confessional and he made towards it with evident signs of disapproval. 'How do you use it?' he asked, and Hope always said he had great difficulty in refraining from saying: 'Just kneel down there and I'll show you!'

'Do you make people go to Confession?' was the next question and Hope replied that it would not be much use to them if he were to do so.

The bishop then marched towards the Lady Chapel, as he had had complaints from people who could not get behind the altar to see the Sidney tomb. He insisted on having the frontal off to see how close the altar was to the tomb and then got down on his hands and knees and put his head underneath. It was a curious posture and anyone coming into the chapel might have thought that another Walsingham custom was being born. When he surfaced again he said that the altar must be brought forward so that people could get behind. Hope pointed out that the Sacrament was reserved there, but that if he moved the altar forward he would need to place it on the High Altar, and would do so if he might tell the people that it had been done by order of the bishop. The bishop paused, but was sharp enough to see the trap and so said: 'No, leave it where it is.'

He then prepared to put Hope Patten into a difficult position and asked whether he had any services in connection with the consecrated elements. He then enquired about the form of this service called Benediction. Hope replied cautiously that there were two hymns, a prayer and a blessing. The bishop immediately asked what sort of hymns, and when Hope paused he said: 'Are they the sort of hymns you would have at a Mothers' Union meeting?' to which Hope was able to answer 'Yes' with a clear conscience, and the subject was dropped.

The bishop made to leave the chapel, pointedly averting his eyes from the Shrine of Our Lady of Walsingham, but Hope pulled at his coat tails so that he stepped back into a box of votive candles scattering them in all directions. This placed him at a disadvantage and Hope was able to say: 'You must see this because it is a reproduction of the image which stood in Walsingham from 1061 to 1538.' The bishop was not impressed. 'Do you teach your people to worship the Virgin, Mr Patten?' he asked. 'Only in the sense that they worship their earthly mothers' was the reply which only drew a grunt from the bishop as he made his escape from the Lady Chapel before it could be suspected that he was making any devotions there.

When he got into the body of the church he said: 'It is far worse than I expected, far worse; all these things which you have put in must be cleared away.' Hope's mouth went into a straight line, which it always did when he was in a determined frame of mind. He told the bishop that the adornments and the services were in line with the Catholic movement in the Church of England, and he would call a meeting of all Catholic-minded priests in the diocese and they would work out a common policy and see how far in conscience they could meet the bishop's demands. In regard to the statue of Our Lady of Walsingham, this was a separate thing; it was never originally in the parish church, but had a chapel of its own, and ought to do so again. If the bishop wished he would try and see that such a chapel was built on private property to house the image, and if he had an objection to statues he would replace it in the church by a picture. The bishop thought he had won a victory and appeared to be quite satisfied with the arrangements, in fact, he allowed himself to say: 'That would be very kind' – a statement which he must later have felt to be a little impetuous. When they got to the door of the church Hope asked for a blessing and was marched back to the High Altar, and there in halting terms the Lord Bishop of Norwich called down God's blessing on a project which was to cause him grave disquiet for the rest of his episcopate. When he got home the bishop was having second thoughts, and he wrote: 'I have not got it quite clear in my mind where the image would be placed . . . not, I suppose, in any consecrated building.'

Hope replied at length assuring him that the image would not be put in any of the other churches, which is obviously a thought which had crossed the bishop's mind. He tells him that land has been given and adds: 'Of course there has been much feeling about the whole business and I have had to handle it very carefully, but I think people who really mind and understand have all been very much touched by your great kindness and consideration in this affair.'

This touched the sentimental chord in the old man, who replied: 'I very much appreciate the goodness of your letter, and I am always so glad that our personal relations together offer a conspicuous illustration of what I always say, namely that good men can differ without quarrelling.'

There can be little doubt that Hope had already foreseen the outcome of the bishop's visit and had decided what action he would take if necessary, for he acted with great rapidity. He called a meeting in London of various influential people who were already interested in the shrine, such as Fr Fynes-Clinton and William Milner, and put his plans before them. He got an encouraging response and some of them there and then promised to put up money for the project. These were the events which led to the foundation of the College of Guardians which he formed while the shrine was being rebuilt.

An appeal was launched and in the spring number of the *Mirror* he revealed that he already had £700, but that much

more was needed. He wrote: 'The name of everyone who con-
tributes will be entered into *The Golden Book of our Lady's Friends*
and sealed in her Altar.'

The architect chosen was Romily B. Craze who had Milner
as his partner in the firm of Milner and Craze, although
Milner seldom got around to doing much designing. He had
caught up Craze in his church interests, so that the firm were
already known for their ecclesiastical work. Romily Craze had
been to Walsingham and was enthusiastic about the job. He
was a skilful architect but, most important, he was infinitely
adaptable and was prepared to translate Hope's dreams into
practical terms. Many architects would have resented the
constant interference and change of plan, but he became
devoted to 'Pat', as he would call him, and indeed admired his
skill. He would often say that architecture lost a promising
recruit when Pat decided to be a priest.

Craze produced two plans, one with the Holy House and
its porch which would cost £1,500, and the other with the Holy
House covered by a larger chapel of the same dimensions as
those given by Willaim of Worcester. The plans were discussed
at length in the vicarage by Hope, Craze and Milner, with Derrick Lingwood there to keep the brake on. It was decided that
they must be content with the cheaper plan, and they all
went to bed. Next morning at breakfast Milner announced that
he had decided to lend the extra money so that the bigger plan
could be put into action. When Hope protested at his generosity
he showed a rare flash of anger and said that it was his money
and he would do what he liked with it. He was able to guarantee
an overdraft at the bank and enable the larger sum to be raised,
which it was in a remarkably short time.

Much legend has arisen over the site chosen for the new
shrine and it has been said that Hope had a psychic feeling
that this was the original position. In fact the kitchen garden of
the hospice on the corner of Holt Road and Knight Street was
the obvious place for such a building without the need of too
much spiritual guidance. Hope's psychic feelings were not
always proved to be correct, for when some bones were dug
up he was convinced that they were those of Nicholas Mileham,
the Walsingham martyr – they were, however, identified as
belonging to an animal.

There is no doubt, for it was well remembered, that before the building began he prayed himself and urged others to pray that, if it were God's will that the Holy House should be rebuilt, the original sign of water should be given. He arranged for the nuns and some monks from Nashdom, who were now living there, to meet every evening upon the spot where it had been decided that the Holy House should be built and to offer prayers.

Before the building commenced Hope was anxious to have some trenches dug in the garden and see what lay under the soil. There was little doubt that he was hankering after the sign of water. He persuaded one of the choirmen and his brother to dig in different places, and they first found what appeared to be a cobbled courtyard; their next hole revealed what was evidently the base of a churchyard cross, and then when they dug in a third place water began to gush out before they had dug down many feet. Further investigation showed that they had discovered a disused well. This was the sign for which Hope had been waiting. He received it as such and his faith in it never wavered for the rest of his life. The well was found to be of Saxon origin and appeared to have been blocked up deliberately, for when it was cleared soles of shoes and other refuse of the Tudor period were brought to light.

It is odd that Hope did not mention any of these things in the current numbers of the *Mirror*, but from that time his mind had identified the cobbles with the 'cobbled court' mentioned by Erasmus, the base of the cross with the 'burial ground of the Canons', where the original house is said to have been situated, and therefore the well must be the spring of Richeldis. The architect was made to alter his plans so that this well might be incorporated into the new building, which he managed to do very cleverly.

It would not be an exaggeration to say that with the beginning of the rebuilding of the shrine, Hope became a new person, and his terrific efforts as a parish priest were now canalised to a fresh objective. He was no longer as accessible to his parishioners. Events like the May Revels were forgotten, for he was totally absorbed in the task not only of getting the shrine built, but of making it live and ensuring its continuance. In the *Mirror* he wrote: 'We are living in historic days again. New beginnings, new prospects, new hopes' (not intended as a pun).

It was at this time that he began to draw up a constitution. He had very much in his mind, as a warning, the example of the Monks of Caldy, who had launched themselves into the Holy See carrying with them all the money and property which had been given for the revival of an Anglican Benedictine Community. He had no fears of his own defection, but he was very conscious of mortality, as can be seen from the letter he wrote to Milner when the property was first obtained. Thus it was that he conceived the idea of the Guardians of the Shrine of Our Lady of Walsingham as a body of Trustees who would hold all the property, so that it could never be alienated except in the unlikely event of them all crossing the Tiber in the same boat.

In the autumn number of the *Mirror* he writes: 'The Sanctuary has been placed in charge of Trustees and a body of Guardians, which is to number, when the ranks are complete, twenty-four men – twelve of each order, lay and cleric. After the trustees had accepted the invitation to act, the present Guardians were nominated by them all, and others will be added to the number upon election of the whole body.' There then follows a list of seventeen names. Several were obvious choices, Bishop O'Rorke, Fr Fynes-Clinton and Sir William Milner, who had now inherited his father's title and wealth. Amongst the clergy were: the Abbot of Nashdom, Dom Denys Prideaux, whom Hope had first met when he was Guest Master on Caldy Island where he had lived as an oblate. He was a brilliant but somewhat unbalanced man who never really knew much about the Church of England, even on its Catholic wing. Someone remembered him looking up from a paper and saying: 'Anyone know anything about a church in Margaret Street?' After the defection of Caldy he was persuaded to head another attempt at founding a Benedictine Order for men in the Church of England, which he did with success against his own inclinations.

Then there was Fr A. H. Baverstock, whose force of personality had enabled him to establish at Hinton Martel, in a tiny country parish, a system of teaching and worship which would have enabled it to be absorbed into the Roman Communion without any of the parishioners noticing that anything had happened.

Another original Guardian, Fr Elton Lury, Vicar of St Peter's, Limehouse, was a married priest, although Hope had written into the constitution that any priest Guardian who married *ipso facto* ceased to be a member. He appeared able to pass an act of oblivion as to how they had obtained a wife if they were already married.

Other Guardians were: Fr Humphrey Whitby, of St Mary's, Graham Street, where it was said that one must be at least the younger son of an Earl to be allowed to carry round the bag; Fr Roger Wodehouse, who would have been allowed to do so as he was the son of the Earl of Kimberley. He had transformed the Church of St Paul's, Oxford, into such a complete replica of a Parisian church that a continental Catholic who was taken to see it, together with the Chapels of Blackfriars and the Pusey House, was quite certain that St Paul's was Catholic and Blackfriars was Protestant, but did not quite know what to make of Pusey House.

The Lay Guardians included the Duke of Argyll and Lord Halifax. The former was to be seen in his element in the Episcopal Church near his castle at Inveraray where he sang complicated plainsong in a high reedy voice from a mediaeval Antiphoner, translating from the Latin as he went along. The latter was an obvious choice as he was the most prominent and saintly of Anglo-Catholic laymen who had given up all his worldly prospects to be president of the English Church Union. He had an unlimited interest in all things connected with the Catholic religion and a Belgian Abbot, after staying with him at Hickleton, said: 'I live in a monastery and naturally there is some talk of religion, but at Hickleton – mon Dieu, there is nothing else!' He was interested in Walsingham from afar as he never visited the shrine, but in 1926 he and Sybil Thorndike had both sponsored an appeal for the new hospice.

Sir John Shaw, a naval officer, son of a priest and enthusiastic about the Catholic religion, together with a small band of locals, the churchwardens and Derrick Lingwood, who was becoming indispensable, completed the number of the first members of the College of Guardians.

From this time forward Hope used the Guardians very much

as a stick with which to beat the bishop. With the aid of Fynes-Clinton he developed an impressive customary and they were given mantles, like members of the Order of the Garter, and he presided as Master wearing a splendid chain of office. They were entirely his creation, and when later they opposed him over certain matters which they thought unwise, he ruefully considered himself a kind of ecclesiastical Frankenstein.

The summer number of the *Mirror*, 1931, records that 'A Novena of prayer will be made from and including 14 August to 22 August, asking that the bishop of the diocese may license the new Pilgrimage Church and Shrine'.

The bishop, however, was becoming more and more determined to have nothing whatever to do with it and not to allow it to appear that he did.

It was at this time that he called on Lady Gurney at the Abbey and asked for a pair of field-glasses. He went upstairs and spent some time gazing at the building operations on the other side of the high wall. He would not even stay to be cheered by a cup of tea, but went away muttering: 'Deplorable, deplorable!'

A foundation stone was laid for the Holy House with a Latin inscription stating that it had been restored in the pontificate of Pius XI, Bertram being Bishop of Norwich and Hope Patten parochus of Walsingham. This got into the press and was commented upon unfavourably by the *Catholic Herald*. Someone sent a cutting to Bishop Pollock and he sent it on to Hope with the following message: '*If* this is true, is there any need for *my* name to appear? Would not the date be adequately given otherwise, without my appearing as a kind of Consule Manlio!!'

To this Hope replied:

The inscription has been rightly copied and well interpreted, but the people who did it and published it have swallowed the hook together with the bait.

'It has been inserted in the wall as a witness to the claim of Anglicans, which claim our English Roman 'friends' will not allow, namely that we (the donors) believe that in this year of grace 1931 the rightful parish priest of Walsingham is Hope

Patten, *not* Fr Grey of Fakenham – and that the true bishop of the diocese is Dr Pollock and not the Bishop of Northampton. But while maintaining these facts we also record our belief and affirm that we are not members of a separate body, cut off from the rest of Christendom, and to emphasise this fact we state that in this year 1931 Pius XI was Chief Bishop. We Catholics are wearied at the perpetual jibes of English Romans and their taunt that we are no ministers of the church, just as in the same way our patience is almost exhausted by the agitations and blasphemy of the militant protestant section represented by Bishop Barnes and the followers of Mr Kensit.

In years to come we hope that, whatever people may say of us, good or bad, they will be able to say 'Well, these "English Catholics" did believe profoundly in their own ministry and at the same time in their place in the rest of Western and Eastern Christendom'.

The very fact that we associate ourselves as ministers of the true church in the same breath, as it were, with Pius XI, declares our belief in the English Church and our own right in the sun! I felt sure from the first that the Roman feathers would be ruffled!

Thank you so much for sending the cutting, I had not seen it before.

The bishop was not to be deflected and insisted that his name should be removed from the stone, and the line in which it appeared was filled in with plaster and obliterated.

It was extremely unwise of Hope to have had the name of the Pope put on to the stone for he cannot have been ignorant of the emotive effect that the very name of the Bishop of Rome still had in England, and he must have realised that in using it he was asking for trouble. He certainly got it, and the stone became known as 'the rock of offence'.

As he suspected, the Roman Catholics certainly did not like it, and before long they had set up a rival shrine and issued literature which pointedly ignored everything that Hope had done.

The *Church Times* adopted its most 'maiden-auntish' style in a public rebuke and from this time was very sniffy about everything connected with the shrine. It frightened the more moderate Catholic parishes who felt that Walsingham was out of their sphere, and for a long time it was only definitely 'papalist' parishes which supported the shrine. This tended to reduce its influence and to suggest that it was the preserve of a very limited number of Anglicans, which was not in the least what Hope himself wanted.

The new shrine was blessed on 15 October 1931, a mellow autumn day, and the image of Our Lady was carried through the flag-decked streets and escorted by 3,000 people, for a special train had been run from London. Bishop O'Rorke presided in his tallest mitre and the Abbot of Nashdom was there in a flurry of watered silk. It was Hope's first large scale triumph in recreating the Middle Ages in twentieth century England. Monks and nuns and friars thronged the narrow streets of the village, while lay people carried lighted candles and rosaries and forgot for a while that they were self-conscious Anglo-Saxons. It was not quite the removing of the image which Bishop Pollock had envisaged.

He had made it quite clear to Hope Patten that he could not countenance the new building with any sort of licence. On 12 October, before the great day, Hope wrote to him: 'I feel I must write, as you have been so kind all the time I have been in Walsingham, and I hate not being quite open with you. On Thursday morning quite early I am going – as parish priest – to bless the new chapel in the Sisters' grounds (the new Shrine) and I propose celebrating their Mass. Many of my friends tell me I ought to do so and that there is no need to trouble you about it, but I feel I cannot do that. I am not happy about it as I know you will not personally approve; at the same time I trust you will not positively forbid me and then put us under a ban.

'I think I shall be much blamed for writing – but I just feel I must.'

The bishop replied immediately. It is interesting that he begins 'Dear Mr Patten' and not 'My dear vicar' as he had addressed Hope heretofore.

I am a little surprised to have your letter after our long conversation. It proves to have been rather a waste of time to talk as we did if your mind is made up or if I failed to make it clear that I do not think it proper for the Holy Communion to be celebrated publicly except in a chapel licensed for the purpose. . . . However, this waste of time does not mitigate my appreciation of those respects in which, at a real cost to yourself, you have conformed, and have come into line with the general worship of the Church of England, as set out in the Book of Common Prayer.

It is a little difficult to understand what had drawn this appreciation from the bishop for, to the outward eye, the worship at Walsingham went forward in the same way as had now indeed become 'our custom', and the villagers would have been surprised at anything else. However, in deference to the episcopal wishes Hope himself did not, for some years, say Mass again in the Holy House, but encouraged others to do so.

He was kept very busy with the new chapel, for it had attracted a good deal of attention and he records in the *Mirror* that people from all over the country are visiting the sanctuary. There was much to do in laying out the gardens in which he had the help of William Milner, who was a notable gardener and was already making his own gardens at Parceval Hall in Yorkshire so splendid that, when he died, the *Times* referred to his Rock Garden as one of the most interesting in the country. The work in the shrine gardens was done by William Frary, a villager who had grown up under Hope's influence, and who was enthusiastic about the revival of the pilgrimage. He became Beadle of the Shrine, as well as gardener, and would head processions in a scarlet gown and carrying a mace. His early death was a personal grief to Hope as well as a great loss to the shrine; but his memorial remains in the very beautiful and imaginative gardens he created.

Around these gardens were being erected Stations of the Cross, with a Calvary Hill and a Sepulchre made out of concrete at the far end. It is odd that the *Church Times* should have singled this out for special abuse, calling the idea 'tasteless', for in a few years Easter Tombs became the rage in Anglican churches.

The idea of the 'Maria Park' around the shrine had come from Hope's familiarity with Belgium where there are many. At this time a large crucifix was placed in the sunk garden and called the 'Hatcham Crucifix' because it was claimed to have been outside the Church of St James, Hatcham, where Fr Tooth was vicar, and to have figured in the ritualistic riots which took place there. Oddly enough, Hope does not mention in the *Mirror* the gift of this crucifix nor is there any record of how it came into his possession, but some recent research into the church at Hatcham seems to show that there never was a crucifix outside it.

The whole place began to have the magic touch of Hope's imagination. There was a carillon of bells hung in a wooden frame and rung every evening by William Frary, and the gardens were full of interesting surprises. Inside the Holy House the altar had been constructed of old stones, the wall behind hung with cloth of gold and the image set in a niche surrounded by rays of glory. It was a complete reconstruction of the kind of thing one might see on the continent, and the casual visitor could be excused for feeling he was no longer in England when he crossed the threshold.

Into the walls of the little house had been built stones from ruined abbeys and holy places all over the British Isles. How Hope managed to obtain such a collection is a mystery. Certainly he wrote around asking and got a good response, but one cannot help feeling that some had been removed by 'cloak and dagger' methods. The Holy Well was by the side of the house and approached by two flights of steps. Unfortunately several people fell down them while gazing at the stones. Fr Fynes-Clinton recalled: 'A woman fell down the steps of the Holy Well and broke her leg. I believe she had come to be cured of something. Very disappointing!' After this it was surrounded by railings, although Hope thought they spoiled the effect.

The number of pilgrimages was increasing, but Hope realised that at the moment they were only possible for the leisured who could be free in the middle of the week. With the discovery of the Holy Well pilgrims wanting the waters were no longer dependent on the Abbey grounds being open to the public, and so he decided to try to persuade parishes to come over the weekend. He produced a leaflet to send to priests giving the story of Walsingham and then adding: 'We are suggesting that you might like to bring your congregation on pilgrimage on either a Saturday, staying until Monday or Sunday afternoon; or, as some are now doing, for one day only, a Sunday.' He had already begun the 'as is our custom' technique with pilgrims, and 'as some are now doing' in the *Mirror* usually meant it was something he wanted them to do.

The leaflet went on to give a suggested programme which contained: 'Benediction and a Second Address' in the afternoon. They were sent out to Priest Associates and to anyone considered as likely to be interested; but obviously there was someone on the mailing list who had a misdirected interest for on 24 June 1932, Hope received a letter from the bishop: 'I have had forwarded to me from London a printed invitation sent to somebody or other to visit England's Nazareth.

'In the last paragraph but one it is said that Benediction and a second address will follow at about 3 o'clock. Would you be so good as to let me hear whether this means Benediction involving the use or the exposure of the Consecrated Bread and Wine. I am asked whether the invitation goes out with my sanction.' (He had obviously learned a little more about Benediction since his visit of the previous year.)

Hope's reply was brief and to the point: 'In answer to your question, yes, Benediction spoken of in the printed paper is the ordinary Benediction of the Blessed Sacrament.'

At that time Benediction was a word which brought the blood surging to the head of most English diocesan bishops, but few of them had much idea what it involved. Later a priest who had been appointed to a bishopric thought he ought to attend the service to see what it was like and said afterwards: 'That seemed to me very inoffensive – from all the fuss I had expected something far more extraordinary.'

A spirited correspondence now developed between Hope and the bishop as to what wording could be put on the papers to make it quite clear that they had not got episcopal approval.

Hope suggested: 'This paper is printed and sent out on the authority of the Pilgrimage Committee and the Administrator of the Shrine', but the bishop was insistent that 'and has no diocesan authority' be added.

Hope was rather aggrieved: 'You know you are rather like the executioner asking the man to cut off his own head!', he wrote, 'I fear if I were to put on the heading of the notice "and has no diocesan authority" people would think we were excommunicated, and I should get into great hot water if I were to send such a notice out without first consulting the other Trustees and the Guardians of the Shrine.' He then suggests that the word 'sole' be placed before 'authority of the Pilgrimage Committee' as making it quite clear that it has no diocesan authority.

The bishop dismissed the idea that anyone might think excommunication to be involved and said, quite reasonably, that if it is evident that there is no diocesan authority, why not express it explicitly? He then suggests 'has no authority of the bishop' might ease the situation. He adds: 'I do not want to be needlessly hard upon you, but I do not want to be needlessly hard upon myself.'

At the end of July he had to write and enquire if his letter had gone astray. Hope apologised but made consulting the Guardians his excuse for not having written; he then suggests that 'the Shrine being private property and extra-parochial' be added to the formula he had already suggested. He then offers to destroy these notices and be more discreet in issuing others.

The bishop had not been a headmaster for nothing and could see signs of submission if he remained firm. He replied:

> I am afraid that your proposal now would not be suitable, for though the Shrine is private property, it is not extra-parochial in the sense that it stands in no parish. Perhaps for the moment the best plan would be for us to try your last suggestion, that is to say, to abandon *these* notices and to issue some further paper. But of course I should wish to see the further paper *before it is issued,* and I am wondering whether it would be easy for you to make *it* more acceptable to me.

Hope replied that he would certainly do all he could to make the new notices as acceptable as possible, but as the summer was so advanced he proposed leaving it till next year.

The headmaster now felt the time had come when he must bring this disobedient boy to heel, and so wrote saying what he would expect to be put in the new paper, but he had pressed Hope to the limit of his patience and on the Feast of Assumption, buoyed up by the ceremonies of the day grandly celebrated in a marquee pitched in the hospice garden and christened 'the canvas cathedral', he took up his pen and wrote to the bishop:

> I have tried to meet you as far as possible about the notices and I can do no more. There is no need for you to consider the new form, as I shall issue whatever invitation I consider best, as it is obviously impossible to satisfy you. It is an unheard of imposition for a bishop to ask one of his parish priests to submit his notices for approval; I foolishly corresponded on the matter as I wished to do all I could to please you. I refuse to do anything more in the matter.

Not surprisingly there was silence for almost a year, till in reply to a letter about confirmations Bishop Pollock wrote:
'Thank you for your kind words; I prefer reading them to those in your letter of 15 August 1932, which naturally concluded our previous correspondence.'

He never commented on the notices again, but he made it quite clear that he was not prepared to give any kind of countenance to the shrine as such.

Other people were more worried about this than Hope himself, for his fertile mind was already engaged on the problems of extending the existing chapel. If anyone enquired about its status he was at this time rather evasive. The experience of building had whetted his appetite and for the rest of his life he was never so happy as when he was planning and building something.

By the autumn of 1932 he had convened the first Guardians Chapter and got them to agree to the building of an extension which, as he says in the *Mirror*, 'will be known as the Choir'. He appealed for £3,000 and suggested it should be a memorial to the Oxford Movement Centenary to be held next year. In dramatic and large print he asks: 'Will 19 July be the day of the laying of the foundation stone of the new buildings? Or will 19 July be the day of the opening of the choir? To a large extent that depends on you!'

The response was not encouraging and in the next number of the *Mirror* he reports that readers have not 'done their bit' towards this much needed extension yet. It was very frustrating but he was already getting Bernard Craze to prepare various plans, including cloisters, a library and a Chapter House.

One thing the Oxford Movement Centenary did produce for Walsingham, beside a sizeable crowd on 19 July, was a large outdoor Altar Pavilion which had been constructed and used for a single High Mass at Lord Halifax's house at Hickleton and then given to the shrine and erected in the gardens. Hope was not amused when a visitor asked at what hour the band played.

In 1934 he achieved a great coup when he secured the ordination of Derrick Lingwood, which would have been impossible in the Norwich diocese. Since he had come to live in the vicarage, Derrick had become almost indispensable: he paid all the bills and organised the pilgrimages, while during the appeal for the building of the Holy House he had managed an office devoted to this. But he never lost sight of the fact that he had a vocation to the priesthood, and Hope's side of the bargain was that he would help him to ordination. The tension with Bishop Pollock made it improbable that he would even consider ordaining a deacon of any sort to the parish, let alone one who had been trained there.

It was a great surprise to many people when Derrick Lingwood was ordained to the diaconate by Bishop Blunt of Bradford, raised to the priesthood four months later and returned to Walsingham to work at the shrine without a licence. Bishop Blunt was a slightly modernist high churchman and had showed little interest in Walsingham, which was not much to his taste. Indeed it is doubtful if he ever visited it. The answer to the mystery is that Sir William Milner lived in the Bradford diocese and was one of the most wealthy and important laymen. It was he who with infinite tact had prepared the way.

Bishop Blunt was encouraged to accept Derrick as a curate for the slum parish of Holy Trinity, Bradford, to serve for two years without stipend, which appeared to him a favourable proposition. He met Hope and was deeply impressed by him, so that when after a few months Hope found that he could not manage without Derrick at Walsingham, and presented to the bishop his plans for a College of Priests to serve the Shrine, Derrick was priested and allowed to return to Norfolk. What Bishop Pollock thought about it all is not recorded, except that he said he might work there with his blessing but not his licence.

So Derrick returned to the shrine and the beginnings were made for the foundation of the College of St Augustine, which was to occupy so much of Hope's time for the rest of his life and prove one of his greatest frustrations.

9

Monastic Dreams and Frustrations

THE MONASTIC IDEAL had gripped Hope Patten's attention when he first came into contact with Anglo-Catholicism and he became convinced that he had a vocation to this life. He did not enter the Caldy Community, nor did he become a novice in any other Order, except the attempt to found an Augustinian brotherhood in Aberdeen. It may be remembered that, when evaluating the lessons learned from that experiment, one of the points he had made was that it should have been clearly understood from the start who was to be the leader or Superior. In later attempts to begin a religious community he certainly took care that this mistake should not recur, for he made it abundantly clear who was the Superior – he was!

It is somewhat unfair to make too much of this authoritarianism in Hope, because without it he would have been unable to accomplish many of the important things which he did. After his death the bishop of the diocese was speaking in private of the wonderful work he had done at Walsingham, but added: 'Of course the trouble was that he was a law unto himself.' It was pointed out that, while this might be true, the 'wonderful work' would probably never have been done if he had not taken the law into his own hands.

From early childhood he had always had his own way and it made him physically ill to be crossed in anything which he considered important. Added to this, he was a very strong personality and it is doubtful if he ever realised how frightened people could be of him. Towards the end of his life he was talking to a friend of long standing about the lack of vocations to work at the shrine and said: 'People say that I am domineering – do you think I am domineering?' The friend hesitated and before he could answer Hope went on: 'You obviously do. Well, I'm not. I know how things ought to be done and I like to see them done properly. But I am not domineering.'

It is possible that he never fully understood the Religious Life and that his approach to it was too romantic. He quite unashamedly said that he wanted to have a Religious Order at the shrine because it would give the right ethos. As will be seen, he tried to get some monks to settle there, and when that proved abortive he was forced to think about an Order of his own. One rather felt that if it had been possible to order monks and nuns from an ecclesiastical shop, an appeal would have been put in the *Mirror,* and they would have been obtained that way. As it was not, he was forced to make a foundation himself as one of many projects. Being Vicar of Walsingham and Administrator of the shrine did not leave much time for the role of Lord Abbot, and it has been discovered by painful experience that one cannot have the Religious Life proper as a part-time activity.

Hope had the presence of a religious Superior and a wonderful control and reserve. He rarely showed signs of anger other than a slight flush and tightening of the mouth, but he was absolutely inflexible about things which he regarded as matters of principle. There was a streak of ruthlessness in him in dealing with anyone who he considered was a hindrance to his main objective of the restoration and continuance of the shrine. He was responsible for acquiring a great deal of property, not only around the shrine but all over the village, although the mechanics of raising the money was beyond him and left to the financial acumen of Derrick Lingwood. He represented this as necessary because he was convinced that Roman Catholics were trying to swamp the village. While they did appear at one time unduly interested in securing houses which came into the market, it is hard to see how this could have been a serious threat; but the management of something which resembled an estate with tenants made an irresistible attraction to that part of Hope which thought in terms of a mediaeval abbot. It is an interesting and remarkable thing that if one saw him away from Walsingham he appeared physically smaller and rather insignificant. In his own domains he was an impressive and powerful figure.

In the letter he wrote to Sir William Milner in 1924 when the hospice and land was bought he had said, amongst other things: 'Now we shall look forward to . . . the cell of St Benet', but it was not until 1930 that he persuaded Abbot Denys to allow a group of monks to come and occupy some of the cottages on the east side of the projected shrine, and now known as St Augustine's. It is obvious that Hope expected it to develop into a Benedictine Priory dependent upon Nashdom and serving the shrine. The monks were led to believe it was a 'holiday home' to which they would go for periods of rest. Abbot Denys was by this time becoming very vague and he may well have been responsible for the misunderstanding. Certainly the monks who were sent there were soon disabused of any idea that it was for a rest cure. The cottages were in a very bad state, without a bath and indoor sanitation, and they discovered that the establishment was to be run as a hospice for men, so that their whole time was taken up with domestic chores, interlarded with periods of duty in the new shrine, to show round visitors. Those who ever stayed in the short-lived Hospice of St Augustine have recorded that its discomfort was almost beyond belief.

When the Holy House was built the monks said their Office there in the Latin tongue, which was a further confusion to visitors and something of an irritation to Hope who, with a strange lack of logic, much disliked the use of Latin in the shrine. From time to time he put up notices in the sacristy saying that priests who intended to use anything other than the vulgar tongue must ensure that their Mass was strictly private.

The poor Brothers were still led to believe that this was a period of relaxation, but Hope had very rigid views about their removing their religious habits, even for recreation, and was deeply shocked when some of them visited the village pubs. He himself, as a secular, would never appear without a clerical collar except on holiday, and then usually only on the continent. Towards the end of his life, when he was going to Spain, he seriously considered the possibility of passing through London in a collar and tie, but finally decided that he might be recognised by somebody and preferred to carry a black suit all over Europe rather than be caught out in what he considered an impropriety. Priests who came to Walsingham without the collar, or indeed without a black suit, were apt to receive a somewhat cold reception from the Administrator. Almost always in the parish he wore a soutane and either a curé hat or an enormous black homburg.

As he was an old personal friend of Abbot Denys he wrote confidential letters to him complaining of the behaviour of the younger members of the Community. When Abbot Denys died suddenly in November 1934 these letters were seen by Abbot Martin Collet, his successor, and other senior monks who, not unnaturally, resented them, and St Augustine's Hospice was closed. There was no row, but a certain coldness did develop between Hope Patten and Abbot Martin. They both had a streak of authoritarianism which did not mix happily. Later, when there was trouble with the Sisters, there is little doubt that the Abbot, by his advice, actively encouraged the Reverend Mother to resist Hope's efforts to assert his own will.

Another member of the Nashdom Community, Dom Anselm Hughes, a great expert on music, came for three months in the summer of 1932 to make special observation of the musical position and possibilities. Hope had a great appreciation of the value and importance of good music and when he first came to Walsingham, Oliver Richards produced a remarkably high standard for a village. Since he left in 1928, to be organist at St Margaret's Liverpool, this side of things had rather deteriorated and as Hope was not musical himself he felt the need of advice and help in this matter. His musical taste was once described as rococo or feeble baroque.

Dom Anselm recommended the founding of a Choir School, which he considered would pay its own way if it were *very* expensive, paying good salaries for first-rate masters and so providing an outstanding education. Hope asked him to run this and Abbot Denys gave conditional consent for the scheme to be explored. Dom Anselm went to America on a lecture tour and during that time he came to the conclusion that he would find it difficult to work with Hope. Abbot Denys died and the idea was dropped for the moment, but the plan had taken root in Hope's mind.

Dom Anselm's decision was a very wise one as far as he was concerned, for anyone who knew both men well would have realised that it would not be long before they arrived at a head-on collision about some point and sparks would have flown in all directions.

The Cell of St Benet having come to nothing, Hope turned his attention to the possibility of founding an order of Augustinian Canons himself, and it was at this time and for this reason that he persuaded the Bishop of Bradford to allow Derrick Lingwood to return to Walsingham. The bishop had written: 'I am quite sure that you are right to begin in a small way and to let the things develop. I always believe that that gives a project the best chance.'

It is strange coincidence that there should have been a House of Augustinians at Walsingham before the Reformation, and although this fact must have influenced Hope's decision, we know that in 1913 he was writing notes about the possibility of an Augustinian revival within the Church of England. With youthful enthusiasm he had worked out at that time the constitutions and customs for such a foundation. During the course of his life he must have written piles of manuscript on this subject particularly on the external observances, which were of special interest to him. Most of these were based on the customary of Barnwell Priory, a translation of which had been published at the end of the last century, and studied carefully by Hope.

The spiritual formation developing from a following of the Rule of St Augustine did not interest him in the same way, – this was a great weakness in any attempt to establish a stable community.

It is difficult to judge another person's spiritual life from external observation. Those who tried their vocations at Walsingham have said that Hope was most rigid and assiduous in the observance of such things as the regular saying of Mass, formal meditation and recitation of the Offices, but that he never seemed to be found at private prayer. He was so obviously a very holy person and had great powers of recollection that one feels that it must have been fed on a deep spiritual life. Derrick Lingwood who lived in close contact with him and often saw him at prayers was surprised that he never knew him to make a retreat. Who but God knows the workings of the human soul in its contacts with him? Yet the fact that he was seldom seen praying was a curious observation made by more than one person who had lived in the College at Walsingham.

The Rule of St Augustine is very vague and not at all like the detailed instructions for an ordered life given in the Rule of St Benedict. Each congregation takes this vague 'Rule' as a guide, and the observances are laid down in the respective constitutions. Soon after 1880 the Austin Canons (of the Laterna Congregation) were revived in England when some French Canons Regular settled at Bodmin in Cornwall, having been driven from France by persecution. Since then they have taken charge of several Roman Catholic parishes in various parts of the country and are well established. It is odd that Hope did not seek advice from any of these houses of Canons Regular in England, but relied almost entirely upon what he could discover from historical records.

The College of St Augustine at Walsingham was begun in the vicarage, and with all the other things which were going on few people were aware that it had commenced as an institution. Hope had always had young men living at the vicarage since his arrival over ten years before, and so the comings and goings were no longer the cause of comment in the village. The only vows taken were of Stability and Obedience to the Chapter. Mattins and Evensong were said in common and there was a chapel in the house, but apart from one or two rules the life was not much different from that of the average clergy house when curates were still easy to get and contracted stomach ulcers from living with their unmarried vicars. There were never more than three or four members at a time and Hope and Derrick were much taken up with the parishes and the growing organisation of the pilgrimages, so that they did not see much of each other except at meals.

Yet the future of the college was very much in Hope's mind, and when he drew up plans for Cloisters and Chapter Houses it was with the thought of Austin Canons using them. At that time he was under the illusion that if you could get the buildings you would get the men.

To begin with there was no distinctive dress, but Hope's attention had been caught by the illustration of an Augustinian Canon in Dugdale's *Monasticon*. It showed him wearing a linen rochet, a black mozetta and for the winter a long black cloak. The whole was topped by a very tall biretta. There is some reason to suppose that this was an artistic exaggeration, but Hope copied it exactly, so that he himself and the Walsingham Canons came to wear the biggest birettas which have probably ever been seen in Christendom.

It is true that the linen rochet is part of the habit, but to wear a cotta over it not only looked odd, but showed that Hope's fetish for what he thought to be correct sometimes interfered with the common sense which so often in other matters prevented him from going too far and making things at Walsingham utterly ridiculous.

At the beginning there was a certain secrecy about the existence of the college and it is never mentioned in the pages of the *Mirror* before the war; later an appeal for men to come and try their vocation is one of the recurrent themes. A small pamphlet describing the life and the customs was produced and given to young men thought to be interested, but marked 'strictly confidential'. The detail and elaboration in this reminds one of the oblate rule Hope drew up for himself and Wilfred Leeds when they were little more than boys. A procession to the cemetery to pray for departed members of the community was provided before they scarcely had any living members. He loved small and punctilious observances as much as he loved mystery and secrecy and these elements always complicated any rule of life he drew up.

After the war Hope left the vicarage and moved into the buildings on the east side of the shrine, which from this time became known as The College. Everything was made monastic and he was fascinated by the idea of enclosure. The downstairs windows on to the street were bricked up and women were made to feel that they faced the greater excommunication if they ventured within the gates. Under these circumstances it was not very easy for the parishioners of Walsingham to see their vicar. Indeed during these years most of the parish work was done by Derrick Lingwood.

Derrick still looked after the finances and was given a lot of responsibility, but he was quite certain that he had not got a monastic vocation. All the while the college remained a glorified Clergy House he was prepared to go along with it, but he opposed the multiplication of Offices and such completely monastic customs as reading at meal times, in which Hope delighted.

An illustrated pamphlet called 'Colleges in Mediaeval days and a modern revival under the Rule of St Augustine' was published. It was written by Hope and its whole tone was only likely to appeal to those who were as much in love with the Middle Ages as he was. Derrick was absorbed in parochial work, for which he had a great gift, but found himself less and less in sympathy with the activities of the college. Vows were taken for a period of three years at a time and so, when one three year period was over in 1953, Derrick informed Hope that he felt he must withdraw from the college as he had no vocation for this sort of life. It was obviously a great blow to Hope as Derrick had been the one stable member besides himself. Readers of the *Mirror* were informed that it was no longer correct to address Fr Lingwood with the initials C.S.A. after his name.

Hope was particularly sensitive about the commonly repeated canard that a lot of people had come to try their vocations at the college but soon left, finding him intolerable to live with. In an article in the *Mirror* written in 1955 and entitled rather grimly 'What will happen when Fr Patten dies?' the exact numbers are given: 'Since the inception of this venture sixteen men have come forward during the past ten or more years, offering to live such a life as would be required by a small band of "fellow workers" with Fr Patten in his task as Founder-Administrator of the shrine and its works. Of those sixteen, there were twelve who decided after six months' trial to continue for a further period, still very much in doubt probably as to whether they were called to do such a work, but willing to have a try. Eventually the number came down to five who felt they had sufficient sense of vocation to remain attached to the new foundation under an arrangement renewable every three years. Of these, two are still persevering.'

Hope's own perseverance in an attempt to found the college in spite of continual disappointment is most impressive. In later years, when one suggested that perhaps it would be wisest to abandon the idea, he would say urgently: 'But God has never left us without anyone, that must mean that he intends it to continue.' He himself was the only member of the community who persevered 'unto death', and richly deserves the initials C.S.A. which are carved after his name upon his tomb.

Looking back it is fairly easy to see one or two things which doomed the experiment to failure from the beginning.

A religious community must be for the love and glory of God and nothing else. Works may grow out of it, but a community cannot rightly grow out of a work. Hope's focal interest was always the restoration of the shrine. He said explicitly on several occasions that the college must be founded because the shrine needed religious, and he brought his community into being with this purpose in view.

The whole constitution of the shrine and the College of Guardians made members of the College of St Augustine uncertain of their own position. When 'The College' was spoken of it was often not clear which body was meant. Hope was a sort of ecclesiastical Poo-bah, for he was Vicar of the Parish, Administrator of the shrine, Master of the Guardians and Prior of the Congregation of St Augustine. Those who joined the college were indeed very uncertain 'what would happen when Fr Patten died'. Their relation to the Guardians was not at all clear. When the recitation of Mattins and Evensong in the shrine was abandoned in favour of the Roman Breviary there were several members of the Guardians who thought that this was unwise, and said so. Hope was very pained and even spoke of the college having to move to some other place where they could lead their life unmolested by outside interference. But it was he who had brought the whole set-up into being.

One wonders if he could have managed to form a community if it had been his only work, and whether he really had what it takes to be a religious founder, which is indeed a very specialised vocation. He certainly had the drive and single-mindedness, but apart from the fact that, in spite of great efforts on its behalf, the college was only one of several irons in the fire, it is doubtful if he had the right gifts for a religious superior.

He himself always disclaimed any wish to be the founder and Prior and expressed the hope that someone else would come along and do the job of restoring the Augustinian Community at Walsingham. Yet this was a pipe-dream, for in reality he must have known that before long the Superior and the Administrator would have been bound to clash.

He had little help with the task. Derrick Lingwood tried to go along with him from personal devotion and gratitude, but he was not really drawn to the religious life and had plenty to do in running the parishes and looking after the finances. Many of those who tried and failed complained that they never had any proper training in the religious life. They saw little of Hope himself who was, and remained, a rather remote figure constantly writing at his desk.

His health still gave out under strain and he was forced to go away for long periods leaving the college to fend for itself. He could never see that people might be surprised at his long and elaborate holidays when he claimed to be living on 10s. a week pocket money. Nor could he understand why the young men living a very restricted life should be unsettled when he returned full of stories of the wonders of continental shrines.

As at the vicarage, he took young men to live in the college who were not members of the community, and this led to friction and two standards, religious and secular, in the same household.

He sought and received a good deal of help and advice from the Superiors of other Anglican Communities for men, and he made immense efforts to get his own community recognised by the Archbishops' Advisory Council for Religious Communities. But even this was mixed with a plan to get the shrine licensed under the Private Chapels Act as a Community Chapel.

He was not a good judge of men and, while at the beginning he was rather choosy as to whom he was prepared to take, when it became obvious that vocations were not plentiful, he began to take anybody who came along. In several cases he had reason bitterly to regret this, and the fact of having unsuitable people in the college made it harder to persuade those who might have come to join.

His love of things monastic stirred up a desire for this sort of life in one or two of the young men, who felt that they must find it in its complete expression and took themselves off to Nashdom Abbey, as a sort of junction before boarding the Rome Express. All these things were a great misery to him as well as a frustration, and he suffered terribly as a result. As he grew older his face showed the marks of tragedy.

One cannot but admire his courage and tenacity and he never shirked responsibility. A lady who felt that she had a vocation to the solitary life placed herself under his direction and lived as an Anchoress in the shrine grounds. For many years he took complete responsibility for her spiritual direction before handing it over to a religious, and he kept her steady in a way of life and prayer of which he himself had little personal experience.

In addition to this he tried to establish an order for women, but in this his limitations in the understanding of the basis of the religious life led him into very troubled waters.

One must bear in mind, when considering the actions which Hope Patten took about the Sisters, that for him the future of the shrine was more important than any other factor. He was convinced at that time that its main chance of survival lay in having a religious community established as a settled and permanent part of the organisation. His great phobia was that he would die before this had been accomplished, that the Sisters would be withdrawn and a new parish priest, appointed by unsympathetic patrons, would manage to close down the whole thing. It was this fear, more than his natural determination to have his own way, which led him to behave as he did.

It will be remembered that the first Sisters to work at Walsingham came from the Community of St Peter's Chains at Horbury in Yorkshire, and were sent by their Reverend Mother Sarah, a lady of forceful character, who was a friend of Hope Patten.

Mother Sarah was an artistic and talented woman, but was one of those rather unfortunate people who provoke very strong reactions in others. She drew out enormous devotion and loyalty, particularly in members of her own sex, but there were others who found her intolerable. This is not a very happy characteristic for the Superior of a religious community. She addressed members of her community as 'Child' – and she meant it.

The community at Horbury had been founded in the last century and had won high respect particularly for their work amongst those who used to be known as 'fallen women'. Mother Sarah was elected Superior when she was comparatively young and junior in the order, because of her obvious gifts. Things,

however, soon began to go wrong and those who disliked her
were given plenty of material on which their natural aversion
could feed itself. The basic trouble was that the community,
like most of the early foundations in the Church of England,
was very old-fashioned, and things in the Catholic movement
had marched far further west than the founders could ever have
envisaged. Mother Sarah herself was an Anglo-Catholic of
advanced views, like Hope Patten, which was indeed the basis
of their friendship and why she had been so ready to send Sisters
to Walsingham.

With brisk efficiency she began to change things in the community and this was a cause of unrest, particularly amongst
the older Sisters. She had strong views about religious obedience
so that they had little chance of expressing dissatisfaction.
However, the Mother House at Horbury did not really belong
to the Community but was held in trust by the Wakefield Diocesan Moral Welfare Society, for it had been founded as the
Diocesan Rescue Home. The members of the committee were
certainly not under obedience to Mother Sarah, and soon an
unhappy situation arose for they began to claim that what happened in the chapel was their concern since it was legally their
property.

Mother Sarah decided there and then that she would change
the Mother House and began taking steps to acquire property
elsewhere. The dispute was given spice and intensity when it
was revealed that she had taken to inflicting corporal penances
on the nuns. In her defence it must be said that she had been
urged on in this by the chaplain and that the Rule of St Benedict, drawn up for a paternalistic society and influenced by
scriptural admonitions not to spare the rod, gave such power to
a religious Superior which would have been recognised in any
ordinary household of that period. The psychological aspect,
which today comes immediately into our minds, was not even
by then fully recognised, but the practice was rightly considered
very unhealthy and provided a more effective rod in the hands
of her adversaries than any she was trying to wield in the cause
of discipline.

A bewildered Anglican world discovered that St Peter's
Chains had broken roughly in halves. Part of the community
followed Mother Sarah and finally settled in a large house by

the side of the Thames at Laleham, and the others remained at Horbury at peace with the Diocesan Welfare Committee.

Soon after the split Mother Sarah spent some time in Spain travelling with Princess Marie Louise and Fr Vernon, an Anglican Friar with a great following who later became a Roman Catholic, through the intervention, he claimed, of the late Mlle Therèse Martin, a nun who won universal recognition of her sanctity under the title of 'The Little Flower'. Hope was particularly devoted to St Therèse and erected a large shrine in her honour in the gardens at Walsingham which caused a Roman Catholic to exclaim, 'Look, they have even stolen our Little Flower!' At this time her enemies said that Mother Sarah also was likely to become a Roman Catholic, but she returned from Spain with trunk loads of baroque ornaments which gave the new convent at Laleham a highly continental flavour.

The nuns at Walsingham, since the controversy was basically a high-low conflict, followed Mother Sarah and so became members of the Community of St Peter, Laleham.

They did magnificent work in the village and once the hospice was opened they took charge and ran it for pilgrims with great charm and imagination. It was natural that those who worked there for many of those formative years should become very personally devoted to Hope Patten, who acted as their confessor and director. They lived at first in very uncomfortable circumstances, but an extension was built on to the hospice and it was the beginning of what it was hoped would develop into a permanent convent.

The war increased Hope's feeling of insecurity, and he determined without delay to put into action a plan which had been fermenting in his mind for a long time, whereby Laleham Abbey should allow the Walsingham house to become an independent priory. In June 1941 he started direct negotiations with Mother Sarah and very soon this was occupying his whole attention, and he began to be slightly impatient with her cautious approach to the question. To him it appeared simplicity itself: she was to supply five or six nuns and consider them permanent fixtures at Walsingham. The place would be called a Priory and, while she would appoint the first Prioress, in future the Sisters would elect their own.

From the first Mother Sarah was very guarded in any undertakings she was prepared to give, and one cannot help feeling that she had consulted the Abbot of Nashdom and probably he had cautioned her to be very careful. In the first letter she wrote to Hope Patten on the subject she made it perfectly clear that the constitutions of her community did not allow for an independent house, but that they might be prepared to go through the motions of setting up such a Priory and detail Sisters who would regard Walsingham as a permanent work. After the war they would then consider changing the constitutions and making the Priory a reality as an affiliated house.

They held a conference at Walsingham in August between Mother Sarah, Hope Patten and the Sisters, at which certain details were settled. Later in life Mother Sarah's memory became very faulty and she could not remember orders she had given ten minutes before. It may well be that she was already beginning to suffer from this affliction, for later she roundly denied having consented to things at this meeting which Hope and the Sisters were certain that she had conceded. She was very cautious in everything she wrote down, but it may well be that, under Hope's influence and the Sisters', who knew exactly what he wanted, at this meeting she appeared to fall in with all his ideas.

In the correspondence which developed from this visit it is obvious that Hope Patten is more and more speaking on behalf of the Sisters. He says that he doubts whether it would be 'acceptable to the Sisters' not to have the power of appointing their own director. 'We here think the Abbot ought to come and install Mother Prioress. When can this be done?' He seems to be pushing things as fast as he can, but Mother Sarah was not to be rushed. She insisted on having a formal petition from the guardians, asking her to take steps for the formation of a permanent community and guaranteeing funds for the Sisters' livelihood and a suitable house as a Priory. On this basis an agreement was drawn up and signed by Hope Patten and Mother Sarah, dated 24 October 1941.

On the Eve of All Saints' Day there was a touching little ceremony at Laleham at which the first Sisters were blessed and commissioned for the new foundation. Hope Patten, who was present, must have felt a great satisfaction that his scheme had at last come to fruition. The first Prioress appointed by Mother Sarah was not a Sister who had worked before at Walsingham, but a very senior member of the community who was aged seventy-six and had rather failing eyesight.

All went well until an aspirant appeared early in 1942 and Mother Sarah demanded that she be sent to Laleham for training in the novitiate. From this moment things began to hum and Hope Patten wrote a very high-handed letter, addressed to the Reverend Mother and Chapter, demanding a clear statement of their understanding of the meaning of a Priory. There was a silence for over a month, and then Mother Sarah wrote saying that while deliberations were proceeding she had received a letter from two of the Sisters, written in a tone and spirit which had shocked her, and asking to be what amounted to an affiliated house, which was a completely different thing from a Priory. She probably was shocked by the tone of the letter as it had been dictated by Hope himself in an effort to get some response to his previous communication. Mother Sarah, however, added: 'I have the highest good for Walsingham in my heart and if it is vital to have an affiliated house instead of a Priory, I am prepared to take the necessary steps to add this to the constitution. It will be necessary to have the signature of the Prioress to every such appeal.'

The last sentence held the rub, for the two Sisters who had written were those who had been a long time at Walsingham and were very much dominated by Hope. The Prioress, as Mother Sarah well knew, was entirely to be trusted to fall in only with her wishes.

Hope's letters now became very wild and he began getting and quoting opinions on what other people thought a 'Priory' meant, which was hardly to the point as the issue was what the constitution of Laleham Abbey defined as a Priory.

Mother Sarah became grimmer and grimmer and he should have taken warning that he was going too far. She wrote: 'I have received letters from the Sisters which oblige me to summon them home at once for consultation with the council . . . the efforts being made at Walsingham to hasten matters are having a disastrous effect on the Sisters, as evidenced by the very wrong letters received from them, and if it is allowed to continue it may make their recall necessary . . .' Hope replied unwisely: 'The tactics of Laleham are truly amazing; they seem, in this matter, to be giving with one hand and taking back with the other. Is it possible, Mother, that the community and council did not properly think out the full implication of this foundation? It seems so, as I have asked more than once for definite and clear statements on various points connected with this House under its present condition and can get no reply . . . I am very sorry but we should be entirely giving the position away if the Sisters go to Laleham to meet the council.' He then goes on to say: 'There is a danger that the members may demand that they be submitted to the indignities concerning which the late and present Bishop of London and others have knowledge – until they did agree.' This appears to be a very indiscreet and backhanded reference to Mother Sarah's flagellatory activities at Horbury. It is not surprising that her replies became more haughty and distant: 'We shall be grateful if any suggestions you have to make may be made directly by you to me and not discussed by you with the Sisters of the Walsingham House either individually or corporately. Such an action can have nothing but a harmful effect upon the Sisters there. The use of such terms as 'self-governing' and 'independent' and so forth, it seems to us, is exceedingly misleading and may cause endless misunderstanding.'

When Hope spoke of 'we' it is not quite clear whom he meant, for the Mother Prioress certainly did not agree with him and so he persuaded her to resign, and put her on a train and sent her back to Laleham, explaining in a letter: 'It was impossible for so small a body of Sisters to look after her; it meant one constantly on the watch for her . . . it disorganised the work here much too much, while she could not do the work of a Mother, according to the constitutions of the community.'

The fat was now well in the fire and Mother Sarah pointed out: 'You have not any religious authority over the Sisters, or in connection with their domestic affairs.' She sets out three proposals from which a choice can be made: (1) The cancellation of the agreement and return to the *status ante quo*. (2) Recall of all the Sisters from Walsingham. (3) The release of those Sisters who really desire it from the Laleham Community for the purpose of founding a separate community.

Soon after this she arrived at Walsingham to see the Sisters and a very painful interview took place in their common room. She began by saying that she wished to point out how very much in the wrong they were in pressing to have a novitiate there. If they had not been so stubborn, self-willed, obstinate, impatient, grasping and insistent on having their own way, the community might have considered it in a few years' time. It is not surprising that in writing an account of the interview one of the Sisters said: 'She railed at us the whole time and concluded by saying, "None of this trouble is my fault. I wish you to know that it is entirely your doing if you are released from Laleham and the community closes down the work here".'

Meanwhile Hope was sitting in his office expecting that Mother Sarah would visit him and hear his point of view, but she drove away from Walsingham like Lady Bracknell leaving the stage in 'The Importance of Being Earnest'. Although years later they were reconciled, she never visited the shrine again.

It was at this point that Hope got into touch with Horbury to discover if they would be prepared to supervise the unfortunate Sisters who had been caught between this battle of Titans. He could hardly have initiated an action which would be more likely to be wounding to Mother Sarah. The Rev Mother of Horbury had been one of the leaders of the 'anti-Sarah party' and she was immediately most sympathetic. She said that she fully understood all the difficulties and had in her time been called all the things the poor Sisters had been called, and more. She would be delighted to take them under her wing; and negotiations began for the release of the Sisters through the intervention of the Visitor of the Laleham Community, who was none other than Dr Geoffrey Fisher, at that time Bishop of London. He dealt with the whole matter with a cool detachment and wisdom which was surprising in one whose somewhat limited career had brought him little into touch with nuns. Hope had submitted a précis of the correspondence he had had with Mother Sarah, but Fisher gives no clue as to what he thought of it. He already regarded Anglo-Catholics as tiresome sixth-formers. He wrote to the senior Sister: 'I have heard from the Abbot of Nashdom telling me that the Chapter at Laleham has granted you and the other two Sisters at Walsingham release and asking for my ratification. This I have given and you will no doubt get an official letter from him in a day or two.

'This was the only solution and I am glad that it has come about. I am now writing to the Bishop of Wakefield asking him to see that all the proper steps are taken for your affiliation to the Horbury House, and I am also informing the Bishop-elect of Norwich. There, I think, my concern in the matter ends. I pray that this may all work out to good under the grace of God.'

Although Hope wrote in the *Mirror* in the autumn number, 1942: 'The life of the Walsingham Sisters is going forward with that quiet regularity and peaceful happiness which are to be associated with the religious state', things were by no means that peaceful. The Sisters seemed to have learned the lesson of independence all too well and it was not long before Hope was writing to their new Warden, who was a Mirfield Father respon-sible for the Horbury nuns, telling him that the new Mother is saying: 'Fr Patten has nothing whatever to do with the community now, and only has anything to do with the Sisters who actually work in the shrine or church.' He adds: 'I am having to walk very carefully, as Mother has so changed since she was Sister – even the village is complaining.'

Hope was not used to putting up with this sort of thing and it was not long before the new Mother felt that she had a voca-tion to the contemplative life and retired to an enclosed com-munity where she ended her days.

This left only two of the original Sisters and one of them, having had a slight accident, was sent to Horbury to recuperate. She arrived there in a terribly nervous state and was obviously on the verge of a breakdown, saying that she felt she was damned for having broken her vow of obedience. The surround-ings of her former convent, associated with unhappy memories of the earlier split, did nothing to tranquillise her. The Mother of Horbury wrote to Hope saying that he should come and see her at once, but meanwhile the Sister herself had got into touch with Laleham and had asked to be fetched home. Hope went rushing up by train, but had been forestalled and the bird had flown.

The strain was obviously telling upon him as well, for rumours were going round that the nuns at Walsingham had been persuaded by him to go into rebellion against their Superior, and many religious communities were showing signs of hostility. On his return from Horbury his body began to produce the extraordinary psychosomatic symptoms which he had experienced as a boy when he was under strain and he appeared to many people to have suffered a stroke.

Up to this point the bishop of the diocese had not been brought into the situation. As far as Bishop Pollock was concerned he had never been asked whether the Sisters might work at Walsingham and he would have disclaimed any responsibility for them whatever. He had, however, resigned in 1942 and Bishop Percy Mark Herbert from Blackburn had been appointed in his place. He did everything he could to be helpful and asked the Advisory Council for Religious Communities to look into the matter. Two Cowley Fathers came to Norwich and discussed the whole situation and decided that a new community might be formed if novices were trained at some well established house and that no final vows were taken until there was a sufficient number to form a chapter of twelve members.

This gave Hope the green light to go ahead with the founding of a Community of Our Lady of Walsingham which he had always wanted. He had only one nun left in Solemn Vows and so he was forced to make her the Superior. This was unfair, as she was the most junior of the Laleham Sisters and through ill-health had herself suffered a very broken novitiate. However, quite a number of aspirants appeared and he soon had a bunch of figures bustling around in religious habits, but the original conflict with Laleham had been about sending novices to be trained elsewhere and he could not bear to let them out of his hands.

It was a great stroke of good fortune for Hope when Fr Raymond Raynes was called back from South Africa to be the Superior of the Community of the Resurrection. He had a great devotion to Walsingham and was prepared to throw his own weight and that of his community into getting a religious order established there. He was a very strong personality and knew a lot about the religious life. His influence led to a great deepening of the monastic spirit in his own community and he had many commitments to the church at large, but he was prepared to spend a lot of time and effort on the affairs of Walsingham, later as a Guardian, but in the beginning by becoming Warden of the Community of Our Lady of Walsingham. He had no illusions about Hope's failings, which had led to the existing confusion, but he admired him greatly and felt that Our Lady's Shrine was worthy of any labours he might expend on its behalf. He tried firmly and kindly to keep things stable. 'As regards the immediate present', he writes, 'I think all the novices and the postulant should be sent to Wantage as soon as it can be arranged.'

This was not done and things went on for two or three years in an increasingly unsatisfactory way, till at last Fr Raynes felt he could do no more, and as the community had dwindled to the Prioress and one novice, he wrote saying that he must resign. Ten days later he wrote again: 'As to my resignation, as I think I tried to make clear to you, this is not due to any irritation nor because I am unwilling to try and help you, but simply to the fact that it seems to me I am not able to help you in the way you wish to be helped and that my advice has not been accepted (here again, you have a perfect right not to accept it), and that my judgement has not been trusted, and finally that, judging from what has happened, various people in the community have not been frank with me; had they been so, a good deal of this might have been avoided . . . I would add that whatever happens my devotion to the shrine and my appreciation of its work will not be in any way lessened nor – I trust – my affection for and friendship with yourself.'

Hope was now faced with the possibility of there being no Sisters at all at the shrine, and there were those who felt that he was reaping the fruit which he had sown when he first encouraged the Laleham Sisters to stand out against their Superior. He went cap in hand to various communities to see if they would be prepared to work at the shrine, but, not unnaturally, he found a reluctance to send nuns to Walsingham. After a depressing meeting of the Guardians in London he went out on a foggy November evening and had one of the strange psychic experiences which seemed at times to direct his life. A voice seemed to say 'Mother Kate' insistently to him. Mother Kate had been the foundress of St Saviour's Priory at Haggerston, an autonomous house in the Congregation of the St Margaret's Sisters of East Grinstead. He took a taxi to Haggerston immediately. He rang the bell and asked for the Reverend Mother, and when they were alone he said: 'Mother, I want Sisters for Walsingham.' She replied: 'It is quite impossible', and then after a pause she added: 'but we must do it.'

Mother Cecily was as good as her word, and sure enough before long Sisters of her community began to work at the shrine. She had taken advice and it was clearly understood that Hope was not to be their confessor nor to have any control over them except in connection with their work for the shrine and parish. This situation might have contained the seeds of trouble, although Hope had to some extent learned his lesson by this time. He wrote in the *Mirror*: 'It is sad when changes take place and yet there are always compensations, and whilst missing our old friends very much, we are more than happy with our Sisters and grateful to the Mother of the Community of St Saviour's for their great venture of faith.'

The new Sister-in-Charge, Sister Margaret Mary, was infinitely tactful and the Sisters worked and prayed hard and there was never any trouble. In 1955 they were formed into an independent Priory and Sister Margaret was installed as the first Mother, so that everything Hope had fought for so violently came to him on a plate without his having to lift a finger.

There were, however, some scars left from the battle. The Prioress of the Community of Our Lady of Walsingham still remained, and steadfastly refused to enter any other Order. For this she can hardly be blamed, having belonged to three in which she had had some fairly harrowing experiences. Hope tried both blandishment and sternness in an attempt to resolve the problem, but she remained unshaken. The Guardians offered her a small pension if she would remove her habit or live within some convent, but she withdrew to her parents' home, which was not far from Walsingham, and claimed, quite rightly, that she had been professed to serve the shrine and would wait prepared to do so if she were given the opportunity. Fr Raynes felt responsible for her and remained her spiritual director, but her presence was a terrible warning to Hope never again to try to use, for his own purposes, those who had taken solemn vows to another Superior.

It is an unhappy chapter in his life and was the cause of great suffering to himself as well as to others, but there were many other things clamouring for his attention at the same time, and in the years immediately before the war he was fully occupied with building the Shrine Church and trying to give it some status in the teeth of determined opposition from Bishop Pollock.

10

Bricks and Mortar

SOON AFTER THE HOLY HOUSE and its covering chapel
had been opened in 1931 Hope Patten began to plan for a
larger building. The reason he gave for this was that the number
of pilgrims had become so great that it was no longer possible
to fit them into so small a space. This was not entirely true, as
he began to make this claim before he had much experience
of the new chapel and the original idea had been to use the
Holy House as a small oratory, while the main services of the
pilgrimage would continue to be held in the parish church as
they had always been. The truth was that, after his slight brush
with the bishop, he was anxious to get everything connected
with the pilgrimage on to private property where he felt he
would be in a stronger position to counter any attempts that
might be made to interfere with his plans.

The first idea had been to build on to the chapel a simple
choir and to make it a thanksgiving for the Oxford Movement
Centenary in 1933. The response to the appeal for this was very
disappointing, but Hope had copies of a proposed plan printed
and published in the *Mirror* and as widely distributed as
possible. This showed not only the choir, but a whole complex
of buildings including a cloister with confessionals all round it
and a whole range of monastic cells.

In 1935 the *Mirror* contains a note of urgency: 'Somehow or
other we must extend the present building or fasten three or
four bays to the 'East' and so make it possible for a modicum
of comfort . . . we now want some kind friend or friends who

have a real love for Our Lady and her National Shrine to come forward and give, or even loan, the necessary money.' The amount required at this time was about £12,000.

One morning in 1936 Hope was opening his letters at the breakfast table and said gleefully: 'I have a cheque for four thousand pounds!' The bursar snatched it from him saying 'You've made a mistake', but there was no mistake, it was in fact for £4,578 4s. od. and had been sent by a wealthy priest who was rearranging his investments, and this was the sum left over which he had vowed to send to Walsingham when he began the operation. He had seen the plans which Hope had published and said that he hoped they would be put into effect as soon as possible.

This windfall decided Hope to start at once on plans for building and to begin to appeal in earnest. He had had a certain amount of practice in collecting the money needed for the original chapel and he knew his public. 'This will be', he wrote, 'the first Votive Church built by members of the Church of England in honour of the Mother of God and to house a Shrine, since the sixteenth century; an act of reparation too for the neglect of the past 400 years.' His mind began to be full of the furnishings necessary: 'Think of all the requirements of an ordinary Catholic Parish Church, where perhaps there are two chapels besides the high altar, and then think of a pilgrimage church with eleven altars.'

Already the simple choir had become elaborated and from this time Bernard Craze, the architect, had constant alterations to make as new ideas sprang to Hope's mind and were roughed out by him on odd pieces of paper. He had a theory that nowhere was too small for a chapel and he had soon devised a plan by which he could fit in fifteen altars for the Mysteries of the Holy Rosary, as he had seen in the Rosary Church at Lourdes. It was well said that his motto should have been 'Multum in parvo'. There were those, one of whom was the bursar, who realised that everything was being designed on too small a scale. They urged Hope to build half of a larger church and leave the finishing of it to the next generation. He would not listen to this, for already he was filled with the compulsion to see it completed in his lifetime and quite certain that if he did not do it then it would never be done. It is ironical that the reason given for building was lack of space for pilgrims, and the new church did little to remedy this after a few years.

There are those who have spoken with great contempt of the building, and perhaps in the eyes of a purist it may seem over pretentious, but it has enormous charm and shows great imagination. No one but Bernard Craze really knew how much Hope had demanded and how little money there was to accomplish it. Some splendid bronze pillars were obtained from the News Chronicle building which was being demolished in Fleet Street and gave a distinguished architectural feature in supporting a gallery behind the high altar. Many interesting devices were used to disguise how small and narrow a church it really was, so that a sense of size and space was given which was quite unreal. A great defect is the lack of light and for this Hope is entirely responsible. For him darkness was mystery and he loved dim corners and flickering candles. In the end he was the greatest sufferer from the artificial gloom he had created, for as his eyesight began to fail he could scarcely see in the shrine and the altars were so low that he needed a missal stand with long legs to bring the book within the focus of his eyes.

When the ground was being cleared there was more opportunity to examine the ancient foundations which had been discovered when the Holy House was built, and they were fully excavated and photographed. Hope wrote a pamphlet entitled 'Some recent discoveries on the site of the Shrine of Our Lady of Walsingham'. He was quite convinced that this was the original covering chapel built over the Holy House, and while he found it easy to forget anything which did not fit in with his theories, there are those who have perhaps dismissed too easily the finds of that time. He speaks vaguely of 'archaeologists' and 'experts' but does not reveal who they were, and it is a pity that he did not allow some impartial authority to examine the whole site. Even an inexperienced eye can see an affinity in their outline to the building depicted on the ancient seal of the Priory.

It was a very happy time in Hope's life for the creative artist in him was having full scope, and there are photographs of him looking over the half-built walls with the eyes of an explorer fixed on new horizons. He loved to see things taking shape before his eyes for his frustrations were so often in not being able to get things moving. When a wall of the original building was taken down a few years ago, to build a Memorial Cloister to Hope himself, a small tin was found bricked up in which were some medals, tracts and the pen nib with which the building contract had been signed. There must be many such deposits built into the walls to be discovered by future generations. He loved small touches of this sort and there are many surprises for anyone who looks closely round the buildings, not least the heads of himself, Derrick, William Milner, Bishop O'Rorke, William Frary and – of all people – Mother Sarah, supporting timbers in the roof.

For some years Bishop Pollock had made no move and the problem of the status of the shrine had been allowed to fall into oblivion. However, the new building projects stirred him again into life and on 15 May 1936, he wrote to Hope: 'Some few years ago you and I had a little correspondence about the celebrating of the Holy Communion in the new Shrine at Walsingham. Would you be so good as to let me know whether you ever celebrate there now, and if you do so, how frequent are the celebrations, and of whom the congregation mainly consists?' Two days later Hope replied: 'I will answer your questions as briefly as you have asked them: Yes, I do celebrate occasionally in the Shrine; I have said Mass there sixteen times during the last twelve months. The congregation consists mainly of pilgrims and a few local members of the Society of Mary. The Shrine is never opened to the general public on these occasions.' Over a month later he received the following reply: 'I have been considering your letter, and from it it appears that though I have not licensed "the Shrine" for the celebration of the Holy Communion you are, contrary to my wishes, still from time to time celebrating the Holy Communion there. Obviously this does not come within the scope of the Communion of the Sick and the parish church is near. I therefore ask you to give up these celebrations altogether and to let me hear that you are proposing to abandon them.'

Hope replied to this, pointing out that he had said Mass there with the bishop's 'knowledge' for four and a half years, and that to stop doing so now would cause much hurt to the increasing number of visitors. He then reminds the bishop that in conversation and in correspondence he had never before actually forbidden celebrations and had indeed given as his reason for refusing to visit the shrine that he wanted to be able to tell people he had not even seen it. He assured the bishop that Mass had not been neglected in the parish church, as for the sixteen times he had celebrated in the shrine he had said Mass three hundred and eighty times in St Mary's. He concluded: 'Taking all this into consideration you will, I feel sure, reconsider your letter, and if you cannot license the chapel just yet, I trust it will be possible for matters to stand as they have in the past.'

A week later the bishop wrote: 'Thank you for your letter from which I am afraid it is plain that you have acted upon my forbearance as if it had been an expressed approval of your celebrating the Holy Communion in a place which has not been licensed. What you tell me about the parish church in which there is, you say, a celebration every day, appears to show that there is quite adequate provision in the parish church for those who wish to attend Holy Communion. I cannot say that I think that it is satisfactory to leave the matter as it stands: for your present practice seems to draw no distinction between a licensed and an unlicensed building, nor between a limited cognizance of what has been taking place and a sanction of it on my part. At the same time I still do not wish to be inconsiderate or to hurry in the matter, and it may be that circumstances of which I am unaware would make it difficult for you to discontinue your present arrangements. I suggest therefore that you should gradually reduce the celebrations in this unauthorised building and bring them completely to an end by the end of the year.'

Hope's reply to this said that there were now many invalids and delicate people staying at the hospice who were unable to get down to the church in the early morning. 'To such, a Mass is a great blessing and joy and it seems a very hard thing to deprive them of that privilege,' he wrote.

This was a strong appeal to the well known soft-heartedness of the bishop, but he was not on this occasion to be deflected by sentiment when he wrote: 'I am glad that I mentioned the end of the year as the date for the discontinuance of these unauthorised celebrations, because it will give you adequate time to give notices that can reach invalids and delicate people desirous of visiting Walsingham who are not vigorous enough to make their way over the little distance to the parish church. Some of these may prefer to postpone a visit to Walsingham until they are stronger.'

In October Hope wrote a long letter blaming the delay in answering on the large number of pilgrimages. He then went on to try to give some idea of a place of pilgrimage, with sick coming to pray for health and wonderful answers to prayer. 'To stop allowing people to receive Our Lord in Holy Communion in the Shrine', he wrote, 'seems to be definitely working against God – in view of all he has done and is doing.' He recorded a priests' pilgrimage at which there were thirty Masses a day, not an occasion which was likely to soften Bishop Pollock's heart. 'A place of pilgrimage is so different from a parish church – and as such needs special privileges', he concluded.

The reply was short: 'The parish church is of course open to visitors and pilgrims as well as to parishioners for the celebration of the Holy Communion. An unconsecrated Shrine, though available for prayer, cannot displace the church for Baptism or Holy Communion.'

Hope replied denying that the shrine had ever displaced the church for Holy Communion and stating that there had never been a Baptism or Marriage there and it had never been suggested that there should be.

The bishop replied: 'I am afraid that I seem inadvertently to have created a little confusion in your mind. I did not for a moment suppose that you had conducted any Baptism or Marriage in the Shrine. Let me then go back to my first letter and repeat that the "Shrine" has not been licensed for the Holy Communion, either to supplement the services in the parish church or for any other purpose, and I ask you, by the end of the year, to discontinue celebrating the Holy Communion in this "Shrine" which is neither consecrated nor licensed.'

Hope made no reply to this, so that in February of the following year the bishop wrote: 'Would you kindly let me hear whether according to my desire the celebrations of the Holy Communion in the Shrine were abandoned at the end of last year? May I hear the date of the last celebration?'

This letter Hope circulated to the Guardians with a copy of

his own reply which was: 'I have not said Mass in the Shrine since December in deference to your suggestion, and as a matter of fact there has been no celebration of the Holy Communion there this year (1937). But, although our correspondence has been kept, as far as possible, strictly private, I have had to place it before the Guardians of the Shrine to whom the chapel belongs, and we are unanimous in the opinion that it is impossible for Mass to be discontinued there, especially in the pilgrimage seasons. Since the Shrine is looked upon and sought by such a large number of Anglicans as a place of healing and spiritual help, and seeing how manifestly it is blessed: to divorce it from the central act of Christian worship is out of the question.' The bishop replied: 'I am glad to hear that you have abandoned the celebration in the Shrine as I requested. If later on more people wish to attend the Holy Communion in your parish you would no doubt be able to multiply and adjust the celebrations in the parish church. I write to you, of course, as a parish priest and incumbent of Walsingham, not as the chaplain of any particular society or college.'

There was then silence for a year, but Hope was already discussing with the Guardians lines of action he could take. Perhaps the most ingenious was that the Duke of Argyll, who was a Guardian, should appoint Hope as his private chaplain and adopt the shrine as his private chapel under some ancient law which allowed noblemen of his rank ecclesiastical privileges outside the jurisdiction of diocesan bishops. Such a solution would have caused a lot of merriment and turned the whole thing into a Gilbertian farce.

Sir Eric Maclagan, son of a former Archbishop of York, who had become a Guardian, prepared a memorandum on the subject for the Archbishop of Canterbury, as the Bishop of Norwich and Mrs Pollock were coming to stay at Lambeth Palace. This he sent with a personal note warning his Grace that some people thought the bishop too much influenced by his wife in these matters.

On 2 March 1938, the bishop wrote to Hope: 'A year has now gone by and I am writing to inquire whether I may take it that the celebrations in the Shrine have been still discontinued during the past twelve months.'

Hope in reply repeats what he had last said about the

Guardians' thinking it impossible to discontinue Mass during the pilgrimage season. He concludes: 'As perhaps you know, the great increase in the number of pilgrims using the chapel necessitated our making considerable additions to the original building; this has been going on for the past year. In the course of work on the site certain foundations have been discovered, which in the opinion of some may place the status of the Shrine on an entirely different basis from that which we thought existed during our correspondence of twelve months ago.'

There are two letters written to Hope at this time by Fr Whitby which show that not all the Guardians were happy at the way things were developing. 'As you know,' he wrote, 'I have never supported the idea of enlarging the Shrine at this juncture. I have always felt it was waving a red flag in the face of the bull. It is bound to strengthen the bishop's suspicion that the Shrine is intended as a rival of the parish church . . . My view of the situation and the results that follow must be qualified by the thought that they have been aggravated by the things I have mentioned.'

The bishop now exploded a slight bomb by putting a notice in the Diocesan Gazette saying: 'The new chapel at Walsingham is not licensed by me and no priest in this diocese or any other has my permission to celebrate the Holy Communion there.' Hope reacted immediately and wrote strongly saying that, since the bishop had seen fit to take this action without consulting him, he intended to exercise his rights as parish priest and say Mass wherever he thought fit in his own parish. He sent a copy of this letter round to the Guardians and Fr Fynes-Clinton replied: 'That is exactly the right way to write to a bishop.'

The bishop himself replied mildly: 'I am sorry if I have seemed discourteous. I wished to put into the Diocesan Gazette just a bald statement. I had already learnt from your previous letter the facts of the case, and there was no reason again to ask for your verification of them. I am puzzled to find any satisfactory connexion between my paragraph and your proposed discontinuance of your present practice. Would you be so good as to consider whether you cannot still continue to adopt the line which you tell me you have been following

through these sixteen months in personal and loyal deference
to my wishes? I should be sorry if you considered that the notice
in the Diocesan Gazette had spoilt the situation.'

Hope proposed that he should come and talk to the bishop
and from now on most of their exchanges were by word of
mouth, and as they were both men of sentiment they wept in
each other's arms. 'It is a happiness to me,' the bishop wrote,
'to think that you and I can talk over these things, even where
we differ, in the spirit of our conversation on Saturday.' Hope
wrote to the Guardians: 'Please "remember me" as this friendly
and personal appeal makes it frightfully difficult, and to me
personally painful.'

Hope now had a strong card in his hand. Fr Whitby had
written: 'There are really two battles to be fought out. One
is quite clear, that you as parish priest have the right to say
Mass where you choose, but I now see that the Guardians might
come in as a second string when it comes to asserting the right
for the site of the old chapel to be used for Mass on the ground
that it is already consecrated.' Hope had clutched at this second
string for he was obviously losing the first battle, and Fr Whitby
suggested consulting Mr Marshall Freeman to obtain counsel's
opinion on this point.

To Hope's great satisfaction Mr Freeman gave his opinion
that as the original shrine had been a 'Peculiar', and as this right
had never been taken away by law, a reconstruction on the
original site might lawfully be considered to have the same
privilege.

It was this that he propounded to Bishop Pollock, who was
a great legalist and so prepared to take the point, which to an
ordinary mind sounds rather like 'Alice in Wonderland'. After
their first meeting the bishop wrote: 'I shall be interested in
due course to see the actual quotation and extracts from the
opinions when you are able to send these along. I shall carefully
consider what you send, which will, of course, be germane to
our talk on Saturday and I am bearing in mind all that you
mention in connection with the foundations that you have
discovered.'

He was too clever to put anything on paper, but this must
have seemed to the Bishop of Norwich a good opportunity to
retreat with dignity and he never made any further attempt to

prevent Mass being said in the shrine. In fact, as far as Walsingham was concerned he kept out of the way until his resignation in 1942.

On Whit Monday, 1938, the new church was blessed by Bishop O'Rorke who came out of retirement in the west country and provided an episcopal flavour to the ceremonies, although an Eastern Orthodox Archbishop ran him a close second for splendour. The village was decorated and thousands joined in the procession from the parish church to the shrine where, after the blessing of the church, Hope defiantly sang High Mass in his own 'Peculiar'. In the afternoon Fr Biggart of the Community of the Resurrection gave an Oration and the bells of the carillon rang out from the new campanile, while Hope considered with exultation that 'the Holy House has been reconstructed and stands in a building almost as big as the parish church and certainly a much larger edifice than originally housed it before the dissolution.' The problem of furnishing the various chapels had been solved by persuading different Catholic Societies to be responsible for them. One or two had been adopted as private chantries and the Priest Associates and Society of Our Lady of Walsingham both now had their own chapels.

The following morning the Eastern Orthodox liturgy was celebrated for the first time at Walsingham, and Hope had already planned to include an Orthodox Chapel in the variety of new buildings he was already envisaging. He was in fact awarded the Medal of Saint Vladimir by the Russian Orthodox Church in recognition 'of your sympathy and noble efforts to organise construction of the Orthodox Church in Walsingham.' Derrick Lingwood was given the same decoration at that time. When it became clear that it would be some time before a church could be built, he constructed a chapel with an iconostasis on a small landing outside the Blessed Sacrament Chapel in the shrine church. For a few years after the war a Serbian Orthodox priest, Dr Najdanovich, lived in Walsingham in a house provided by the shrine and supported by the British Council of Churches to minister to a camp of Serbian refugees in the district. Hope loved the Eastern Church, but he was more interested in their liturgy and customs than in their theology, and of course their great devotion to the Mother of God made a strong appeal to him.

He had for a long time wanted to have an Orthodox house in the village, not only because of his great interest in and veneration for the Eastern Church, but he regarded it as a challenge to the Roman Church which had more or less set up in opposition to him.

It is odd that he himself suffered from exactly the same sort of inferiority complex towards them as that which seemed to afflict Roman Catholics of his generation towards the Church of England, and particularly the Catholic Movement in it.

One might have imagined that the Oxford Movement would have been a joy to the sad recusant remnant in this country, who had waited through three centuries of persecution for the dawn to break. But human nature is a curious thing and does not always react as might be expected. The deep feeling they had about the Established Church was that it had stood aside and watched their miseries, when not actually inflicting them, and then when easier days arrived had begun to claim 'We too are Catholics, we really had the Mass all the time under a different name.' After Newman's secession there were waves of converts who followed him into the Roman church and it became a settled policy to encourage individual conversions from the Church of England. Many of them took this step at great personal sacrifice and with subconscious feelings of guilt, and both these elements embittered them towards their former allegiance. The claims of Anglo-Catholics particularly infuriated them, and as they grew larger in numbers and more important they delighted in delivering snubs whenever possible and producing tracts with such titles as 'Anglo-Catholics: have they missed the point?' An intelligent and sensitive man like Ronald Knox was capable of making such statements as: 'All identity discs in heaven will be marked R.C.' This attitude of mind seems almost incredible in the light of the change in thinking towards other Christians which has come over the Roman church as a result of Pope John XXIII and Vatican II. But one must remember, when recalling some of the unhappy episodes in the early days at Walsingham, that both sides were as yet unliberated from the tyranny of their past.

The interior of the parish church and the new shrine, when

it was built, made some Roman Catholics really angry. They considered it a cheat and a deliberate deception and they made their feelings abundantly clear.

It will be remembered that the Slipper Chapel had passed into the hands of the Roman Catholic church in the last century, but that it had been a cause of conflict amongst them, and while it still belonged to the Benedictine monks of Downside they were unable to use it in any way. It stood in perfect repair but closed and unused. Hope wrote to Downside after he had restarted the pilgrimage to ask permission for it to be visited and prayed in by pilgrims. He received a reply from the Abbot which began 'Dear Sir' and went on: 'It is with deep regret that I feel obliged to refuse permission for public prayer in the Slipper Chapel. There is no need for me to say that I am much interested in your efforts to revive devotion to Our Lady of Walsingham and, if it were only for reason of courtesy, I should have liked to be in a position to accede to your request. But in these matters we have to be governed by our clearly defined principles, and therefore I am obliged to say No when it would have been much more congenial to say Yes.'

The attitude of the Abbot may, of course, have been governed by the fact that there was still a papal ban on any public services being held in the chapel, which is something he was hardly likely to wish to reveal. But it is an amiable letter compared with some which might have been written at that time under similar circumstances. Prinknash Abbey wrote asking Hope to refrain from selling their cards in his Tract Case as being misleading and deceitful. Poor Hope was fighting on two fronts over this, as there were many Anglicans who thought the selling of Roman Catholic books and tracts was unwise and confusing and made their feelings known.

After the Slipper Chapel had been transferred to the Northampton Diocese there were still unfortunate incidents, as when the caretaker refused to let some Anglican pilgrims enter and roundly told them what he thought about 'protestants'. There were deep apologies from the authorities. The Roman Catholic priest at Fakenham wrote: 'I venture to hope that your charity will find a way to forgive the mistaken zeal of the old man which was expressed in such uncourteous terms.'

Of course there were many Anglicans only too ready and willing to say what they thought about 'papists', but unpleasantness of this sort at Walsingham has most frequently been caused by visitors and not by inhabitants.

When the Slipper Chapel was opened as a shrine in 1934 Hope wrote in the *Mirror*: 'One supposes the conditions are not unlike those in the Holy Land where the Orthodox and the Latins, the Armenians and other Easterns, all claim the Holy Sites and live together, treading on each other's toes more or less frequently.'

There are many Roman Catholics who feel that the setting up of a rival shrine in Walsingham was not entirely motivated by a desire to honour the Mother of the Lord. The cult of Our Lady of Walsingham had been centred at King's Lynn for many years and nothing had been done about the Slipper Chapel because of this. There were few, if any, Roman Catholics living in Walsingham so that they had no congregation who needed ministrations. It was not until the Anglican shrine was built that they felt it necessary to refute the claims of Anglo-Catholics and set up their own shrine. It has been pointed out that there were so many ancient shrines in England crying out for restoration that it was a pity to settle upon a place where it was already being done. It was very unwise to entrust the work to an ex-monk of Nashdom Abbey who had worked in Walsingham as an Anglican and who was bound to be regarded with resentment and suspicion.

Having set up the shrine in the Slipper Chapel propaganda was issued in connection with it, which either ignored everything that Hope Patten had done and stated that pilgrimages had restarted when Cardinal Bourne came in 1934, or spoke in rather patronising terms of well-meaning efforts by misguided persons who were outside the Catholic Church. All kinds of 'first time' claims were made and an R.C. layman once said that he would never be surprised to read a headline in the church press: 'First Catholic cigar smoked in Walsingham'.

It is not surprising that Hope and others resented this attitude and he was apt to make snide remarks and comments about Roman Catholics in the pages of the *Mirror*. There can be no doubt that his vehemence in upholding the Saxon foundations as the original site of the shrine was because he knew that it would annoy the Romans. And in this he judged rightly.

Stupid and rather petty stratagems were employed to outwit each other. Finger posts were put up reading 'Shrine O.L.W.' and promptly ones pointing the other way, which had 'Slipper Chapel' and a papal tiara before 'Shrine O.L.W.' were erected. Apparently the use of the initials 'R.C.' was considered a sacrifice of principle for when, after vigorous complaints that it was not made clear enough that the Anglican shrine was Church of England, Hope offered to put up an explicit notice if one was put in the Slipper Chapel reading 'This is the R.C. Shrine of Our Lady of Walsingham', the offer was refused.

Having far greater resources than Hope, the Roman Catholics produced very large pilgrimages which simply swamped the village. For Anglicans in those days these great occasions tended to be 'day of wrath and doom impending', for the more intolerant of the pilgrims were apt to make ugly scenes in the Anglican shrine and parish church. Roman Catholic laity wished to live near their shrine and so bought up houses in the village forming a fairly sizeable parish, and the local paper more than once referred to their clergyman as 'parish priest of Walsingham', which made Anglicans climb on to their Established 'high horse'.

Because of these things Hope developed a certain scratchiness towards those he would refer to as 'our Roman brethren' and kept himself very aloof from them. If imitation is the sincerest form of flattery they ought to have been very flattered, but it did not strike them that way. They really were in visible communion with the Pope, for whom he had so great a veneration, and they did not let him forget it, so that he sometimes was made to feel like a poor and unwanted relation. On the Feast of the Assumption in the Marian Year there was a vast Roman pilgrimage in the Abbey grounds and a golden crown sent by the Pope was placed on the head of the image. Someone remembered Hope sitting in the garden of the Hospice, where a small parish Fete was being held, and listening to the function going forward on the other side of the wall, and they recorded that he seemed a rather sad figure, for he was the man who, in many ways, was responsible for it all and he had no part to play.

The difficulties which Hope had experienced were in some

ways repeated in the history of the Slipper Chapel. For many years the Bishop of Northampton was a very autocratic and rather cross-grained conservative whose diocese became known as 'the cruel See', so that it was ironical that, after the departure of Bishop Pollock, the priest at the Slipper Chapel suffered much more obstruction from his bishop than the Administrator of the Anglican shrine. There were various upheavals and comings and goings; but at last Fr Gerard Hulme came as priest in charge. He was a man of great humility and tact, so that from this time any tensions came entirely from outside, and a measure of goodwill was restored which blossomed easily under the warming influence of Pope John XXIII.

Hope did not live to see the advent of Pope John and one wonders how he would have reacted, for he had this strange dichotomy in loving the Roman Church passionately but very much disapproving of and even disliking Roman Catholics. However, one cannot help feeling that he would have melted before the charm and simple holiness which even won over quite bigoted protestants.

Once the new shrine church had been opened Hope began to see the possibility of a great expansion in the work and influence of the shrine. He and Fr Fynes-Clinton would be closeted together for hours and Derrick Lingwood would tremble in his shoes, for he knew only too well that the likely outcome would be some new scheme for which he would be expected to raise the money. They saw the organisation of the shrine as becoming something similar to the Woodard Corporation, having schools, patronage and all manner of works under its control. What might have been the outcome, if things had proceeded without interruption from that point, one cannot tell. In fact war was declared in the autumn of 1939 and very soon Walsingham, like many places near the coast, was made a prohibited area and organised pilgrimages virtually came to an end for the duration of hostilities.

II

The War Years

'SURELY THE TIMES IN WHICH WE LIVE should make the use of the Shrine of Our Lady of Walsingham appeal to the imagination of all Catholics,' Hope wrote at the beginning of the war, and he was convinced that his war work must be to keep the shrine running and as unchanged as possible. He records that 'the Pilgrimage Church has been entirely "blacked out".' This cannot have been very difficult as little light had ever been allowed to get in from the outside in the first place, and now it was in almost perpetual darkness. Evening Services from the parish church were all moved to the Shrine, and some of them never moved back.

His policy of keeping things going was certainly not without point for many people actively involved in the turmoil of the war years were greatly encouraged by the thought that things were going on quite normally at the shrine, and intercessions were kept up for those in the armed forces. If there were no pilgrims to light votive candles Hope lit them himself, so that the whole atmosphere was unchanged.

Writing to someone overseas in 1940 he said: 'These days we generally keep a Triduum each or nearly every week for victory and peace at the Shrine. The programme is daily Holy Communion – visit to all the altars and the fifteen Mysteries of the Rosary – the Stations of the Cross – visit to the Holy House – Evening visit to the Holy Sacrament. Then a special Mass is said in the Holy House each day and Benediction given in the evening. All go to their Confession during the

Triduum. Quite a number of people from the village keep them. Every evening we have either night prayers in the Shrine or half an hour Exposition between 6.30–7.30. On Tuesdays Benediction and every Friday Holy Hour before the Most Holy exposed for peace.' It does not sound exactly like a shutdown.

The only person who was not altogether happy about the policy of 'business as usual' was the bursar, who had to pay exactly the same bills with offerings from pilgrims and visitors having almost completely ceased.

When Hope spoke of 'people from the village' it now included quite a number of elderly ladies who had moved to Walsingham for what used to be known to readers of the *Church Times* as 'Catholic privileges'; and they certainly got a lot of them. In his early days at Walsingham Hope had tended to encourage people who wanted to come and live near the shrine, but towards the end of his life he admitted that it had been a great mistake. While some of the 'squatters', as he called them, were very generous and helped in many ways, they were a disturbing element in the village. He always maintained that he had never had any trouble with the village people themselves, but that at times the devout ladies had nearly driven him crazy with their squabbles and feuds.

One rather wealthy lady bought the Martyrs House and opened it as a café. Having spent a lot of money on it, with Hope's deep approval, she engaged some tenants to run it, but very soon fell foul of them and ordered them off the premises. Feeling that they had been unjustly treated, Hope, as parish priest, championed their cause, and had some cottages opposite the shrine adapted and put them in to run it as the Knight's Gate Café. The lady, who had come to live in Walsingham as a great devotee of his, was wildly incensed and announced that she would run the Martyrs Café herself. With a misplaced sense of humour Hope included her name in a list of local tradespeople he put as an advertisement at the end of a guide-book to the shrine. It was a particularly shrewd thrust as she was very sensitive about her origins, and she at once altered her will, and not only cut out the shrine entirely, but made it impossible for Hope to obtain her house which she knew he particularly wanted. It was not only an expensive joke, but it

revealed a slightly feline streak in Hope's nature which often
deflected his better judgement.

He tended to see the war years mainly in terms of the shrine
and the church. 'Over fifty of our boys have joined up,' he wrote
to a friend in America, 'which makes a great difference to the
village and also serving, choir, etc.' He had no personal fears,
but he was worried lest bombs should be dropped and destroy
everything which he had built with such labour. He wrote to
Canon Peterson, the Rector of St James', Cleveland, Ohio,
and a wealthy and influential American: *'Please remember* – if
we are all knocked out and the Shrine is destroyed – it's *got to
be built up* again – *right away*. Please do all you can by letters to
the press, etc., if that happens, to stir up folk to get a move on
and build it up again – That's my legacy to you!!'

Just before the war began he had launched into a new venture. In the spring number of the *Mirror* he announced: 'It
has been suggested that there ought to be a charity connected
with the shrine and so the decision has been made to have a
home for poor and destitute children. If support justifies this
work then perhaps the scheme may develop into a series of
homes. As a preliminary to this plan we hope Fr Bernard
Walke's home at St Hilary will shortly be transferred to Walsingham and that it may eventually be incorporated into our
scheme.'

The tiny Cornish village of St Hilary, near Penzance, had
been much in the news in the 1930s. The talented and imaginative vicar, Bernard Walke, had accomplished there much the
same sort of miracle that Hope had worked in his early years
at Walsingham – except that he had had the advantage of a
wife, who was an artist, to help him. The village had been
won over to Catholic worship and the church decorated with the
work of local artists, such as the Dod Proctors, who were friends
of Annie Walke. Like Walsingham it acquired an extraordinary
sense of holiness and a feeling that time had stopped still and
the Reformation never happened. It was very remote and might
never have attracted much outside attention had the B.B.C.
not decided to broadcast the annual Nativity Play at Christmas
time.

Broadcasting was in its early days and the play managed to

convey an atmosphere of simplicity and devotion in a wonderful way, which provoked great enthusiasm in listeners. But of
course the play was unrelentingly 'high' and words like 'Mass'
and 'Our Lady' were said quite naturally in winning Cornish
accents. This drew the attention of militant protestants to the
village and they were lucky to get the support of a slightly
demented parishioner. She had a personal grudge against the
vicar and allowed herself to be used by a protestant society as
the legal objector to Romish practices in her parish church.
There followed a most hideous squeal of persecutions which it
would be difficult to justify under any interpretation of Christianity. Coach loads of objectors were introduced who prevented
Mass from beginning by bawling 'Abide with me' at the top of
their voices. A series of legal actions were brought in church
courts, and when the removal of certain ornaments was required
and Fr Walke refused to comply, a hired gang came and broke
up the church themselves.

Fr Walke was a convinced pacificist and had taken a public
stand about it during the Great War so that he would not allow
the villagers to retaliate in the only way they knew by flinging
out the demonstrators with force. Thus they saw their church
wrecked without being able to lift a finger. Bernard Walke
resigned and a priest was appointed who did everything he
could to satisfy the objectors. He restored the Prayer Book
entirely and gave up Benediction and extra liturgical devotions,
but the riots continued, sponsored from outside the village, and
he too finally resigned and today the church stands with the
stone altars hacked out but the reredoses still in place, while
the shrines are untended. It has not only a negative and desol-
ate air but an active feeling of evil, so that to visit the church is
a painful experience.

Bernard Walke had a strong social conscience and had
gathered a group of unwanted children into a home which he
called 'The Jolly Tinners'. Hope wrote:

As we all know, the church has suffered grave persecution
there, and the impossible conditions of church life which have
been introduced since the resignation of the last incumbent
have made it out of the question for the children of the home
to remain. We hope Walsingham will take them to its

heart and that they will be real children of Our Lady. Two
cottages have been bought for this home by Fr Walke's
Committee.

So St Hilary's Home first came to Walsingham and settled
temporarily in the High Street with five girls and six boys
comprising the family. The girls did not interest Hope as much
as the boys, because they could not become servers, and he
was rather anti-feminist in any case. No more girls were taken
and before long it became a boys' home. This was not acceptable
to some of the Guardians and Fr Fynes-Clinton insisted on
raising a small sum of money for a girls' home which might
stand in the accounts as a reminder that this had been the
original intention.

The cottages bought for the home were never occupied by
them, because the war began and they moved from the High
Street and took over half the first floor of the vicarage. This was
a time when children were being evacuated from London and
the big cities and it seemed to Hope that it would be better
to have his own children in his house than those who might
be billeted by the authorities.

In 1942 a house was bought on a hill just outside the village
and there the home moved and remained, while after the war
the village extended so that it was not left isolated for long.

In the early days there was a constant turn-over in matrons
and regular notices in the *Church Times* advertising for
applicants. On several occasions when there was a crisis the
children had to be looked after by local people who came to
their aid. It was not until after the war that Miss Bartholomew
and Miss Williams, who had met working in the Land Army,
deciding to take on a job they could do together, settled at
St Hilary's. They have done a remarkable work and given it
the stability it needed.

The children's home was to Hope, of all the things he founded
in Walsingham, more of a consolation than a worry. He loved
children, in the way that bachelors so often do, and several of
the boys, as they grew older, gave him real companionship and
affection, which was enormously important to someone like
Hope, who could not bear to be alone or unattended. He also
had teams of servers at his beck and call, but in many ways

it was a mistake to let them replace the village boys, as from this time the extraordinary influence he had exerted through a keen band of local servers tended to decline. When he first came to Walsingham he had gathered boys around quickly and they liked him and were always ready to do things for him. He was not at all athletic, but he gripped their imaginations so that they never thought of religion as something to be left to girls. It was the same with the boys at St Hilary's. They were asked to do a lot of serving in the shrine and parish, but they never complained or said later that they had had too much religion when they were young.

He rather erred on the side of over-indulgence with the home boys and there were grumbles from some quarters in the village that they had far more done for them than the locals. He tended to have favourites amongst them and the matron complained that in any dispute he almost always took the boys' side. Yet St Hilary's flourished and did a splendid work in providing a really happy home for children who had no family background. It was perhaps more successful when they were very young than when they grew older and there were great problems in keeping in touch with them after they left school. There were few jobs, except connected with agriculture, in that part of Norfolk, so that boys had to go away to get work, and it was only too easy for them to feel rootless. For a while a hostel was opened in the village for those working in the district or returning for holidays, but they tended to get married too quickly for it to justify the expense it involved.

The whole project of the home reveals another side of Hope's thinking which shows that he had a wider vision than might have been supposed. He realised that there was a great danger in having a place given over entirely to worship without having some active work of Christian charity connected with it. He was unashamedly interested in the externals of religion, which he considered very important, but he wanted to dig the foundations of the shrine much deeper than that, and it is because he did this that it survived.

In 1942 Bishop Pollock resigned the see of Norwich which he had held for over thirty years and ended his days a rather sad old man. It is probable that he never understood in the least what Walsingham was about, in spite of Hope's impassioned letters on the subject of shrines and pilgrimages, but he was historically, however reluctantly, one of the founders of the Holy House. One of Hope's most potent threats, which always intimidated the bishop, was that the shrine would be replaced in the parish church. It is one of the ironies, of which history has so many examples, that Bishop Pollock will be best remembered because of his connection with something he opposed, and of which he most strongly disapproved.

His successor was Percy Mark Herbert, the Bishop of Blackburn. What Hope had heard about him is not clear, but he wrote to the Rev. Mother of Horbury: 'Seeing that Blackburn is likely to come, I fear we Catholics in this diocese are in for some stormy times.' Nothing could have been further from the truth, but Hope, like many of his generation, had a rooted suspicion of bishops in general and, like people who cannot bear to be in a room with a wasp without making a dab at it, he felt that he was not really upholding the faith unless he was engaged in a conflict with the bishop of the diocese. There can have been few people harder to provoke than Percy Mark and the only chance he gave to Hope was when, stirred up by the schoolmasterly figure then at Canterbury, he tried to make some regulations about Reservation and Benediction in his diocese in 1950. Hope promptly sprang into action and took the lead in opposition, writing round to all kinds of people gathering ammunition. A line of counter attack was proposed by urging the bishop publicly to dissociate himself from 'such blasphemy and heresy as is uttered by ✠Birmingham and ✠Truro'. If he would not do so, then he was to be told that his motives were suspect and his regulations considered the sort of persecution to which Catholics were well accustomed.

Percy Mark mildly suggested that members of the Federation of Catholic Priests should come to see him at the palace, and he assured them that he had no intention of taking any action in the matter. The whole question of regulations was allowed to drop, so that Hope's great bomb ended as a rather damp squib.

In every other way the new bishop showed himself kind and helpful towards the shrine and, when Hope wished to get a young man who intended to join the college released from national service, the bishop supported him, although he did not agree with the policy.

When Percy Mark first arrived in the diocese he was faced with the trouble over the Sisters at Walsingham and, as has been seen, he acted with wisdom and consideration towards all concerned. His own personal feeling, having read the very large file on Walsingham and having also spoken to one or two people, was that Hope Patten had had something of a raw deal from his predecessor. He therefore proposed himself for a visit early in 1943. Hope wrote in the *Mirror*;

> We have all been made very happy by a kindly visit to the Shrine and Sisters of our new Diocesan, the Bishop of Norwich, who showed great interest in all he saw. He stayed the night and attended the Mass in the parish church the next morning at 8 o'clock. This is the first time for over twenty-one years, that is during the present incumbency, that the Chief Pastor of this Diocese has attended a service of any kind in these parishes, and the first time since the sixteenth century he has visited the Shrine.

Fortunately, or unfortunately, the bishop was not able to see all that he might, for as the result of a power cut the Shrine was plunged into more than usual darkness, and he had to be led round by the light of a candle!

He did not himself feel that his gesture had been much of a success, and although Hope was as charming and delightful a host as he could always be, yet the bishop was never invited again and was fully conscious that there was a reserve and lack of trust in his reception. Being a wise old man he realised that Hope's experience with his predecessor had caused the iron to enter into his soul and that it was too late to expect any easy intimacy. He stayed the night in the college, but nothing was said about Mass the following morning as Hope was obviously not particularly keen to have him see what went on. He got up and found his own way over what Bishop Pollock had called 'the little distance to the parish church'. His comments were rather amusing for he said: 'I couldn't hear very much of the service, but what I did recognise seemed to be in a very unusual order and I was surprised at the number of times he managed to say "The Lord be with you".'

However, he continued to be affable and was prepared to fall in with any plans for the college or the Sisters which needed his consent. One thing he did not feel able to do anything about was the status of the shrine. On 21 April 1944, he wrote to Hope:

> I have considered the question which you raised privately with me, and now write to say that I do not think I should find it possible to consecrate the Shrine. It is obviously unsatisfactory to consecrate a place over which the bishop subsequently has no control, as he could not in the case of a building which is private property, the owners of which would hardly wish to have its uses controlled by the bishop.

Yet the whole thing had his cordial goodwill and in 1952, when he discovered that Hope was anxious about the future, he wrote:

> I am writing to state that on any change of incumbency I should be ready to regard the college and the Shrine as coming within the provisions of the Private Chapels Act, 1871, and to license as warden a priest of the Church of England nominated by the trustees and approved by me in the usual way.

And he was as good as his word.

With plans for the college and the trouble with the Sisters, Hope had a good deal to deflect his attention from the war-time lack of pilgrimages. Yet ways of extending knowledge of the shrine were always at the back of his mind and so through these years he encouraged the making of spiritual pilgrimages to local shrines of Our Lady of Walsingham, and the formation of cells of members of the society who would band together in their particular district to promote and spread interest in the shrine.

The setting up of shrines of Our Lady of Walsingham in churches and religious houses all over the world has been an extraordinary outcome of the restoration of the Holy House. As early as 1926 an American priest named Fr Curtis had a copy of the image carved in Oberammergau, blessed in Walsingham and set up in his church at Sheboygan, Wisconsin, by the side of Lake Michigan, where it has been a centre of pilgrimage ever since. Many other shrines have been erected in America, Africa, India, Australia and wherever the Anglican communion exists. Perhaps the most remote shrine is on the island of Tristan da Cunha, recognised as one of the most isolated places in the world. It was a great consolation to Hope to reflect that this second era of Walsingham had spread its fame far wider than the first.

As the war began to draw to its close small pilgrimages were again organised, but transport was still difficult. Hope became rather impatient. 'It was intended,' he wrote in the *Mirror*, 'to have a pilgrimage of Thanksgiving after V.J. Day, but there seems to be very little request for this.' He drew up plans for a war memorial chapel and a valuable picture by Sodoma from the Mond collection was given as a reredos, but the response was very small and Hope had so many other projects in hand that, apart from an occasional irritable note in the *Mirror* on the subject, he had no time to beat the big drum about this memorial and it was quietly forgotten.

Unusual pilgrims were parties of Italian and German prisoners of war, who were mostly Roman Catholic, but found the Anglican shrine far more like those to which they were accustomed in their own countries than the rather austere Slipper Chapel, and could not be prevented from using it. Both nationalities painted pictures which they presented to the shrine and which were hung in the Holy House. It was getting very full of swords, medals, rosaries and other votive offerings left there by pilgrims, including a pair of surgical corsets. All these things were soon covered in soot from the large numbers of candles and provided the right atmosphere of holy dirt which Hope loved so much.

Before the war ended Hope had the opportunity of launching another scheme which had been germinating in his mind over the past ten years – the formation of a choir school. It will be remembered that Dom Anselm Hughes had recommended this step as a solution to the problem of music in the shrine and it could, of course, have been invaluable. The last year of a devastating war was hardly the most propitious time for such a venture, but Hope was nothing if not intrepid. He had the opportunity of acquiring an almost ready-made school, which was the sort of luck which he had always been hoping for with regard to a community, but which in that case never seemed to happen.

Quainton Hall School, Harrow, was founded in 1897 by Agnes Eyden, who had very high ideals of a school which would express the virtues of a Christian family. Her son became a priest and in time took over the school and built a chapel so that it had a definitely church character in the Catholic tradition. He was a passionate believer in the Boy Scout movement and he liked to say in jest that Quainton Hall was really a Scout Troop with a school attached.

When the war began provision was made for those boys whose parents wanted them to be out of the London area, and about fifty boys were evacuated to Long Marston Vicarage, near Tring, with the music master and his wife in charge. In 1944 the buildings they were using were requisitioned and they needed to move. Fr Eyden very generously suggested at this point that they should move to Walsingham and become the choir school, about the possible foundation of which Hope had had occasion to consult him. A new charitable and religious company was formed called The Walsingham College Affiliated Schools Ltd. using the Guardians as shareholders.

The boys who moved to Walsingham were accommodated in the buildings on the east of the shrine which Hope had earmarked as the future college. They used the Pilgrim Refectory as a diningroom, classroom and play centre. It was all very primitive, but they enjoyed it. The whole arrangement suited Hope very well because 'educational purposes' was one of the few magic words which at that time got building permits and impressed local authorities, so that he was able to get a lot of work done on these dilapidated cottages which would otherwise have been impossible.

Hope was at the height of his troubles over the Sisters and his newly formed community had to try to keep the boys fed on top of everything else, so that they certainly had no time to go away and be trained as novices, and few of them had much knowledge of cooking, as the prevalence of tummy trouble amongst the boys seemed to indicate. Cooks were not easy to find, but Fr Eyden heard of a possibility and returned in triumph to announce the news to Hope. Instead of exclamations of satisfaction, Hope asked immediately: 'Is she a practising Catholic?' and, when Fr Eyden said that he had no idea, said it would be quite impossible to employ her unless she were. He was certainly acting up to his claim in the *Mirror*: 'The School is being run as a definitely Catholic school.'

For the first year Fr Eyden acted as headmaster and his intention had been to hand over to his deputy, who was an expert in music, which would have been very suitable in a choir school.

Unfortunately while Fr Patten was on holiday they changed all the tunes sung at Benediction as a surprise for him on his return. It was certainly a surprise, but not one he appreciated, and in a heated exchange the deputy headmaster told him that he would rather teach the boys to tell dirty stories than to sing the kind of music then in use at the shrine. The result was that the deputy headmaster and his wife left, for, as Hope wrote in the *Mirror*: 'They have had a most difficult year under very trying conditions.' He announced at the same time that the school was moving to the vicarage and would be known henceforth as the Sanctuary School. The new head-master was to be Mr Thomas Tapping. This should have been a success as Thomas Tapping had been one of the young men who had lived in the vicarage when Hope first came to Walsing-ham.

One of the great difficulties which began to manifest itself from the beginning was that Hope had never been to school himself, except for one year at Christ's Hospital, and had no idea how a school should be run, nor any realisation of the fact that the headmaster had to be in control. Fond of him as Mr Tapping was, he got more and more irritated when the boys were constantly required for functions in the shrine and the timetable was thrown into confusion. Tapping tried to be firm, but this was not something which Hope was prepared to tolerate in what he regarded as his own domain. Added to this the headmaster was not altogether in sympathy with every-thing that went on in the shrine and in which the boys were forced to participate.

Hope was at the height of his enthusiasm about relics, having recently added greatly to his collection. Readers of the *Mirror* were told:

A letter came from a devout client of Our Lady of Walsingham offering us a relic of St Hugh B.C. St Hugh is the chief
patron of the Administrator. One of his great ambitions has
been to have relics of St Hugh and St Thomas of Canterbury.
The latter was sent to the Shrine last year from America, and
now one of the great Carthusian Bishop of Lincoln has come.
It seemed to be beyond one's wildest dreams ever to have
these treasures at the Shrine. They are most unusual and
difficult to come by. Of course, in both cases they are properly sealed and accompanied by the letters of authentication.

He had no sense of humour about this rather 'cigarette card
collecting' approach, and when some of his young men in the
college enclosed a feather in a reliquary and labelled it 'St
Michael', so that a rather innocent nun placed it on the altar,
he was furiously angry.

The boys at the school were constantly being required to
venerate this and that, and when the headmaster objected Hope
became convinced that he was not the right person for a
'thoroughly Catholic school'. Although the Guardians were
governors of the school they had little idea of what went on and
the decision to make a change, although done in their name and
communicated by the unfortunate Derrick Lingwood as
secretary to the company, was entirely Hope's. He wrote in the
Mirror: 'They were both very keen, and it was a real sorrow
that a change had to be made.' It was more than a sorrow; it
was a disaster. In three years Tapping had begun to build the
school into something considerable and he was popular with the
parents who were very upset by the change. Hope, on the other
hand, never bothered much about the parents. In fact few of
them had had much chance of meeting him, so that they naturally took Tapping's side and when he opened a school in the
vicinity many of the boys left the Sanctuary School.

It was not until another headmaster had come and gone
under similar circumstances that the Guardians really woke up
to what was happening and insisted that Hope must give the
new man an entirely free hand. By then it was too late, for more
boys had left to follow the last headmaster, and the school had
been given a feeling of instability from which it never recovered.

It went on till 1956, but once rumours started that it was going to close, it became harder and harder to get parents to send boys. It began losing money to such an extent that the Guardians could not afford to go on subsidising it and were forced to cut their losses and let it close.

As it got more and more into difficulties Hope made frantic efforts to save it. He raised money, but not enough; he wrote vast numbers of letters begging people to use their influence to get boys. It was sad that he was entirely unable to see that he was in any way responsible for the situation. He wrote peevishly: 'The Sanctuary School has closed, much to the great regret of all, but Catholics evidently do not want a church school of definite teaching and practice, and so it is they who have virtually shut it down.'

There is little doubt that the school could have been a success and would have proved a great asset to the shrine. As with his community, Hope began by being very choosy about whom he would take both in boys and staff, but as things became more difficult he clutched at any straw and standards lapsed.

Quainton Hall School at Harrow, under Fr Eyden, grew and developed and became exactly the sort of school Hope had wished to have at the shrine, but although it belonged to the Walsingham Guardians it was a hundred and thirty miles away.

Before the school closed Hope had brought to birth another scheme which had been waiting for a long time to come to fruition – a home for retired priests. He did not call it the Home of St Francis Borgia, which had been his intention in 1924, but contented himself with the less exotic patronage of St Thomas of Canterbury.

On the east side of the shrine there were rows of cottages with a builder's yard. Some of this property had been acquired in the original purchase of the hospice, but some cottages came into the market subsequently and Hope urged the bursar to buy them, having a wonderful gift of being able to see what could be done with unlikely buildings. It sprang from his enormous powers of imagination. He would look at a ruinous house and his eyes would take on a shrewd but far-away look, and he would produce a little measuring rod and make a few calculations, and then say: 'Yes, that would be perfectly possible.'

Most of the property was in very bad condition and had been condemned by the local authority. The architects whom he consulted all said that restoration was out of the question and that everything must come down. This Hope would not accept and so he decided to do the job himself with the aid of the local builder, his friend Tom Purdy. From day to day Hope would decide what was to be done and very often Tom Purdy would protest that it was impossible, but Hope was very firm that there was always a way to overcome the impossible, and nine times out of ten he was proved right. Tom Purdy always said that it was a wearing experience for him being in the hands of such a ruthless task-master, and that if he had known what it was going to involve he would never have consented to undertake it. However, from the ruined cottages and the junk-laden yard Hope created an enchanting range of buildings round three sides of a quadrangle, with a very attractive garden in the middle.

The buildings are full of amusing details and in his own sittingroom, which was constructed out of three cottages, he had made a large open fireplace faked out of cement which fooled many people that it was an original find. He bought what seemed an unlimited supply of old bedposts, which he utilised in a variety of ingenious ways as pillars, candlesticks, riddel posts, and of course beds. The transformation of this rather unpromising jumble of derelict buildings into the college as it is today was a work of unmistakable genius, and it gave Hope plenty of outlet for his restless energy and creative urge. As each part was completed he had plans and ideas for the next section. Of course it cost a good deal, but he relied on Derrick Lingwood to produce the money and seldom enquired how it had been done.

In 1949 Sir William Milner made it possible for the Guardians to acquire his estate in Yorkshire and a new company called the Walsingham College (Yorkshire Properties) was formed to run it as a charitable trust for religious purposes widely defined. This made much more work for the bursar, but it produced some more capital from which loans could be made and it was in this way that Hope found it possible to restore the derelict cottages to the north of the college as an Old Priests Home. It seemed to him that it was all the same company and he could never understand why it was necessary to pay back the money loaned. He also managed to use the Yorkshire Properties to acquire one or two houses in the village which he thought should be under the control of the shrine.

When the first part of the college was completed he had moved from the vicarage and had become an increasingly remote figure to his parishioners. He was able to direct the restoration of the north wing on the spot, but this time Bernard Craze co-operated as a new cloister was to be built. He constructed five bed-sittingrooms while the cloister was to be used as a commonroom. Outside there was a terraced garden of great charm, and on the first floor a door was made into the college refectory where the elderly priests were to take their meals. This refectory was one of Hope's most successful transformations, made out of several rooms and producing such a mediaeval-looking hall that several experts thought it might well have been one originally and only later broken up into cottages.

His idea of a home for retired priests was purely romantic. He saw them as stately becassocked figures moving with dignity between the shrine and their apartments and spending their whole life either saying Mass or reciting their Office. In his heart he saw it as a means of accomplishing what he had always longed for, the constant and regular use of the many altars he had constructed in the shrine. But the retired priests did not materialise. The majority of clergy on retirement wished to be near shops and cinemas and were somewhat frightened of the climate on the north Norfolk coast. Also by this time the rumour that Hope could be something of a despot had circulated, and made those who had led an independent life pause before committing themselves. One elderly priest of a retiring nature settled and others came for short periods, but the venture was never a success.

It had not occurred to Hope that the aged get more infirm and very often bed-ridden, which produces a problem in itself. He had not really considered who was to care for them. He would say airily: 'Members of the college', but they were expected to do so many things and he already had plenty of work connected with the shrine for their limited numbers. The empty rooms were a great frustration to him, but he began to fill them with priests bringing pilgrimages or coming to stay at the shrine. Fr Lingwood occupied a cottage by the gate and other members of the college were housed in St Augustine's, where the Benedictines had run a hospice and where, although it still had no bathroom or lavatory, Hope had established a library. In the old scullery he made a tiny Chapter House complete with seven stalls and a lectern, constructed, inevitably, out of a bedpost.

In 1954 the Sisters of St Margaret began to build a permanent convent. This was the first building in the shrine grounds for which Hope had no responsibility whatever and he was rather reserved about it. He would certainly have planned for them something picturesque, probably in the Spanish mission style, but that was not at all what was built. The Reverend Mother was accustomed to say: 'Isn't it lovely, it looks just like a council house, and so we live in exactly the same sort of house as most of the people.' This was a noble point of view, but not one which was likely to commend itself very strongly to Hope.

As he grew older he became in some ways more difficult and impossible to deflect when he had made up his mind about something. Derrick Lingwood had been like a son to him and more than anybody able to manage and reason with him. When Derrick refused to remain a member of the college a certain strain entered into their relationship. Derrick still remained living in the cottage by the gate, but the old intimacy began to fade and he was not always consulted about things. A basic trouble was that Derrick had learned the Catholic religion from Hope, but had not moved from the position which he had then received. Hope, on the other hand, had, over the years, been much influenced by his papalist friends and had gone back on much of his policy, particularly in connection with the Prayer Book.

Derrick had been left with the charge of the parishes, and he was in touch with the way things had been changing in the church at large since the war, but he did not have an entirely free hand. A new housing estate had been built not far from St Peter's, Great Walsingham, and he had begun to use this church more and hoped to encourage the newcomers to attend

Mass there. It seemed to him that for pastoral reasons it ought to be far more recognisably Prayer Book than at St Mary's and St Giles', but Hope absolutely refused to allow Mass to be said differently anywhere in the parish.

After Christmas in 1955 Derrick wrote Hope an official letter saying how distressed he was as a Guardian that the Prayer Book had been replaced by the Roman Breviary for the public Office of the college. He pointed out that this was likely to prevent the shrine from spreading its influence amongst ordinary members of the Church of England. He records that a prominent member of the Church Assembly had said to him: 'With the present set-up this shrine can never become *England's* Nazareth', and he ends by saying: 'With so much going on I have not yet had time to work out my own position, but when the festivities are over I must get down to it.'

The possibility of leaving Walsingham had been on his mind for some time, as the pressure of parish work plus the financial responsibility for the shrine and all its dependencies had become an intolerable strain. The collapse of the Sanctuary School had in itself been a nightmare for the bursar, as the guarantors were forced to pay up and he felt very responsible for this. He had an assistant who had been brought up at St Hilary's home and who had been trained as an accountant in the army, and he felt the moment had come when the services of a full-time bursar were necessary. He was offered the living of St Peter Parmentergate in Norwich, but at the same time the Bishop of Exeter offered him the church of St Martin's, Barton, Torquay. Barton was away from Norfolk and presented the greater challenge and so he accepted the charge and left Walsingham, where he had lived for the whole of his life except for the short stay at Bradford at the time of his ordination.

12

The Last Years

WHAT HE REGARDED as 'the desertion' by Derrick Lingwood
was a terrible blow to Hope and from this time he began to
become an old man. When Derrick made his decision to leave
there was one other priest member of the college. He was not
much use, but was another pair of hands. Derrick went away
for a short holiday and on his return discovered that Hope had
got rid of the priest and was entirely on his own with a few lay
brothers. It was as if he wished to emphasise his abandonment.

The remarkable thing is that he was forced once again to
take up the reins as parish priest, and in the few years that
remained to him he won back the personal love and devotion of
his people more strongly than ever. Some of the older villagers
who remembered his first coming to Walsingham rallied round
him, and he managed to keep things going without relaxing
any of the traditions he had built up. At Christmas he insisted
on having all the Masses in the shrine as well as in the parish
churches, although he had to say them himself. On Remembrance Sunday he had always had a Requiem after the Parish
Mass, and now he was on his own he solemnly came into the
sacristy and changed into black vestments and celebrated Mass
again for a remnant of the same congregation.

So much had been accomplished, and yet the future was so
uncertain and he felt horribly insecure. It was reported to him
that at a meeting in the north of England a question had been
asked about the 'extremity' of Walsingham and a Mirfield
Father, who was the speaker, had answered that when Fr Patten

died all that would be changed. He was deeply grateful for the help and support he had received from Fr Raynes in an attempt to establish a Sisterhood, but this made him very suspicious of the Community of the Resurrection and he thought that they were expecting to 'take over' at his death. It was at this time that he raised the alarm by printing in the *Mirror* the article, 'What will happen when Fr Patten dies?' It says the Guardians may appoint an Administrator but 'it will never be quite the same of course, because a new man could not possibly maintain a tradition which he had not helped to create, and after his term of office had expired, a new man, a new tradition, will replace the old.' There is then a stirring appeal for recruits for the college stating that it is in its birth pangs and not, as some suppose, in its death throes. It concludes: 'Walsingham's future is in the hands of Mary's children. God calls: are there none with sufficient love to answer?'

It is strange that one of his spiritual maturity was not prepared to leave things in the hands of God, but he had needed to fight hard to get the shrine established and he could not see that the battle was won. To the end of his life he was haunted by the terror that, in spite of all his efforts, it would fall to pieces as he had seen the Sisterhood and the Sanctuary School do.

Then he received perhaps his bitterest blow when it was announced that Fr Lingwood was to be married. He felt this as an act of personal treachery, for he had been responsible for Derrick's religious upbringing and could not believe that anything which he considered as important as clerical celibacy could be regarded as a matter of opinion. What made it worse was that he convinced himself that this was the reason that Derrick had left Walsingham and that he had been the victim of gross deceit. Fr Lingwood vigorously denied that there was any understanding between himself and the lady he married while he was still living at the shrine. On the other hand, he made no secret of the fact that when he left he had for some years been out of sympathy with the rigorist approach to celibacy, and the idea had crossed his mind that if the opportunity arose he might get married. The loneliness and isolation of living alone, as he began to do in Devon, soon convinced him that it was a necessary step for him. He knew that Hope would not approve but he hoped that he would understand.

H

There was nothing much that Hope could do except maintain an icy silence, but Derrick was a Guardian and in the constitution, which Derrick himself had helped to draw up, it was clearly stated that: 'Should any Priest Guardian marry (subsequent to his election to the Guardianship) he shall *ipso facto* CEASE FROM FELLOWSHIP' (sic). This clause of the constitution Hope insisted should come into force forthwith, and he refused even to discuss the subject. It was sad that he was unable to separate his personal relationship from his public disapproval and he refused to have any personal communication with Derrick and wrote saying he had not opened a birthday gift.

The Guardians were deeply divided upon this issue. Sir William Milner had become a close and affectionate friend of Derrick's and had been taken into his confidence when he first considered marriage. Sir William urged him to go forward and expressed his opinion that once it was an accomplished fact Hope would accept it and agree to a change in the constitution to enable him to remain as a Guardian. He had judged very wrongly in this, but the Guardians were also a limited company and Derrick had been made a life director, and the Companies Act does not concern itself with the problems of clerical celibacy. Hope thought that he should resign, but he was urged by Sir William and other Guardians not to do so, and the strange situation arose that he was a director of the company, but not a Guardian.

As always in moments of stress and crisis, Hope's health began to give cause for alarm. His eyesight had been getting worse for some years and he was convinced that he was going blind. To some extent this was a nervous disorder, as it tended to vary and become much worse when he was emotionally disturbed. Since the war he had suffered several breakdowns in health and had been forced to go away for months at a time. His old haunts in Belgium and France were difficult to visit because of the devastation left by the war, and so he took to going to Malta, where he felt very much at home on that most Catholic of islands. He refused to go by air and had always hated the sea, so that the journey was something of a penance. Even crossing the Channel he insisted on taking a cabin and lying flat no his back in mortal terror until reaching dry land again. The *Mirror* became full of articles about Maltese shrines and he made great friends with an aged Maltese priest called Canon Catania, who came to cherish a great veneration and respect for him.

One of the difficulties about his illnesses was that he was very reluctant to do anything which the doctor prescribed except going away. He was fascinated by unorthodox treatments and was a great believer in 'the black box'. He spent a great deal of money on such things, for they were very close to his lifelong interest in the supernatural. Had the Catholic religion allowed spiritualism, he would probably have proved to be a medium for he easily, when very tired or slightly feverish, passed into a trance-like state. There were times when Derrick Lingwood had feared that people who did not understand him might think that he was drunk; but he retained this psychic streak to the end of his life and he would far have preferred using a relic or a holy thing to effect a cure than any antiseptic the doctor might provide.

There continued to be projects in hand which sustained his interest as the hospice was being extended with a new building and an impressive gate-house. It was made possible by a large anonymous donation. The family of a rich benefactress of the shrine were convinced that their mother was the donor and became very restive as they thought they saw their patrimony disappearing, but they were mistaken. Hope was in some ways obsessed by bricks and mortar, because he was convinced that the more that could be built, the less possible would it be to close the place down.

He found buildings far more easy to manage than human beings. The second generation of Guardians did not seem as content to leave things entirely in his hands as had their predecessors. Some of the new lay Guardians were not the stately figureheads that Lord Halifax and the Duke of Argyll had been, and they became a little restive when they discovered that, after coming all the way to Walsingham for chapter and passing various resolutions, Hope then did exactly as he had intended in the first place. He was not a committee man and was a bad chairman who became very ruffled if he was opposed. He once said in an icy cold voice, when a proposal he had put forward was defeated: 'When I founded the Guardians in 1931 I imagined that they would pay some attention to my wishes. I see that I was mistaken.'

John Upcott, a retired Eton housemaster, was particularly incensed at the way things connected with the school had been managed and did some very direct speaking to Hope about the rights of headmasters. He was a bluff, rather John Bullish figure, who was very unlike the conventional picture of those thought to be interested in Walsingham. When on his first visit Fr Patten had asked him: 'Can you answer Mass?' he had replied: 'I didn't know there was an answer.' He became personally devoted to Hope, as was the case with all the Guardians, but it did not prevent him speaking his mind. Hope had not been used to this sort of thing, and although he said as a joke to the ex-naval officer, Sir John Best-Shaw, 'I refuse to be spoken to as if I were a defaulter on your quarter deck', this did indeed reflect what he felt like at times.

Several of the guardians felt as strongly about clerical celibacy as he did. Canon Maryon-Wilson had let it be known that he would resign immediately if the constitution were to be changed. Lord Norton, amongst the lay Guardians, although retiring and unassertive, was equally positive on this point. Several of the Guardians, while not feeling at all strongly, did consider that Fr Lingwood was a special case, as the shrine owed so much to him for the skill with which he had piloted its finances through the rocks of Hope's extravagance and restive imagination.

A motion for amending the constitution was put down for debate at Chapter, and Hope was in a frenzy as it seemed that there might well be a majority of Guardians who were in favour of this. He got someone hastily to write a tract on celibacy and sent it round to members of the Chapter, but its effect was some-what marred by the fact that 'celibacy' was spelt wrongly throughout. He worked himself into a highly nervous state and Fr Fynes-Clinton was seriously alarmed that if the motion was passed he might well have a stroke. There is little doubt that the majority of Guardians went into the Chapter room determined to vote for a change in the constitution. The debate was not in the least acrimonious and was very much dominated by Bishop Vernon, who was himself in favour of a change. It was an example of the Holy Spirit working through a corporate body and bringing it to a common mind. Although Hope said little, most members of the Chapter were fully conscious of how strongly he felt and that it would be a great reproach if the body which he had created should bring his grey hairs in sorrow to the grave. There was, however, a matter of principle involved. The Guardians were a private society and it was possible to make any requirements for membership without making a universal judgement. If it were thought desirable to have only people with one leg, it was their own affair. But the requirement for Priest Associates to resign from the society if they got married did imply that they had done something disgraceful, and this a majority of the Guardians considered both unrealistic and unjust for those who claimed to be members of the Church of England. The final resolution was that this should be dropped and the guardians' constitution remain unchanged, and it was agreed to by the Chapter with a large majority. This did something to allay the haunting fear which had gripped Hope's mind that the guardians were preparing to tear down everything which he had built up with such pain and labour.

What he did not realise was that some of the later Guardians represented the new spirit which was stirring in the church and which had completely altered the approach to Walsingham and the shrine. When he had restarted the pilgrimage it seemed an outrage to average Anglican churchmen, but that prejudice had passed away and the thing which he had always longed for, to make it open to as wide a section of the Church of England as possible, was now a reality. He had fought such battles that, like many priests and indeed laymen of his generation, he could not realise that they had been won on an unexpected front. He had seen something of the liturgical revival on the continent, but it did not make much appeal to him, and apart from providing some very full gothic vestments, which he himself characteristically wore with a lace alb, he did little to change the worship of the parish church or the shrine. He remained adamant against any but the server joining in the responses when he was saying Mass, but he did admit towards the end of his life that he had made a great mistake when he abolished the audible saying of parts of the Prayer Book in the parish church. He could not go back on what he had done, but he realised that it had isolated the parish from the main flow of the

Church of England. This had been made clear to him during the war when the boys who went into the forces, having lived their whole lives in Walsingham, found it quite impossible to adapt themselves to service religion, and so lapsed.

Not all the Guardians' Chapters were fraught with tensions and mostly they were happy and very companionable occasions with much fun and laughter.

They would gather for Vespers followed by a large dinner in the college refectory, and next morning the priest Guardians would say Mass in their own chapels and after breakfast there would be a Chapter Mass, and then they would get down to business. Fr Fynes-Clinton would act as a sort of sergeant major, going round the younger Guardians, telling them they were improperly dressed or should have been standing at some point in the Liturgy. Almost always there was something very funny as when Hope, holding a large envelope in his hand, told of the new reredos for the Holy House which had been designed by Sir Ninian Comper. 'And this is the result', he said, drawing out and holding up a photograph of the Walsingham football team. There was a pause and then a shout of laughter which brought a flush of anger to Hope's face until he realised that he had got the wrong envelope.

The shrine was expanding and there was so much to be done, for pilgrimages were increasing rapidly and there began to be very few weekends without them. At last he secured an assistant in one of the earliest members of the college who had left to be ordained in the West Indies and who returned to work at Walsingham. It was only just in time for Hope's health was becoming very precarious and he was forced to go away more and more. This had been a familiar pattern for so long that it did not cause undue alarm.

He became very dependent upon those about him and needed companionship constantly. He could not bear to be left in a room alone. He had always had something of a morbid fear of illness and death, but this became more marked and he was rather impatient if anyone enquired too particularly about his health.

Most of the burden fell upon the new bursar, Stanley Smith, who was forced to accompany him everywhere. As Hope's eyesight deteriorated he felt a passion to go and see things he had always longed to see before the darkness he dreaded completely overtook him. Stanley drove him across Europe and around Spain, escorting him with great patience in search of things in which he himself had little interest. As he was engaged to be married these long absences from home, when he had to act as chauffeur, valet and secretary, were a real sacrifice.

After Derrick Lingwood's departure Hope's 'Benjamin' was another boy from the village who, under his influence, had developed a vocation to the priesthood. It was a great joy to him that this boy joined the college, and after being away at Lichfield Theological College was ordained deacon by the Bishop of Norwich. Thus there came to be more help with the work of the parish and the shrine at a time when it was getting more and more necessary. After Stanley Smith got married and moved out of the college, Hope depended more and more on the new deacon, John Shepherd, who seemed to have been raised up to replace Fr Lingwood.

The year 1956 was the Jubilee Year of the rebuilding of the Holy House. It was indeed impressive to consider all that had been accomplished during that time. There had been disappointments, but there was an almost incredible achievement in the bringing to life and building up of a mediaeval place of pilgrimage in twentieth century England. Casual visitors were amazed to discover such a thing as the shrine functioning in an ordinary Norfolk village.

To celebrate the Jubilee there was a gathering in London and in October a series of functions at the shrine on the anniversary of the translation of the image from the parish church. The campanile was floodlit and inside the shrine hundreds of extra lamps flickered above the stalls and on the screen at the east end. It all had the unmistakable mark of Hope's genius for making a fiesta exciting. There was a torchlight procession to the parish church, a High Mass at the shrine at midnight with Exposition of the Holy Sacrament throughout the night, while Mass was said at half-hourly intervals in the Holy House. Bishop Vernon sang Mass next day and the Abbot of Nashdom preached in the afternoon before a procession through the village circling the precincts of the shrine. Yet even in the midst of these jubilations Hope was full of worries and frustrations about the things he had not yet established. He was more and more conscious of the passing years and his declining strength while so much of his vision remained unfulfilled.

The Sisters built a new chapel which was dedicated by the bishop of the diocese so that it seemed in some directions that the longed for stability was being achieved. And yet Hope never ceased to be baffled by the remembrance of things he had not been able to create because they needed human beings who slipped out of his hands in an unpredictable way. He had always wanted a Crafts Guild centred upon the shrine, but of all the various likely people who had from time to time worked at Walsingham the only one to persevere was the artist Enid Chadwick, whose skill he had used in many directions from the painting of murals in the church to designing labels to stick on the myriad bottles in which water from the Holy Well was carried away by pilgrims.

Till this time whenever money from a bequest became available Hope immediately planned how it could be spent, but the Guardians at last managed to convince him that it would provide far greater stability than bricks and mortar for the shrine to be properly endowed and therefore capable of paying realistic stipends for priests. It was decided to try to raise £50,000, and various laymen undertook the organisation of an appeal. To get it launched, the Master of Lauderdale, a very active lay Guardian who was a Member of Parliament, arranged a press conference at the House of Commons at which Hope was to speak. He was very nervous about this and had been sternly briefed that his 'devoted clients' technique would not be suitable. He did appear somewhat small and old surrounded by the larger-than-life gentlemen of the press who were obviously a bit puzzled by him and treated him slightly as if he were a 'witch doctor'. He was very guarded in what he said, for they were thirsting for sensational copy about miracles, but he would commit himself no further than to say that, having lived at Walsingham for nearly forty years, he was convinced that there was a power at work there, and he said it in such a way that he produced an atmosphere of the supernatural in those unlikely surroundings.

There was, in fact, a cell of the Society of Our Lady of Walsingham at that time in the House of Commons and the

Speaker's Chaplain had said Mass for the members in St Stephen's Chapel in the house.

Yet Hope was becoming very weary and a lot of his old drive was no longer there. Stanley Smith had married and moved out of the college and he was left with only two members of his Congregation of St Augustine, and one of these he had already decided had no vocation. The prospects for this cherished institution looked bleak indeed. When the pilgrimage season of 1958 commenced, in a letter to John Upcott he wrote: 'The grind of Walsingham begins again.' What had been to him a joy and an excitement had become a grind.

It was the year of the Lambeth Conference of bishops and it was decided to arrange an Episcopal pilgrimage in August. There was not a large response, but Hope urged the Guardians to come and support him on this occasion. He had been showing signs of tiredness and had complained of a pain in his heart more than once, but 'Father's turns' had become familiar so that they were not taken too seriously. But there were ominous signs for those who could read them. In June he decided not to have daily devotions to the Sacred Heart, and it was most unlike him not to maintain something which had been a tradition since he first came to Walsingham.

Twelve Guardians arrived on 11 August to welcome the small party of bishops and a very large dinner had been arranged at the Knight's Gate Café, over which Hope presided with exceptional charm and grace with a U.M.C.A. bishop sitting on either side of him. It was a particularly hot and heavy evening, and as they struggled into their heavy mantles for a procession one of the Guardians said in jest: 'We are being butchered to make a Roman holiday!'

From photographs which were taken during the procession it was obvious that Hope was in great discomfort for his face was contorted with pain. He gave Benediction on returning to the shrine church and carried the Blessed Sacrament back up the stairs to the chapel in the gallery behind the High Altar. This final effort must have been too much for he closed the Tabernacle and, with a characteristic impatient gesture, rearranged the veil which had become untidy, stepped out of the sight of the congregation and collapsed into the arms of the servers.

He was helped over to his cottage and died a few moments later on his enormous four-poster bed, surrounded by bishops and Guardians. With his great love of the dramatic he could hardly have arranged a more sensational death if he had sat down and planned it, as he had planned so many other functions. The Guardians themselves helped to clothe his lifeless body in the sacerdotal vestments which he had been careful to mark as those in which he wished to be buried.

It was decided, in view of the fact that the Guardians were mostly already there and the Feast of the Assumption was in two days' time, that the obsequies must begin the following evening, and even at that late hour *The Times* was contacted so that a notice could appear next morning.

The Bishop of Norwich was about to leave for his holiday and the suffragan Bishop of Thetford was already away, so that there was only the Rural Dean to represent the diocese in which Hope had worked for almost forty years. The comment in the village was: 'They didn't do anything for him in his lifetime and it is just as well they should stay away now that he is dead.' This was unfair, as the climate had changed in a dramatic way, and not only had Bishop Herbert done much to show friendship and sympathy, but a recent book written by Hope and called *Mary's Shrine* had received a flattering notice in the Diocesan Gazette, where twenty years before Bishop Pollock's little paragraph had denied any connection between the diocese and the shrine.

On the evening following his death Hope's coffin was carried into the shrine and left open while the villagers came to pay their last respects. It was a very moving sight as they filed past in large numbers sprinkling Holy Water on the body of their parish priest, without whom they might never have known such a fluid existed. Some of the older ones could remember him arriving in the village as 'the boy' and cycling around with great gusto, but any under forty had never known any other vicar and to them he was simply known, and always would be, as 'Father'.

During the day priests had been arriving from all over the country and it was possible to have Mass said every half hour during the night in the Holy House, as it had been at the

Jubilee. A long procession of priests headed the cortège through the village street and to the parish church where Fr Lingwood sang the Mass of Requiem. It was a happy thing that some relationship had been restored between them and there is no doubt that, had he lived longer, Hope would have been able to bring himself to a full reconciliation. He and Mother Sarah had both forgiven each other some years before and Hope was incapable of nursing a grudge for long.

Fr Colin Gill, one of the Guardians, preached a panegyric and Hope was finally buried by the west door of the church which he had loved so dearly and served so well.

He died very much at the end of an era, for within a year Pope John had entered upon his short and momentous reign and things in the whole of Christendom began changing so fast that it left many of the causes for which Hope had stood so firmly appearing very dated and slightly ridiculous, but in spite of all his fears the shrine continued to grow. Someone not in the least sympathetic towards him wrote in a private letter: 'Considering his many limitations, it is amazing that A.H.P. managed to create the whole Walsingham racket and that it should have survived his decease.' And this is his final vindication, he did make the foundation and it did survive.

Many people thought of him as a saint, but there were sides to his character which did not fit into the conventional pattern of sanctity. There were delusions of grandeur, but there was also a very profound humility which hated any sort of self publicity. There was a sternness and in some ways a ruthlessness when he was crossed, but there was also an almost feminine tenderness to those in trouble. There was a loneliness and detachment, but a frantic desire for companionship and understanding. He was always conscious of his priesthood, and being a perfectionist he demanded of himself in this respect the high standard he required in others.

Perhaps his most remarkable characteristic was the power he had of communicating his enthusiasm to other people and achieving extraordinary things through them. If one considers the record of his life, it becomes clear that the things he tried to do alone were the things which were a failure. The attempt to found a Sisterhood was a good example of this. And there is every reason to believe that he was fully conscious that he was acting as an agent of divine grace. He never had any doubt whatever, after his first hesitation, that God was calling him to restore the Shrine of Our Lady of Walsingham as England's National Shrine of the Blessed Virgin Mary. Those who thought that he was likely to become a Roman Catholic and take the shrine with him simply did not begin to understand his deep loyalty to the Church of his baptism. He received no recognition from the official Church of England, but shortly before his death at a Church Union Rally in the Albert Hall, his name being mentioned, there was a spontaneous burst of applause which grew into a thunderous standing ovation. He was genuinely moved and astonished by this and said, quite simply, that he had had an Image of Our Lady carved and God did the rest.

Epilogue:
The Story of Walsingham Continued

IT IS NECESSARY to step outside the curtains if the story of Walsingham is to be continued to the present day and to write a final chapter from my own personal experience.

In the great theme of the birth, destruction and rebirth of the shrine at Walsingham, it will have been seen how God works through people, often overruling their mistakes in the fulfilment of his purpose, and in this drama I have had a small part to play.

I first went to Walsingham in 1936, having responded to a letter written by Fr Kenrick, a well known Anglo-Catholic priest, to the *Church Times* asking for companions to join him in a pilgrimage on foot.

I had heard of the Shrine when I was at school as my cousin, who later became a monk, sent me a card when he was there in the late 1920s, and I had kept it in my bible ever since.

Only six pilgrims set out from Holy Trinity, Hoxton, at the beginning of that September, and I was by far the youngest. One priest was in his late seventies and he walked every step of the way. He was the father of the future Bishop of Thetford, the suffragan of Norwich, who was there when I came to live in Norfolk many years later.

Like Hope Patten, I had learned the Catholic religion in the churches of Brighton, and I too was entranced by the idea of restoring the Church of England to an outward form of what it might have been had the reformation never taken place.

Fr Kenrick was a papalist, which was a position in churchmanship which I had never consciously considered, but I was a ready pupil and during the long days on the road I drank in all that he had to say, so that by the time we arrived at the shrine I was ready to accept the whole thing in the most uncritical fashion. Walsingham was so exciting and stimulating to me that when I left I found it difficult to believe that I had not dreamed up the whole thing, and I could hardly wait to go again as soon as possible to prove to myself that it really existed.

On that first visit I met Hope Patten and was enormously impressed by him. He liked young men, and the circumstances of our pilgrimage appealed to his imagination so that he was particularly kind and gracious to me. I fell completely under his spell and from that time until his death I was in constant touch with him. At one time he was hopeful that I might join the college, but something restrained me and I think it was an apprehension of the authoritariansim which lay beneath the charm.

I saw Walsingham as an outsider and was conscious of the tensions, but like many other people who came there at that time, I was fully aware of the genius of Hope Patten and the fact that everything seemed to depend upon him. One realised the terrific efforts he was making to get the shrine established and the constant strain under which he lived. No detail was too small, and I was much amused at one time to discover that he himself was advertising in second-hand book catalogues for out of print Walsingham publications in order to get them circulating in those quarters and so advance the prestige of the shrine.

After the war, when I was vicar of St Mary Magdalen, Oxford, I was elected to be a member of the College of Guardians and so became much more closely involved in the politics of the Shrine. Already the Guardians had begun to assert themselves and there was some complaining that Hope did not pay much attention to resolutions passed in Chapter unless he agreed with them himself.

Amongst those forming the college there were strong personalities such as Fr Raynes and Bishop Vernon, who had both had a lot of experience, one in running a religious community and the other a diocese, so that they were not content to let things be entirely governed by the Master with the Chapter as nothing more than a ratifying body.

Fr Raynes in particular had a very great influence as he had managed to interest several of his friends who became Guardians, and although Hope sometimes spoke of the 'Mirfield Clique' with impatience, he was fully conscious that they had done a lot to widen the scope and influence of the shrine.

When Derrick Lingwood left Walsingham and ceased to be a Guardian both the offices of bursar and registrar, which he had held, were left vacant. It had been decided to have a bursar who was not also a Guardian, but when the position of registrar was discussed Fr Raynes suggested my name and I was elected.

One of the Guardians has since said to me: 'Did you realise that when we elected you, we were consciously choosing Hope Patten's successor?'

I can only say that I had no idea whatever of these undertones, nor did I really understand what the office involved. It was said vaguely that it was more or less the position of vice-chairman and that if Hope was ill, as he was beginning to be more often, I must take the chair in his place. It was not mentioned that if he fell dead, as he did soon after, I should have to carry on.

In the early morning of 12 August 1958, I went to my bed, having assisted in the vesting of Hope Patten's lifeless body, and conscious that a great part of the weight which had rested on his shoulders had been transferred to mine.

During the next few months the main problem was how the shrine was to be run, and my first idea was that this was the moment when it should be taken over by an established religious community. I got in touch with most of the main communities for men in the Church of England, but none of them felt able to take over the work at that time. If Fr Raynes had been alive I think it is possible that the Community of the Resurrection would have done so, although the possibility of this had been one of Hope's greatest phobias, but Fr Raynes had died only a few months before him.

The Guardians elected me as Master at a meeting held in

London and the problem then presented itself as to who was to be Administrator. I was under a good deal of pressure to undertake it myself, but I had no wish to leave my parish in Oxford and was fully conscious that in any case administration was not my strongest suit.

The combination of the parish and the shrine had worn out Hope, and in his last years he had on occasions been left with little or no assistance. I felt quite certain at that time that the two things should be separated, and the patron of the living was most co-operative and anxious to find someone who would maintain the traditions of the parish and be acceptable to the Guardians. I therefore made it clear that I could only manage the shrine alone, as I had no immediate prospect of help, and trying to do both things had recently killed the former Administrator.

I am now sure that I made a mistake, and that if I had had the courage to take on both things help would have been forthcoming from somewhere. The shrine had grown up in the parish and, although it was not much used by parishioners, yet they felt that it belonged to them and a lot of them were involved in the secular side of the pilgrimages. The separation left them uncertain where their loyalties lay and has proved a disadvantage to both shrine and parish.

About this time I had an interview with the Bishop of Norwich, whom I had never met and did not know. I went to see him in a very adamant frame of mind for I secretly hoped that he would try and make all manner of difficulties so that I should be forced to take a strong line which would give me the excuse I wanted to be able to say to the Guardians that it would be more suitable if I were to remain outside his diocese.

I was very blunt with him and said that I had been for the whole of my ministry in a diocese where I was in good standing, and where we were not fussed about the sort of services we provided for our people. I said that if I were to come and work at the shrine at Walsingham I should expect to be properly licensed and that it would be made clear that I was part of the diocese as I had no intention of being forced to be a nonconformist.

To my surprise the bishop was most sympathetic and understanding, and he readily agreed to everything I asked. When I left he patted my shoulder and said: 'My dear man, I can see that everything can be quite safely left in your hands.'

So it was that on 1 April 1959 I moved to Walsingham and began to work there.

The pilgrimage season had begun and I was soon trying to cope with it all on my own and able to realise something of the strain of Hope's last years.

On Saturdays I would go into the shrine at 2 p.m. to start sprinkling the day pilgrims at the Holy Well. Before they had made their last visit the weekend pilgrims would have arrived and had to be welcomed. When I finally got to bed, after the torchlight procession and sitting in the confessional for a long time, I was more completely exhausted than I have ever been in my life.

The second big mistake which I made was to accept without question Hope Patten's unshakable conviction that the college should be run in the context of a religious community. The buildings had been constructed with this in mind and it seemed a pity to waste them. Obviously one cannot develop a religious vocation to order, but I had for some years been an Oblate of the Benedictine Community of Nashdom Abbey and there do exist in Catholic Christendom groups of Oblates living together in community so, after taking advice, I decided to try and form such a group.

Although I did not realise it at the time, I was reconstructing the sharpest rod which had tormented the back of my predecessor.

I learned many lessons, most of them the hard way, and I found myself more and more facing the same situations which had caused Hope Patten so much misery.

If you are a community you are dependent upon people feeling a vocation for the life, and so you have to wait for them to come forward, which means that you cannot engage and get rid of assistants as in the ordinary parochial situation.

At that time the shrine had very little money, and while in the first flush of enthusiasm those wanting to come would say that they understood this, once they were installed they tended to grumble and be dissatisfied. We never managed to work out a satisfactory arrangement of community of property which left us very much living together as individuals.

The work was very heavy in the pilgrimage season and negligible outside it, which was difficult to adjust, and the constant coming and going of visitors made any community life almost impossible.

It has always been found difficult for human beings to live together except under vows, and we were not under vows so that friction and clash of temperament created constant problems.

Several people made a heroic effort to live the life, but in some ways it seemed that the oblate ideal, of maintaining the religious spirit while living in the world, did not fit in with being part-time monks living in community. Most serious of all, visitors to Walsingham thought that we were a religious order, as we were a scapular, and in fact we were not, so they weighed us in the wrong scales and finding us wanting, went away in disapproval.

If we had been closer to Nashdom and had been able to have more instruction in the religious life, things might have worked better. As it was we were in a remote corner of the country, engaged in a very exacting work, and perhaps saw the inside of the monastery to which we were supposed to be attached only once a year.

Most of the mistakes made were mine, but I had no experience of being a religious Superior and no wish whatever to be one. Things tended to get out of hand when I was away, but I was forced to go around the country on the business of the shrine knowing that on my return I should probably have to deal with an accumulation of irritations. After three months in America I came home to find the college in a very unsatisfactory situation and I decided there and then that the only solution was to give up all attempt at being a house of oblates, and to run the place as a clergy house.

My experience of this made me wish that I had had the sense at the beginning to see that this was the best solution, but I had been blinded by exactly the same sort of romanticism from which Hope himself had suffered.

I felt that one of my first tasks was to reconcile the shrine with the Diocese of Norwich and to make it more widely known and appreciated in the Church of England at large.

When I first came to live in Walsingham I was surprised at how completely the shrine was regarded as a thing apart by the surrounding parishes. Antagonism had largely died, and Fr Hope Patten, if known at all, was regarded with awe, but Walsingham was considered a different religion entirely from 'ordinary C of E'. I began at once to help in local parishes and it caused great astonishment at first that I was prepared to do exactly what they were accustomed to, and if need be say Mass without vestments using nothing but the Prayer Book. But the old suspicion still remained and one church warden when I said that I hoped I had given them what they usually had, replied: 'It was very nice, but of course we aren't as high church as you and don't usually have the ten commandments.' In another parish where we were helping during an interregnum someone was told: 'We are being looked after by Roman Catholics, but we like them very much.'

It was the experience of personal contact which made all the difference. Hope Patten had been a very remote figure to those living outside the parish of Walsingham. In the course of the ten years that I worked there we had helped during a vacancy in every parish in the rural deanery, and made many good friends, who began to regard the shrine in a different light. I was much moved when I discovered someone who had lived most of their life in the vicinity praying in the shrine one day who said to me: 'I often come over now and have found enormous help here, but I am haunted by the shame of the awful things I have said about Walsingham in the past.'

The ruri-decanal chapter of clergy began meeting regularly at the shrine, so that before long every member, whatever their churchmanship, had said Mass there.

Soon after I came to live in Norfolk, Bishop Herbert resigned and his place was taken by Lancelot Fleming, who was translated from Portsmouth.

He proved to be a man of immense charm, with no particular ecclesiastical party affiliation, but a desire to understand and appreciate different traditions as widely as possible. He brought a new friendliness and warmth into the relations of Walsingham with the diocese and his great pastoral concern made him realise at once how a group of priests, such as the college, could be used. Thus he gave his support to the idea of the shrine taking over the care of several small country parishes in the vicinity, which provided the clergy working there with a good spiritual antidote for the constant rather exotic worship of the pilgrimage church.

Whit Monday had become the day of the largest pilgrim gathering of the year, which came to be called the National Pilgrimage. In 1959 the Church Union decided to join in as part of their centenary celebrations and the High Mass was celebrated in the grounds of the Abbey. The Bishop of Thetford represented the Bishop of Norwich, and so for the first time an official representative of the diocesan took part in the chief pilgrimage of the shrine.

Pat Leonard, Bishop of Thetford was, as I have said, the son of one of the priests with whom I had first come on pilgrimage to Walsingham. For the rest of his life he came every year to the National Pilgrimage and it was the last public function he performed before his untimely death.

His help and interest has been continued by the Bishop of Lynn who came to live at Stiffkey, close at hand, and who has in many ways replaced the redoubtable Bishop O'Rorke as 'the bishop down the road'.

In all these ways the shrine has become very much part of the Diocese of Norwich and is included in the Diocesan Calendar of Prayer, being prayed for by name in the cathedral together with the clergy at the college. When one remembers how comparatively recent were the machinations of Bishop Pollock against the shrine's having any official recognition, it is amazing that priests are now licensed to work there in the Holy House itself.

The fact that I was made an Hon. Canon of Norwich and elected by the priests of the diocese to represent them as a Proctor in Convocation shows that Walsingham is no longer something apart.

During the ten years that I was Administrator I must have travelled many thousands of miles talking and lecturing about the shrine, not only in every part of England, but during two tours of America, one of which lasted four months and covered almost every part of that vast country. This has helped in widening the support and interest for Walsingham which now comes from a larger and more varied section of churchmanship within the Anglican Communion.

This has not always taken place without tensions and difficulties. In 1966 the Bishop of Southwark consented to come and preach at the National Pilgrimage and this was much resented by some extreme Anglo-Catholics who regarded him as a persecutor of Catholics from his rather heavy-handed attempt to enforce some sort of liturgical uniformity in his diocese. I received the most surprising letters of protest from people who obviously regarded Walsingham as a sacred enclave of one type of churchmanship. The vicar of an advanced, but not very well attended, London church threatened to bring a party to make a demonstration. There were, in fact, rather more people than usual at the National Pilgrimage that year and the presence of an English diocesan bishop who was not likely to be in sympathy with some aspects of the cult, did demonstrate the wide appeal which a Shrine of the Incarnation can make to members of the Church of England if they can only overcome some of their irrational prejudices.

This has become the more important because of the amazing and rapid growth of the Ecumenical Movement which has led thoughtful church people to realise that the position of Mary in christian theology is one of the matters about which the Church of England must make up its mind if it is to be able to take part in a fruitful dialogue with both the Church of Rome and the Eastern Orthodox Church, which have a very important place for the Mother of Christ both in theology and devotion.

In 1961 I was invited to a private audience with Pope John XXIII, who was deeply interested in the Anglican shrine at Walsingham and wished to know more about it. It was for me a very moving experience for it obviously made the Pope happy to hear about this Anglican shrine and I could not help thinking how pleased Hope Patten would have been to see the Holy Father looking with appreciation at photographs of the buildings which he had planned and decorated with such love and care. When I left I asked the Pope if I might take his blessing to those who worked at the shrine, and he said: 'I would wish my blessing to descend on all who visit your shrine;' and then after a pause he added: 'not as exerting authority, but in all simplicity.'

Since his pontificate and the second Vatican Council it has been possible to co-operate far more with Roman Catholics and the vestiges of old rivalries have almost completely disappeared. There have been joint pilgrimages on the parochial level and a mutual participation by the clergy at all importanl functions. The growth of tolerance and charity on both sidet has removed something which many people found distastefus in what was supposed to be a holy place. A small pilgrimage came from Spain to pray for unity through Mary and their leader, a Dominican friar, led the Rosary in Spanish at Shrine Prayers in the Anglican Holy House.

The Orthodox, who formed an early link with Walsingham, have continued to come in increasing numbers. The Greek Metropolitan Archbishop, who is an Honorary-Guardian, presided over a Pan-Orthodox Vespers at which a Walsingham Fraternity was officially established in the Orthodox Church. A small group of the Russian Church in Exile have formed a Brotherhood and adapted the now disused railway station at Walsingham as their house and chapel. They also use the shrine for worship and so the Orthodox Chapel there has the Liturgy regularly celebrated. For some time a Roman Catholic Carmelite nun, who had a great passion for unity, lived in the village with the permission of her superiors and worshipped in all the churches. The Methodists also have shown an interest in Walsingham and have not only brought parties to visit the shrine, but the ministers of the East Anglian Synod paid an official visit and prayed there. At Christmas time the Salvation Army Band have played carols within the Holy House.

In 1967 there was a Marian Conference held in Walsingham which included Roman, Orthodox and Methodist speakers, as well as Anglican Evangelicals; and it became obvious that all were much closer to each other than they had supposed. A Roman Catholic layman, who has been closely connected with Walsingham since the reopening of the Slipper Chapel, has been instrumental in founding an Ecumenical Society of the Blessed Virgin Mary which has had wide support, and which continues to foster and extend the contacts which have been made with various denominations in this field.

When I first became Administrator in 1959 the last parish pilgrimage of the season was always reckoned to be a large one from St Augustine's, Tonge Moor, which came at the first weekend in September. So great has been the growth of parish pilgrimages that they now extend until the end of October. It is difficult to record numbers of pilgrims exactly, but the office estimates that at the moment about a hundred thousand come on pilgrimage to the Anglican shrine each year and many thousands come to the Slipper Chapel so that the full total is not a negligible figure in a country which is supposed to be fast abandoning religion.

This great increase in numbers has meant that a big building project has had to be undertaken as the feeding and accomodation of pilgrims in this quantity taxed the existing capacity to breaking point. It could not have been managed at all without the great and almost sacrificial labours of the Sisters. To ease this situation a new refectory and kitchens were built, while the Pilgrim Hospice has been completely remodelled to provide more sitting space, bathrooms and other things which a new generation of pilgrims expect to find at a place where they stay.

This has in some ways destroyed the quaint old hospice known and loved by early pilgrims, which had very great charm in its day, but it had fallen so far below the accepted standards of comfort in the modern world that it seemed unreasonable to impose this type of penance on pilgrims. Special rooms are being provided for the sick and disabled, and more light and space introduced into the shrine church.

In 1961 the parish church of Little Walsingham was almost completely destroyed by fire. In some ways the interior of St Mary's bore the stamp of Hope Patten's genius more winningly than the shrine itself, and its destruction seemed very much the end of an era. The parish was lucky that Walsingham had such a wide appeal and money was soon raised for it to be rebuilt. But the interior, however beautiful, is very different from the immeasurable charm of the old St Mary's which had for a brief period been the pilgrimage church and had never entirely lost the atmosphere of those years. If one looks closely at the fine stained glass of the new east window, one can see a tiny figure of Hope Patten. Ironically Henry VIII is three times the size and shows up clearly from the back of the church.

I found Walsingham a fascinating place in which to live. Hope Patten had made his mark upon it and the atmosphere he left was nothing but good. Certainly his parishioners very much venerated his memory, and they were the people who had lived alongside him for many years and were in the best position to judge. He left in Walsingham a high regard for the priesthood, and I am convinced that it was his example more than his teaching which had accomplished this.

I never encountered any of the ghosts which had played such a considerable part in the new legends of Walsingham, but I was conscious of an extraordinary sense of the supernatural which at times could be disconcerting. One felt that things were taken out of one's hands in a very strange way. I soon discovered that there was no need to worry about the financial side of things, because if something was needed the money just came. Soon after I arrived, being concerned about the lack of capital, we launched a disastrous planned giving campaign, but the moment we stopped it money flowed in from legacies and other sources, so that we were able to build what was needed and improve the property without any special appeal.

It was the same with people to work at the shrine; when there was a need they just appeared. Walsingham owes a great deal to many people, those who have given artistic, business or manual skills, and those who have laboured just washing, mending or scraping up the grease from the burning of countless numbers of candles. If one began to try and name them it would be an almost impossible task, but they have all played their part in the revival of the shrine and there is something almost uncanny in the way they have always been there when they were wanted. Added to this feeling that things happened at Walsingham in a way in which they do not elsewhere were the cures at the Holy Well, and the constant remarkable answers to prayer, too frequent to fulfil the laws of coincidence.

There is no doubt in my mind that Hope Patten was raised up to set in motion this whole work of restoration. He was most insistent that he was not the 'Founder', but the 'Restorer'. Like all human beings he had imperfections and limitations, but he was constant in his conviction that this was his vocation. It was his faithfulness in this which has bequeathed a legacy of a living growing thing which is the Shrine of Our Lady of Walsingham, England's Nazareth. During and since his lifetime it has again become dear to the hearts of a vast number of people and it has an increasingly important role to fulfil in the Church

today, for never has the truth of the Incarnation been in greater
need of visible demonstration before the eyes of men and women
and this is perhaps why God has allowed Walsingham's shrine
to live again.

> *Except the Lord build the house:*
> *Their labour is but lost that build it.*
> (Psalm 127)

Index